AGAINST THE GRAIN

A Historian's Journey

JEROLD S. AUERBACH

Quid Pro Books
New Orleans, Louisiana

Copyright © 2012 by Jerold S. Auerbach. All rights reserved. No material in this book may be reproduced, copied or retransmitted in any manner without the written consent of the publisher.

Published in 2012 by Quid Pro Books.

ISBN 978-1-61027-122-6 (pbk)
ISBN 978-1-61027-133-2 (hc)
ISBN 978-1-61027-123-3 (eBook)

QUID PRO, LLC
5860 Citrus Blvd., Suite D-101
New Orleans, Louisiana 70123
www.quidprobooks.com

Publisher's Cataloging-in-Publication

Auerbach, Jerold S.
    Against the grain: a historian's journey / Jerold S. Auerbach.
        p. cm. — (Journeys and Memoirs)

1. Auerbach, Jerold S. 2. History—United States—20th Century. 3. Jews—Cultural Assimilation—United States. 4. History—Israel I. Title. II. Series.

E187.T6.A971 2012   971′.03321′066—dc20
                                                                               201253378

For my children

and grandchildren

. . . and theirs

From generation

to generation

with love

CONTENTS

Introduction i

I. Law and Society 1

   1. The Best Men 3

   2. Lawyers and Clients 19

   3. Lawyers in the Depression Decade 27

   4. Law and Acculturation 41

   5. A Plague of Lawyers 51

II. Promised Lands 59

   6. Liberalism and the Hebrew Prophets 61

   7. Rabbis and Lawyers 67

   8. Zionism as Americanism 77

   9. "Exodus" and Return 83

   10. *Altalena*: The Pariah Ship 89

   11. American Home or Jewish Homeland? 93

   12. Americans in Israel 99

   13. The Long Shadow of 1977 103

   14. Zionism Without Judaism 109

   15. Israel's Shadow Line 115

   16. Zionism vs. Judaism 123

   17. Welcome to Palisdan 129

   18. Are Settlements Illegal? 133

   19. Hebron Letters 139

   20. Inventing "Palestine" 145

III. Rewriting History 151

   21. Woodrow Wilson's "Prediction" 153

   22. New Deal, Old Deal, or Raw Deal 161

   23. Means and Ends in the 1960s 169

   24. Thomas Friedman's Israel 177

   25. Edward Said's Silence 187

   26. The Corruption of Historians 193

   27. American Holy Land 201

IV. Reflections 213

   28. Jacob's Voices 215

   29. American Jew 221

   30. A Community of Jewish Memory 225

   31. Anti-Semitism with White Gloves 233

   32. The Clock and the Scale 239

   33. My Desk: Archive of My Victorian Self 243

   34. Victory Lap 247

   35. At Home 251

   Author's Note 253

   Permissions 255

   About the Author 257

Introduction

Historians emerge from their meanderings along paths of serendipity. December 7, 1941, "the day that will live in infamy," provided my earliest enduring historical memory—if only because my parents and grandmother were riveted to our radio, not to me. World War II framed my childhood. There were nighttime air-raid sirens and blackouts. A cousin in the Marines was killed in the battle of Tarawa. Neighborhood children contributed to the war effort by collecting tin foil, growing vegetables in our schoolyard "Victory Garden" and selling government war bonds. (With my father's partnership, I was crowned the most successful salesman in my grammar school.) My favorite uncle, who served on a hospital ship, gave me a first-aid kit filled with genuine army gauze, tape and band-aids that made me the envy of my friends. Just before my ninth birthday, I learned from photos in *Life* magazine about the Holocaust.

But history really began for me with baseball. The wondrous moment of my boyhood came one September morning when newspapers prominently displayed the photo of a jubilant player crossing home plate to accept handshakes from his joyous teammates. He had just hit a grand-slam home run in the ninth inning of the final game of the season that clinched the American League pennant for the Detroit Tigers. He was Hank Greenberg. And, as my father proudly informed me, he was our cousin.

That epiphany transformed my childhood. It instantly plunged me into a world of statistics, comparisons, and interpretations that were constantly challenged and revised by new evidence and counter-claims from boys no less obsessive than I. We agreed that Babe Ruth was the home-run colossus, Ty Cobb was the best hitter and base-stealer, and Cy Young was the stellar pitcher of all time. But, we debated endlessly during our teen-age years growing up in New York City, who was the best center fielder: Willie Mays, Mickey Mantle, or Duke Snider? Life-long bonds of friendship emerged from our competing claims, historically referenced, statistically documented, and passionately argued. Baseball taught me that conclusions must be supported by evidence.

Baseball knowledge also encouraged me to challenge authority and even to imagine myself as a sportswriter. My favorite Manhattan restaurant—owned by Al Schacht, once a major-league pitcher who became better known as "The Crown Prince" of baseball for his whimsical antics—was filled with baseball memorabilia. There, from menus as round as baseballs (although considerably larger), diners could select entrees named after star players. Once, beneath the dessert list, I discovered a glaring statistical error: Walter Johnson, who (I knew) won 417 games in his stellar career, was only credited with 414. A consultation with the waiter brought Schacht to our table; he graciously acknowledged the mistake and promised to correct it.

In my mid-teens Bruce Catton deflected my reading from baseball books by John R. Tunis to the Civil War. I was riveted by his Army of the Potomac trilogy, which immersed me, for the first time, in American history. There I encountered George McClellan's frustrating hesitation, Ulysses Grant's ferocious aggression, Robert E. Lee's serene nobility—and, of course, Abraham Lincoln's tragic greatness. Catton so vividly captured the tumult and chaos of battle that I persuaded my father to drive with me to Gettysburg and Manassas. Riveted by the "Lost Cause," I spent hours exploring the Confederate Museum in Richmond.

But it was an experience during my freshman year at Oberlin College that sealed my future as a historian, although I could hardly have imagined it at the time. To meet our English Composition requirement, we were required to write a term paper. For the only time that year, the library stacks were opened to freshmen for research. Inspired by Catton and awed by the opportunity to be alone, surrounded by books, and free to read whatever I chose, I discovered General McClellan's postwar memoir. It was carefully (and critically) hand-annotated by Jacob D. Cox, an Oberlin graduate who had served under Lincoln's notoriously cautious general.

Here was a fascinating century-old dialogue, punctuated with Cox's scribbled marginal notes and exclamation points. To read his comments, sharply contesting McClellan's account, challenged the authority of the printed page and opened a wondrous world of possibility. I had never before imagined that history was anything but fixed factual Truth, faithfully recorded by disinterested chroniclers. But writing history, I began to realize, meant asking questions of the past.

Gifted teachers in various disciplines reinforced that lesson. Whether in history, literature, political science or philosophy, they taught me that critical thinking trumped conventional wisdom; from them I learned to question and analyze. Along the way a frosty curmudgeon, who still boasted that he had voted for Herbert Hoover in 1932 (the only person I ever met who proudly made that claim), introduced me in his constitutional law class to Justice Oliver Wendell Holmes, Jr. Famously declaring that shouting fire "falsely" in a crowded theatre constituted unprotected speech, Holmes inspired me to imagine that some day I might argue First Amendment cases before the Supreme Court.

But the reality of first-year legal education was Torts, Contracts, Civil Procedure, and Criminal Law, converging in unremitting classroom torture. The more I was told that I was learning to think like a lawyer the less I wanted to become one. I endured one semester, followed by a week when I was verbally lacerated in every class. Confronting two more years in law school, or the army and a future in my father's jewelry business, I chose instead to embrace Clio, the ancient Greek muse of history.

Graduate school, in truth, was not much better than law school—and it lasted twice as long. But a handful of courses engaged me. One actually began, rather than ended, in 1900 (beyond which none of my undergraduate history classes had ventured). Assigned an arcane research topic—a labor law enacted during the Progressive era—I plunged into the depths of the Columbia library stacks and the New York City Municipal Archives to write my first doctoral seminar paper. There I rediscovered my intellectual home. I managed to transform the sow's ear of the *Congressional Record* into the silk purse of my first published article. Sharply challenging the progressivism of Progressivism, I became a historian. Once historical research opened my mind, the past became my future. Even my father, skeptical of my career choice but duly impressed that I had received a fifty-dollar honorarium for my publication, was reassured.

When my professional apprenticeship ended I found my first scholarly niche along the border between legal history and the sociology of law. As a visiting scholar in—of all places—the Harvard Law School, I began to scrutinize the history of the profession that I had abandoned a decade earlier. For a year, I wandered between the archives and (once again) the library stacks, from the fascinating private correspondence of Roscoe Pound, Felix Frankfurter, Zechariah Chafee, Jr. and other legal luminaries to dreary state bar association reports and deservedly obscure legal treatises.

From that inquiry emerged *Unequal Justice*, my history of lawyers and social change in modern America. The first social history of the legal profession, it recounted how professional opportunity had long been allocated according to religion, ethnicity, race, and wealth (to say nothing of gender). This, I concluded, did not produce equal justice under law, but unequal justice under lawyers. Along the way, I discovered that aspiring Jewish lawyers had long been the most blatant targets of professional prejudice and discrimination. Their unsavory attributes—"following the methods their fathers had been using in selling shoe-strings"—had discomforted the legal elite, suddenly forced to confront Shylocks in their midst (or imagination). Years of professional energy had been devoted to developing strategies designed to exclude or marginalize Jews.

So, ironically, I devoted nearly a decade of research and writing to the profession that I had abandoned. Nearing the end, I began to wonder whether there might be less adversarial alternatives to legal dispute settlement and to "the plague of lawyers" that by the 1970s had descended upon American society. A courtroom, after all, could be as bizarre as Alice's Wonderland (where some of her strangest adventures occurred). Trials often were Kafkaesque. Who knew better than Franz Kafka, trained in law?

In the American experience, I wondered, had there ever been justice without law, even without lawyers? I finally discovered it, buried and overlooked in the histories of immigrant (and, revealingly, utopian) communities. For many decades Scandinavian conciliation, Chinese mediation, and Jewish arbitration had resolved disputes outside the formal legal system, the better to preserve non-adversarial communal norms.

It surely was not coincidental that my attention, once again, was drawn to the (unanticipated) Jewish dimension of my subject. My own Jewish identity, ever since my bar mitzvah, had meant little to me. For so many Jews of my parents' generation, as the children of Eastern European immigrants, Judaism had all but vanished, to be redefined as American liberalism. From personal experience I was familiar with such evasive forms of self-protection, designed to encourage assimilation and fend off allegations of un-American disloyalty.

But I only began to understand that process of acculturation—both personal and historical—while living in Israel. Until a sabbatical year in Jerusalem, prompted by an exciting trip to Israel designed for "disaffected Jewish academics," Judaism had been little more than a minor inconvenience, easily disregarded. But once I inhabited Jewish space and time, questions about Jewish identity began to refocus my historical inquiry (and, indeed, transform my life). Over time, my experiences as a wandering American Jew refocused the trajectory of my research and writing, pulling me inexorably from American law to American Jewish history and, ultimately, to the history of Israel.

As I navigated my way—geographically, emotionally, and intellectually—between the United States and the Jewish state, I encountered the Jewish identity dilemmas of modernity. In the United States rabbis and lawyers had developed a persuasive synthesis of Judaism and Americanism that promised to erase any semblance of contradiction between a good Jew and a loyal American. But Israel had threatened to undermine their security as Americans. Was their American home compatible with the Jewish homeland? Were American Jews "one" with Israel? To be sure, Israelis struggled with their own Jewish and national identities. Was Israel a state like any other (as Theodor Herzl had dreamed), a Jewish state, a state of Jews, a democratic Jewish state? These issues engaged my attention as a historian because they had emerged at the forefront of my own life.

Jerusalem became my surrogate home but a fortuitous journey brought me to Hebron. In this most ancient Jewish holy city in the biblical land of Israel, where the patriarchs and matriarchs of the Jewish people are buried, I felt the extraordinary power of Jewish memory. There I also encountered the most relentlessly reviled Jews in the world, the "zealots" who comprised the vanguard of the Jewish settlement movement following the Six-Day War. My encounters on the newest Zionist frontier redirected my scholarship once again, eventually yielding the first published history of the 3,000 year-old Jewish community of Hebron.

Along the way, I was exceedingly fortunate to teach (for forty years) in an elite undergraduate college, where I could mentor intelligent young women who were eager to learn. But Wellesley, still a bastion of Christian privilege a century after its founding, continued to experience (and demurely tolerate) dismaying episodes of anti-Semitism. How ironic that Wellesley and Israel, each in its own distinctive way, had converged to liberate me from my past as a non-Jewish Jew.

Regardless of the subject—law, modern American history, Pueblo Indians, American Judaism, Israel—deference to the conventional wisdom never had been my style. I always enjoyed the stimulation of writing against the grain: discovering hidden meanings, challenging historical and political pieties, and exposing the self-serving ideology that often lurked beneath self-evident truths. Providing intellectual catnip, it also enabled me to reach readers far beyond the narrow confines of academic journals.

My creative work always was done in the solitude of my study, my sanctum within my home. Enclosed within the treasured artifacts, maps, photographs, prints, and books accumulated during decades of research and travel, I explored the historical past that both inspired and reflected my own intellectual trajectory. Virtually every book I have written, to my genuine surprise, contained within it the seed of its successor. That, of course, is discernible only with hindsight—which, after all, is the distinctive attribute of a historian. I invite my family, friends, and interested readers to accompany me to some favorite destinations during my journey.

I · Law and Society

The writing of legal history once was an arcane specialty reserved for a handful of reverential chroniclers. But law has come to be recognized as a social institution, reflecting the values of the society in which it is embedded. As a historian for whom this understanding was formative, my challenge was to locate the modern American legal profession in its historical and social context: the emergence of an urban industrial society, with an economy increasingly dominated by large corporations; a population dramatically transformed by unprecedented waves of immigration; and the increasing power of the regulatory state. These sweeping social changes between 1890-1940, which jarred American society loose from its Protestant, agrarian and small-town past, profoundly impacted the structure and values of the American legal profession, and opportunities for success within it.

The legal profession has long provided a vital channel of social mobility in American society—but not for every aspirant. Pluck and luck might have elevated Horatio Alger from rags to riches, at least in popular mythology, but well into the 20th century professional opportunity was closely correlated with family background, social (and financial) capital, and elite educational certification. Who one was—Protestant or Jew, white or black, man or woman—largely determined educational and professional possibilities, fields of legal specialization, professional status, and the power, influence, and wealth that accrued to those who succeeded.

The sources and consequences of professional stratification attracted my attention and framed my writing. As I moved backward and forward in time through the 20th century, my focus included corporate lawyers who formed the self-defined professional elite, law teachers who trained its aspirants, and the ethnic and social underclass that was long consigned to the professional margins. Scrutinizing the internal mores of the legal culture I discovered a profession that was exceedingly reluctant to moderate its entrenched elitism with democratic opportunity—and often fought off that challenge. Bar critics, in turn, wondered whether specialized service to wealthy corporate clients could be reconciled with the public interest.

The American legal profession has reflected the values of the culture in which it is so deeply embedded. Whether the result was equal justice under law, or unequal justice under lawyers, was the question that the following essays addressed. The answer, as in any legal encounter, was sharply contested.

1 · The Best Men and the Best Opportunities

As the United States moved uneasily but irrevocably from its homogeneous, rural, agrarian past to its heterogeneous, urban, industrial future, its legal institutions were afflicted with cultural lag. In impassioned language which captured the cadences of turn-of-the-century professional rhetoric, Dean Roscoe Pound of Harvard Law School described in 1912 a legal system already shackled by principles suitable only to small-town life. The principles endured, but the society that once had been comfortably governed by them no longer existed. It was virtually impossible, Pound wrote, to apply traditional legal doctrine "in a heterogeneous community, divided into classes with divergent interests, which understand each other none too well, containing elements hostile to government and order, elements ignorant of our institutions...." This was especially true of a community "where the defective, the degenerate of decadent stocks, and the ignorant or enfeebled victim of severe economic pressure are exposed to temptations and afforded opportunities beyond anything our fathers could have conceived...."

The professional implications were ominous. Like American society, the legal profession abided by nineteenth-century values; indeed soon after the twentieth century began, it vigorously reasserted these in its Canons of Ethics. Like that society, it had become more heterogeneous and stratified; hence its reverence for antebellum simplicity and its effort to recapture it. If social tranquility was undercut by corporate power and by a proliferating *lumpen* class of immigrants, professional harmony was likewise destroyed by the emergence of corporate law firms and by a professional underclass drawn from the immigrant communities. As society confronted conflict and disorder, members of the legal profession voiced unease over the declining force of law—and the declining stature of lawyers. Profession and society: each wrenched by change; each crippled in its choice of means to cope with change by its tenacious hold on the past. Until lawyers could discard their myths and memories, their profession would teeter precariously between the world that was lost and the world that was becoming—unable to relinquish one; unable, therefore, to enter the other.

Even before the nineteenth century ended, the legal profession seemed far removed from any golden age. Lord Bryce, another aristocratic visitor to the United States, found a weakened sense of professional dignity and "a latent

Unequal Justice: Lawyers and Social Change in Modern America (1976), 17-39.

and sometimes an open hostility between the better kind of lawyers and the impulses of the masses." In contrast to its stature in an earlier day, he concluded in 1888, the bar "counts for less as a guiding and restraining power." At one extreme, the growth of a moneyed class had diminished the prestige of professional men; at the other, mass education had narrowed the distance between the multitude and the profession. Tocqueville's America had disappeared; worse yet, during the last decade of the century social cataclysm seemed imminent. American society was rent by a severe economic depression, agrarian and labor unrest, attacks on corporate power and private wealth, a vigorous third-party challenge, labor-management conflict, and a violent defense of the new industrial order waged by private and public armies in behalf of business interests. Legal instruments of social control, ranging from injunctions to the police, were pressed into service. The judiciary vigorously defended private property against the regulatory efforts of legislative majorities. Supreme Court decisions voiding the federal income tax law and upholding an injunction issued against workers during the Pullman strike in 1894 precipitated a "conservative crisis" which split the legal profession. Bench and bar divided over the Court's sweeping assertion of judicial prerogatives and its application of law as an instrument of class advantage.

With McKinley's victory over Bryan in 1896 the national crisis subsided. But the crisis in the legal profession had barely begun. Fed by converging currents of ethnic and economic conflict, it swept through professional life during the first three decades of the twentieth century—until the Great Depression jolted the profession into new concerns. Ethnic homogeneity had been one of the salient characteristics of the legal profession during most of the nineteenth century. Daniel Webster, defending the interests of the Second Bank of the United States before the Supreme Court, might share little in common in his daily professional life with the rambunctious country practitioner so evocatively depicted in Joseph Baldwin's *Sketches of the Flush Times of Alabama*. But as native American Protestant lawyers, they not only shared a heritage defined by centuries of Anglo-Saxon legal development but a common national cultural experience. Embodied in social and legal institutions, it was—in a distinctly proprietary sense—*theirs* to honor and to perpetuate. It was the cement that held otherwise disparate attorneys fast to each other. Stratified by education, wealth, power, and style, Tocqueville's aristocrat and the country lawyer nonetheless belonged to one society, one culture, one past. But by 1900, lawyers no longer could inhabit such a homogeneous national and professional culture because it no longer existed.

With accelerating momentum in the second half of the nineteenth century, the traditional, cohesive social structure was threatened with disintegration. Industrialization, urbanization, and immigration were the forces weakening the foundations of agrarian, rural, Protestant America. There were varied and complex responses to this process of social and cultural subversion. Some Americans vigorously reasserted traditional values. Others experimented with new instruments of social control and order. Still others created privileged sanctuaries for the "best" people and their progeny. Legal institutions and the legal profession were profoundly affected by these developments.

The city and the immigrant frightened respectable, middle-class, American-born professional and business people. The city was the sordid home of criminality, corruption, vice, disease, and delinquency; the immigrant was the presumed carrier of these contagious social germs. Both needed cleansing with the values of rural Protestantism. New controls over deviance were devised to assuage xenophobic fears. Incarceration was one response. Prisons, reformatories, asylums, and almshouses became "a dumping ground for social undesirables." They were filled with a disproportionate number of inmates drawn from the foreign-born and urban lower-class population—the "dangerous classes." Children from urban slums were "saved" by removing them to rural reformatories where thrift, discipline, and hard work were taught. Delinquency was "invented" and child-saving was practiced to preserve parental authority, family stability, and the work ethic as defined by native-born middle-class Americans. Here, perhaps, were the most extreme nativist responses to foreign ideologies. But even "progressive" reforms were tinged with xenophobia: women's suffrage might counteract the immigrant male vote; prohibition would circumscribe immigrant pleasures; good government could defeat immigrant bosses and restore the "best men" to political power; vice control imposed censorship in the name of rural innocence; and education reform socialized the children of the immigrant poor. Quite aggressively, native Americans attempted to retain the values of a pristine, arcadian past destroyed by immigrants in an urban industrial society.

Besieged Americans not only created coercive institutions for recalcitrant outsiders; they built sanctuaries from which they could assert their own values against the infidels, and retreated to them. Capital eased the task for some. As mass immigration and urbanization inundated the dominant Anglo-Saxon culture, the fortunate few moved to the safety of selected social institutions—Eastern schools, for example, and careers in business and finance—which could protect, or extend, their power and status. As immigrants gained political control in cities, native Americans took refuge in business careers. Big business served as "a new preserve of the older Americans, where their status and influence could continue and flourish.... The social patterns established within Big Business bureaucracies at the turn of the century helped to close off key areas of the economy and to keep them virtually impenetrable to even the most gifted outsiders."

The emergence and proliferation of corporation law firms at the turn of the century provided those lawyers who possessed appropriate social, religious, and ethnic credentials with an opportunity to secure personal power and to shape the future of their profession. These lawyers were not conspirators who subverted either law or society. They were propelled by the same social and economic forces that were transforming American civilization. They capitalized upon historical circumstance to hitch professional values, which they were advantageously located to define, to the service of social stratification and corporate profit. The corporate law firm was their fortress. Its priorities—more precisely, the priorities of its clientele—shaped professional education, career patterns, ethics, mobility, and the availability and distribution of legal services—indeed, the very meaning of law and justice. It functioned as a prism, refracting social change upon the professional culture and back again to the larger society.

Only lawyers who possessed "considerable *social* capital" could inhabit the corporate law firm world. Born in the East to old American families of British lineage, they were college graduates (a distinct rarity) who followed their fathers into business and professional careers. They molded the law firm to resemble the corporation; both restricted access to those who presented proper ethnic and social credentials. According to folklore, the doors of access to the legal profession always swung open to anyone stung by ambition; lawyers might prefer a restricted guild, but democratic realities required them to settle for less. But this is a half-truth, which conceals the fact that doors to particular legal careers required keys that were distributed according to race, religion, sex, and ethnicity. Myths notwithstanding, mobility was not a ladder whose rungs all could climb; for outsiders a career in a Wall Street, State Street, Market Street, or LaSalle Street firm was "more like scaling a wall than climbing a ladder." Immigrant and farm boys who became corporation lawyers in prestigious firms, like those who became business leaders, "have always been more conspicuous in American history books than in American history."

By the turn of the century corporate law firms were edging to the pinnacle of professional aspiration and power. Structurally the legal profession still was, and would long remain, "mostly a cottage industry of single practitioners." But the emergence, rapid proliferation, and growth of corporate law firms, their impact upon patterns of recruitment and styles of practice, and their appeal to ambitious young attorneys invested them with significance (and their partners with professional power) that far exceeded their number and size. As early as 1900 the corporate firm expressed the palpable stratification of professional life and the application of professional expertise to the service of particular values and interests in an urban industrial society. It is necessary to understand the values it defended, the services it provided, the opportunities it created, the power it accumulated—and the concern that it elicited.

Corporate law firms were creatures of an age of organization. They reflected the needs of the most powerful institutions within the new urban industrial society. With business enterprise growing in size and complexity, and government by legislation and administration accelerating in tempo, the resolution of disputes required the preventive techniques of the counselor who spoke to the future rather than the forensic skill of the advocate who litigated the mistakes of the past. Business corporations needed efficient organizations to service them, a need which nineteenth-century law firms could not meet. Few in number, the older firms were indistinguishable in organization and competence from the traditional two-man law office. Dimly lit, lacking telephones and typewriters, staffed at most by a stenographer and a clerk, they were suited to unhurried times and to small claims. Corporate law firms—organized, departmentalized, and routinized—filled the vacuum. To contemporaries they were as appropriate (and, to some, as menacing) an expression of the age as their most conspicuous clients. In an era whose dominant impulses were rationalization, specialization, and professionalization they epitomized the search for order in a complex society.

Corporate lawyers became the new professional men of the new century. Their "flair for figures, passion for facts and more facts, and insistence on realistic economic analysis rather than polished rhetoric, literary allusion or poetical quotation" set them apart. Renowned for their mastery of the intricacies of corporate finance, they earned their reputations for work done at their desks and in conference rooms, not in court. Attuned to the accelerated pace of business activity, they were described even by admirers as "high-strung, tense, and driving personalities." The prototype of the new breed was Paul D. Cravath. As clerk to Walter S. Carter, an early titan of the corporate bar, Cravath had grasped the responsibilities and opportunities of law practice in a new era. When Cravath left Carter to join the Seward firm in 1899, he instituted the "Cravath System," which quickly spread as the model for other firms.

Until Cravath arrived, the Seward partners worked independently of each other; the firm, less than the sum of its parts, lacked members with sufficient business acumen to serve its corporate clients adequately. By molding the firm into a "cohesive team," and by providing for an ever-replenished source of talented specialists in newer fields like securities, taxation, and reorganization, Cravath built a dynamic, efficient firm from a sputtering partnership. Systematic recruitment and training formed the lynchpin of the Cravath system. Cravath learned from Carter the advantages of hiring recent law-school graduates. As Carter explained: "I thought the best way to get a good lawyer was to make him to order, instead of getting him ready-made." No longer did friendship with a client or a partner automatically qualify a lawyer for firm membership. New recruits followed a carefully prescribed path: college (perhaps Phi Beta Kappa); Harvard, Yale, or Columbia law school; preferably a law review editorship. In addition to academic credentials they were expected to possess "warmth and force of personality" and "physical stamina."

Once inside the firm, Cravath men were trained methodically as generalists before being entrusted with the responsibilities of specialty practice. According to the firm historian, they were "not thrown into deep water and told to swim; rather, they are taken into shallow water and carefully taught strokes." Those who swam with demonstrated competence were rewarded with responsibility until, after approximately five years, they earned the ultimate reward of partnership. Cravath's insistence upon selecting partners from within the firm reflected his conviction "that the office and its clients would get the best service from men confident of unimpeded opportunity for advancement"—and, doubtlessly, his belief in the efficacy of strenuous competition. Cravath men were made to understand that the practice of law must be their "primary interest" and that all business transacted in the office was Cravath business. The nature of this business was clear: "The practice of the office is essentially a civil business practice.

Cravath desired a staff equipped to serve corporate and banking clients in any of their legal problems." By 1910 the Cravath system, widely emulated, dominated the expanding world of corporate law firms.

Underlying the Cravath system was the assumption that business practice within a law firm would attract and hold the ablest graduates of leading law schools. The assumption was valid. Young lawyers responded with alacrity to the challenge and income that awaited them in metropolitan corporate practice. The rewards were ample. Within five years after their graduation from law school lawyers in the larger cities, where corporate work was concentrated, were earning considerably more than their less urban brethren; an alumnus of Harvard reported that the lawyer who derived satisfaction *"from merely being in touch with big things and big business"* had no excuse for unhappiness in New York practice. There was always the possibility, Elihu Root told the graduating class at Yale Law School in 1904, that the truly successful lawyer might win "some prize of business life" and become a corporation president. Even those who remained in corporate practice could derive solace from reports that William D. Guthrie earned a million-dollar fee—at a time when two-thirds of the lawyers in New York City earned less lean $3,000 annually and two thousand Chicago lawyers had incomes lower than union brickmasons. As Charles Evans Hughes observed of the New York bar at the close of the nineteenth century: "These highly privileged firms seem to hold in an enduring grasp the best professional opportunities...."

Only the best men, however, were permitted to seize the best opportunities. There was, as Hughes also noted, "little room for young aspirants outside the favored groups." Barriers to access became more formidable as the desirability of access increased. Young men, doubtlessly nurtured on the belief that success rewarded perseverance and integrity, learned that professional opportunity depended upon ethnic, social, religious, and educational credentials. A Columbia graduate (later an appellate division judge) realized that "the doors of most New York law offices were closed, with rare exceptions, to a young Jewish lawyer." Even John Foster Dulles, who in time would qualify for partnership in Sullivan & Cromwell, vainly applied for a position with eminent New York firms only to discover that a law degree from Harvard or Columbia was preferred to his own from George Washington University. Impoverished applicants were advised to avoid combining day work with night law classes because only university law schools offered access to desirable professional positions. Certain areas of practice receded into the professional shadows cast by corporate work. "It is a reproach in our profession and in the community," wrote Samuel Untermeyer, "for a man practicing law in the city of New York to be regarded as essentially a criminal lawyer.... Unlike the custom of former days no man with large corporate interests to protect would think of going to a man however eminent and learned in the law, whose reputation had been achieved as a criminal lawyer." The point was succinctly made by a Cravath partner, who told a neophyte interested in litigation not to come to New York: "The business connected with corporations and general office practice is much more profitable and satisfactory and you will find that the better class of men at our Bar prefer work in that line." Another attorney described the stratification of the New York bar into constitutional lawyers, corporation lawyers, and collection lawyers. Cromwells and Cravaths rose to the top; "Hebrews" sank to the bottom.

There were, of course, conspicuous examples of nonconformity. Felix Frankfurter spurned private practice after brief exposure to it because it meant nothing more than "putting one's time to put money in other people's pockets"; he complained that "the intellectual process involved does not sufficiently appeal to me to make me forget the ultimate end." Similarly, Henry L. Stimson grew disenchanted with the business transactions that consumed his energy in Elihu Root's firm. When the accelerated pace of federal regulation under Theodore Roosevelt's Square Deal expanded the need for government lawyers, Stimson left the firm to become a United States attorney. "The profession of law was never thoroughly satisfactory to me," he told his Yale classmates in 1908, "because the life of the ordinary New York lawyer is primarily and essentially devoted to the making of money...." New York practice doubtlessly exacerbated such feelings, but the phenomenon knew no geographical bounds. Progressive reformer Frederic C. Howe, partner in a Cleveland firm whose clients were drawn primarily from railroads, banks, and manufacturing companies, deserted law practice entirely; he wrote in his autobiography, "I never overcame my dislike of the profession and got little enjoyment out of such success as I achieved."

Yet those who left, no less than those who remained, testified to the growing professional dominance of the corporate firm. When Stimson left the United States attorney's office he was reassured that "a high stand in private business is worth more than too much public office," and he was reminded that "more happiness and money" surely awaited him in practice. A law student's magazine, commenting upon James Beck's departure from the Justice Department for a Wall Street firm, casually dismissed notions of public service: "Most any man can hold a government position.... If the government wants good men let it pay for them. That is business." One of Frankfurter's Harvard professors reminded his eccentric pupil that "most young men have a right to have in mind the pecuniary needs of later life," which government work could not satisfy. But a friend, taking the opposite tack, urged Frankfurter to remain in government at least temporarily—and justified his suggestion with the prescient observation that public service might translate itself into a larger income upon return to private practice.

The Anglo-Saxon Protestant retreat to corporate enclaves was facilitated by changing patterns of legal education, which enabled corporate firms to camouflage their prejudices under the cover of academic achievement. By the turn of the century university law schools were assuming a substantial share of the burden of legal education. Law teaching was professionalized, and a standardized curriculum, emphasizing the staples of business practice, was instituted. Most significantly, corporate practitioners accepted student certification and ranking by law teachers—especially after grades became convertible into law review experience. Once Harvard blazed the trail in 1887, the proliferation of law reviews helped to certify a professional meritocracy and to systematize hitherto random hiring practices. In special circumstances lawyers like Stimson and Frankfurter communicated directly with law teachers to obtain the pick of well-stocked university law school talent pools. A strong nexus developed between law firms and law schools. An inexorable channeling process directed those lawyers designated as "best" into law firms that served the new corporate elite. Lawyers, by serving that elite, joined it.

If academic merit alone had defined "best," the result would have been a truly democratic meritocracy in which elites circulated to reflect the shifting social base of American society. But this hypothetical model did not accurately depict reality, although most lawyers doubtlessly believed that it did. None defended it more vigorously than Felix Frankfurter when he reminisced about Harvard Law School, where he was a student between 1903 and 1906, a law review editor, and then a member of the faculty for a quarter of a century. Frankfurter sang paeans to "the democratic spirit" of the institution and to its ranking process:

> ...rich man, poor man were just irrelevant.... The thing that mattered was what you did professionally.... The very good men were defined by the fact that they got on the *Harvard Law Review*.... All this big talk about "leadership" and character, and all the other things that are non-ascertainable, but usually are high-falutin' expressions for personal likes and dislikes, or class, or color, or religious partialities or antipathies— they were all out.... There was never a problem whether a Jew or a Negro should get on the *Law Review*. If they excelled academically, they would just go on automatically.

By restricting his scrutiny to the academic basis of selection to the Harvard Law Review, however, Frankfurter overlooked *social* filters which functioned at antecedent and subsequent stages to deplete drastically the pool from which the *Law Review* meritocracy, and law firm partners, were chosen.

Frankfurter described Harvard law students with alluring simplicity: "They were rich and poor." Yet, ironically, Harvard was the worst example Frankfurter could have chosen to make his point because it was, until 1916, the only law school to require a college degree for admission. Among Frankfurter's American contemporaries, born between 1885 and 1889 and likely to enter law school between 1905 and 1910, fewer than 4 percent finished high school *and* college (while approximately 20 percent finished high school). Harvard's admission requirement effectively eliminated 96 percent of the eligible population from *consideration*; admissions policies at less exclusive university law schools eliminated 80 percent. Restrictions based upon sex, race, ethnicity, class, and family background permeated the admissions process. The school excluded women. The financial expense of undergraduate and legal education, in addition to the substantial loss of income during the seven years required to earn two degrees, eliminated the most impoverished, among whom racial and ethnic minority group members were disproportionately concentrated. In theory, professional education was open to all who qualified. In fact, rich and poor enjoyed

"Anatole France equity" (both being forbidden to beg or sleep in public parks). University law schools, like their undergraduate branches, remained "especially open...to children of northern European origin whose fathers did not work with their hands." Frankfurter, the Austrian-born son of Jewish immigrant parents, was the conspicuous exception, not the prototypical product of a democratic meritocracy. His analysis was correct as far as it went, but it stopped too soon. The Jew or black who excelled academically *would* become a law review editor. But the critical question was whether a Jew, a black, a woman, or the Polish Catholic son of a day laborer could first qualify for admission to the school.

Even assuming that equal opportunity for a law review editorship existed—a false proposition—possession of the coveted honor was not legal tender for every holder. Frankfurter overlooked the law firm selection process just as he ignored the law school admission process. Again, with some conspicuous exceptions to the contrary, Jewish law review editors were excluded from partnerships in the prestigious corporate law firms until after World War II; blacks and women were outsiders until their token entry in the late 1960's and early 1970's; and other ethnic minority group members have barely begun to gain entry. Consequently, Protestant partners in these firms comprised the professional elite; comprising it, they defined it; defining it, they excluded non-whites, non-males, and non-Christians. Academic achievement was necessary, but insufficient, for entry. Social origins, together with racial, gender, and ethnic identity, determined both the possibility of academic achievement and the opportunity to reap its rewards. The Wall Street firm, and its counterpart in other cities, was the crucial link between corporate capitalism and social elitism within the legal profession.

Harvard Law School and legal education were neither synonymous nor coextensive—although the Harvard model dominated university law training. Similarly, there was more to the legal profession than corporate lawyers; indeed, only "a handful" of lawyers held large-firm partnerships around the turn of the century, and nearly half a century *later* the bar remained "a profession of highly individualistic practitioners," organized in 1940 as it had been organized in 1840. But the newer corporate firms, as legal historian Willard Hurst has observed, "symbolized a new role of the bar. They reflected the demands of big business clients." If their numbers were small, their power—economically and professionally—was considerable. As yet, they barely resembled the Wall Street firms that would dominate corporate practice in later years. The dangers of retrospective projections of size, organization, and efficiency are obvious. In 1903, when, James Beck left the government for Shearman and Sterling, which became a giant among giants, he described the advantages of a partnership in a "small firm." That same year Samuel Untermeyer complained of the chaos in Guggenheimer, Untermeyer & Marshall. With a trial pending one afternoon he discovered "absolutely no preparation"—no statement of facts, no brief, no list of witnesses. "I find to my amazement," he told his partner, "that there is not a soul in the office who knows anything about this case...." Yet measured by the experiences and expectations of contemporaries, these firms and their partners represented a sharp break with the past and an omen for the future. In Richmond, Virginia, where only one firm in 1901 had as many as three members, the organization of a four-man firm elicited comparison with "the larger New York law concerns that are equipped for handling all legal matters." Evidence of their small size, occasional disorganization, or minuscule numerical beachhead within the profession could not eradicate concern that one age had ended and a newer, menacing era of concentrated economic power had begun.

The invective directed against corporate lawyers and their firms was embellished by rhetoric that doubtlessly exaggerated their presence. But the fear that generated the rhetoric was deeply rooted in the realities of twentieth-century life. The size of law firms did not matter; it was the service they provided, and the clientele they served, that elicited distress. The looming presence of the metropolitan firm made many lawyers uneasy because no other institution so accurately reflected the altered contours of professional and economic life in the new century. With nostalgic fervor they harked back to an earlier day of presumed professional esteem—a day invariably located in the pre-urban, pre-industrial past. The independent small-town lawyer, whose clients were his friends, acquaintances, and townsmen, could not comprehend the mores of the austere partner who counseled corporations, not people. Even some city lawyers echoed that discomfort. A Detroit attorney advised the graduates of Michigan Law School in 1902 to seek employment in a country lawyer's office. "You will learn more there in a year than you will in a city office in five years." City practice, he cautioned, was a "great mistake." A New York judge insisted that for training and self-reliance the old-time lawyer "is as far superior to the average modern lawyer as the self-sufficient pioneer is above the dweller in the city." In a revealing metaphor the modern firm was described as "a money-making mechanism, inelastic, rigorous, unsympathetic; into which the young man, just from his studies, fits...like a fresh adjusted cog into a well-oiled machine."

Corporate lawyers presented the most visible target for critics within and outside the profession. As the symbol of change this new legal elite drew the fire of those whose notions of professional propriety were shaped by images, whether real or imagined, derived from an earlier era of professionalism. Critics used the legal profession as a surrogate for society. By attacking corporate lawyers and a commercialized profession they could displace some of the anger, fear, and resentment stirred by their perception of the declining quality of life in an urban industrial age. Once the corporation became the object of public scrutiny and then the target of public hostility, as it increasingly did after the turn of the century, the new professional elite was vulnerable. The private corporation, a legal "person" entitled not to be deprived of its liberty or property without due process of law, owed its legal existence and therefore much of its social power to the innovative skills of lawyers and judges. Their reworking of the Fourteenth Amendment into a shield for corporate power had met the wishes of a society whose brief concern for freed slaves had yielded to a more enduring concern for free enterprise. But lawyers became identified in the public mind with the corporate clients whose interests they served. It was hardly possible to pillory malefactors of great wealth yet ignore those who counseled the malefactors.

The lawyer as surrogate for the corporation presented an alluring target. Thorstein Veblen, writing in 1899, concluded that the profession of law was nothing more than a form of employment "immediately subservient to ownership and financiering.... The lawyer is exclusively occupied with the details of predatory fraud, either in achieving or in checkmating chicane, and success in the profession is therefore accepted as marking a large endowment of that barbarian astuteness which has always commanded men's respect and fear." Journalist Herbert Croly, describing the betrayed promise of American life, insisted that the lawyer was no longer qualified to interpret and guide American constitutional democracy because he had abdicated his role as representative citizen to defend special interests. Perhaps the unkindest cut came from President Theodore Roosevelt, once a student at Columbia Law School, who delivered an address at Harvard in 1905 sharply critical of the new professional elite. "Many of the most influential and most highly remunerated members of the bar in every centre of wealth," Roosevelt charged, "make it their special task to work out bold and ingenious schemes by which their very wealthy clients, individual or corporate, can evade the laws which are made to regulate in the interest of the public the use of great wealth." These lawyers, Roosevelt concluded, were encouraging the growth of "a spirit of dumb anger against all laws and of disbelief in their efficacy."

An acute sense of loss pervaded the legal profession during the early years of the new century. In a representative complaint, John R. Dos Passos described "a transformation from a profession to a business." For Dos Passos the Civil War divided the old order from the new. The postbellum years represented not only an era of change but of "intellectual decadence" in the bar. The lawyer's "aristocratic and social prestige" had disappeared; his "moral and intellectual standard has been lowered;" dignity, learning, and influence had declined. Once the lawyer had been a cultured man who was treated with deference, observed Theron G. Strong, member of a Connecticut family of lawyers dating back to the Revolution. But "the incursion of the money-making power" had robbed the lawyer of his stature and self-respect. Furthermore, "many of the best-equipped lawyers of the present day are to all intents and purposes owned by the great corporate and individual interests they represent, and while enormous fees result they are dearly earned by the surrender of individual independence." James Hamilton Lewis, who mourned "the end of lawyers," observed sadly that "the lawyer who is but a lawyer, however talented, learned, and refined, must take second place beside the director of the company for which he is counsel or beside the client who is rich."

With independence undermined, influence must deteriorate. Lawyers were richer, corporate attorney Edward M. Shepard told the New Hampshire Bar Association in 1906, but their public influence had diminished. In the nineteenth century, Shepard claimed, lawyers had wisely refused to commit their professional skills to the interests of any single client or type of client. But corporate needs imposed irresistible pressures upon the profession. The more lawyers counseled corporations the less public esteem the bar retained. Harlan F. Stone, delivering the Hewitt lectures at Columbia University, referred to "a deterioration of our bar both in its personnel, its corporate morale, and, consequently, in the public influence wielded by it; and...this deterioration has been very considerably accelerated during the present generation." Stone expressed unease over the leadership of the business lawyer, skillful and resourceful at his best, but at his worst "the mere hired man of corporations." Woodrow Wilson, speaking to the American Bar Association in 1910, contrasted the golden past with the sordid present. Principled lawyers had once offered disinterested service to the community. But American society, Wilson observed, "has lost something or is losing it...." The constitutional advocate, once the pride of the profession, had virtually disappeared. In his place stood "lawyers who have been sucked into the maelstrom of the new business system of the country.... They do not practice law. They do not handle the general, miscellaneous interests of society. They are not general counsellors of right and obligation." The modern lawyer, Wilson declared, counseled individuals, not the community. "He does not play the part he used to play. He does not show the spirit in affairs he used to show. He does not do what he ought to do." Worse yet, lawyers did what they ought not to do: as corporate counsel they applied their skills to the destruction of the old order. They were "intimate counsel in all that has been going on. The country holds them largely responsible for it. It distrusts every 'corporation lawyer.'" Wilson hoped to "recall lawyers to the service of the nation as a whole," but his remarks offered scant solace to those who may have shared his wish.

No lawyer articulated this sense of concern with greater precision than Louis D. Brandeis. In an address to Harvard undergraduates in the spring of 1905, he attributed declining popular esteem for the bar to the lawyer's fall from independence. "Instead of holding a position of independence, between the wealthy and the people, prepared to curb the excesses of either, able lawyers have, to a great extent, allowed themselves to become adjuncts of great corporations and have neglected their obligation to use their powers for the protection of the people. We hear much of the 'corporation lawyer,' and far too little of the 'people's lawyer.'" For nearly a generation, Brandeis claimed, leaders of the bar had opposed constructive legislative proposals in the public interest, while failing to oppose legislation in behalf of "selfish interests."

Wilson and Brandeis: moralists in politics and in law. Both men had launched public careers whose rallying cry would be a new freedom based upon the restoration of old values. Community cohesion, stability, and fixed principles of "right and obligation" characterized the old order, which the "new business system" had undermined. The destructive power of corporate capitalism fed their unease and drew their fire. Corporation lawyers incurred mistrust, not because they were inherently venal, but because, in contemporary reform rhetoric, corporate interests were *ipso facto* antithetical to social interests. By definition, lawyers who counseled corporations were derelict in their social obligations. The language varied, but the meaning remained despairingly constant. Tocqueville's aristocrat, to say nothing of the country lawyer, was unrecognizable as Stone's "hired man," or as Brandeis' "adjunct." The omnipresent corporation seemed to hold the lawyer's professional soul in its grasp; he no longer commanded the respect that accompanied professional detachment. In the heyday of the new corporate lawyer, when James C. Carter, William D. Guthrie, and Paul Cravath served as models for aspiring neophytes, an old-timer sadly complained that "the American Plutarch will find little material for his pen in the lives of modern lawyers, but among the lives of bankers, manufacturers, pioneers, railroad men and other men of business, material of the richest sort awaits him."

Corporate lawyers were not indifferent to these jeremiads, but neither were they persuaded by them. In their struggle for professional acceptance they enjoyed important advantages. Above all, they rode the rising tide of national economic development. In addition, their corporate clients, facing the common enemy of governmental regulation, demanded the efficient services that cohesive law firms were best able to provide. Furthermore, just as they shared bonds of social origin, education, religious affiliation, and club membership with corporation managers, their relationship with university law schools assured a perpetual flow of talent to meet the needs of their clients. Finally, bar associations, in which they wielded power disproportionate to their professional numbers, provided an organizational base for their interests, a forum for their views, and leverage for the implementation of their programs. Unwilling to be confined to nineteenth-century molds, unafraid of corporate power, and eager to confront the challenges of organization and control in modern society, they committed their professional energies to the service of industrial capitalism. At bar association meetings and in professional journals they flung the gauntlet of criticism back at their detractors.

James B. Dill, a prototype of the new corporate lawyer (he enjoyed a lucrative New York practice, drafted the New Jersey holding company and incorporation statutes, and advised Theodore Roosevelt on trust policy), asserted that the successful modern lawyer no longer was the last resort of a businessman facing destruction, but his constant consultant at every stage of business enterprise. Consequently, "the more nearly the lawyer brings his profession into touch with business methods the greater will be his success, and the profession is to-day [1903] beginning to realize the fact and to act upon it." The corporation lawyer had evolved as the necessary counterpart of the corporation manager. "Yes," Dill concluded, "law is a business, and if the young man wants to practice it, the sooner he makes up his mind to do so with an eye single to some particular branch of it, the better lawyer will be become." Defenders of the old order might chastise Dill for deflecting aspiring lawyers from traditional professional ideals, but Dill's call for specialization and business methods found many echoes in professional circles.

In one city after another, corporate lawyers repudiated the notion of professional decline, asserting that never before had talented practitioners enjoyed such abundant opportunities. None of them disputed the *fact* of change; their disagreement was over the *quality* of change. "Let the flamboyant orator and the sensational newspaper writer say what they will," declared Henry Wollman of New York, "there never was a time when lawyers, as a class, were so genuinely respected and looked up to and trusted as they are now." A commercial age inevitably produced commercial lawyers; instead of lamenting this development the bar might point with pride to lawyer-presidents of the Union Pacific Railroad, United States Steel, United States Rubber, and the International Paper Company and conclude, with Wollman, that "there never has been a time when so many lawyers have been called...to fill so many places of enormous responsibility." Levy Mayer of Chicago asked a familiar question: "Is the lawyer of today a mere material tool of commercialism, narrow in mind, lacking in logic, and deficient in legal acumen?" His answer, like Wollman's, was vigorously negative. The modern lawyer was indeed more businesslike than his mid-nineteenth-century counterpart, but he also was better educated, better equipped, and more skilled.

Many attorneys stood the argument of the Cassandras on its head, asserting that the role of the lawyer in business affairs reflected his *ascending* position and power. They saw new opportunities for the lawyer who could cope with modern conditions. Charles W. Needham, assistant solicitor for the Interstate Commerce Commission, observed that "new conditions in social and political life demand new types of men, or at least, men of special training and equipment." A New York lawyer reassured Cornell law students that the change from advocacy to counseling did not signify professional deterioration; rather it meant that lawyers had learned to adjust their skills to changing social conditions. Edward P. White, another New Yorker, spoke unselfconsciously about the "law business," asserting that lawyers had much to learn from businessmen. The commercial spirit, he declared euphorically, "transforms barren abstractions into fruitful realities. It is essentially just...and it is inspiring because it deals with things and not theories." White implored his professional brethren to "get in touch with business men and in sympathy with business methods so that we can be of real assistance in carrying on business enterprises." Few lawyers were as indecorous as White, who bluntly asserted that "the profits of the business [man] are our most practical concern." But many, aware of changes in the lawyer's role, refused to equate change with decline.

Knowledge of opportunities in corporate practice spread quickly through the profession. Within a decade, declared Dean Harry S. Richards of the Wisconsin Law School in 1914, "an entirely new field of usefulness for the lawyer has been created, and its boundaries are not yet fixed." Professional opportunity was greater than ever, he concluded, even if "the character of the business" had changed rapidly. The generational appeal of corporate practice was evident. "It is significant of the development of the Bar of our generation," wrote Julius Henry Cohen, "that the successful lawyers—the men who have attained supremacy—are men who combine business skill with the training of the law." The modern office lawyer, Cohen observed, must be both administrator and executive; in sum, "a business manager as well as an adviser to business men." In a society whose economic and political life increasingly reflected the power and values of corporate enterprise, the professional dominance of corporate lawyers was assured. So, too, was the evolving diversity of their roles: they were attorneys who were also business counselors, lobbyists, and public relations men. "Their new importance by the turn of the century," concludes one historian, "reflects the growth of bureaucratic managements typically in need of help in navigating legal and political labyrinths and in conciliating public groups often made hostile by the results."

The ascendancy of corporate lawyers marked a critical turning point in the emergence of the modern American legal profession. Capitalizing upon advantages conferred by corporate growth and ethnic stratification, they exerted professional leverage quite disproportionate to their numbers. As a pyramidal social structure based upon the ethnic identity of lawyers and the class interests of clients emerged within the legal profession, corporate lawyers, at the apex, associated professional responsibility with group interest. Responsive to the economic opportunities of the new age, they thrust themselves into professional leadership as the legal profession experienced the growing pains of modernization. Once in the ascendancy, the best men began to set their professional house in order and to set themselves resolutely against challenges to their own professional authority or to the political and economic power of their clients. Especially at the metropolitan bar, where corporate lawyers were concentrated, traditional folkways were unsuited to the changing demographic patterns, accelerating commercial pace, and shifting values of an urban industrial society. Within a generation the profession pulled away from the old moorings. Bar associations expressed an impulse toward professional cohesion. Bar admissions standards were tightened, and ethical norms were promulgated to define and deter deviance. University legal education, especially the case method, elevated academic excellence above practical experience and encouraged the professionalization of law teaching. Systematized recruitment patterns channeled the talent flow to corporate firms which provided comprehensive services to a restricted clientele. The transformation in structure and values was completed as the new elite guided the profession through the disruptive fluidity of the late nineteenth century to the uncertain stability of the early twentieth century and forged a new professional identity that would profoundly affect law and the administration of justice for decades to come.

2 · Lawyers and Clients

Toward the end of the nineteenth century, when Charles Evans Hughes and John W. Davis decided to practice law, the American legal profession had begun to experience the growing pains of modernization. ... Hughes and Davis ascended to eminence within the new professional culture. No professional honor and barely a high public office escaped their grasp. Hughes was Governor of New York, Associate Justice of the Supreme Court, Secretary of State, and Chief Justice of the United States. Davis was a congressman from West Virginia, Solicitor General, and Ambassador to England. They were presidents of the American Bar Association a year apart and, had a Republican been elected in 1916 and a Democrat in 1924, Davis might have followed Hughes to the White House. No Chief Justice after Marshall did more than Hughes to preserve the Supreme Court from attack upon its institutional power. No advocate after Webster argued more cases than Davis before the Court or won more glowing plaudits from its members. Hughes and Davis were the consummate statesmen of the legal profession in the first half of this century. Not only did the appellation "lawyer's lawyer" describe them; their personal and professional attributes virtually defined the accolade....

Hughes, the son of an upstate New York minister, was a precocious child and a voracious student who was driven relentlessly by his parents to excel. Equipped with a formidable intelligence, a law degree from Columbia, and letters of recommendation from his father's well-placed friends, he entered the law office of Walter S. Carter, the architect of the modern law firm who institutionalized its symbiotic relationship with university law schools and business corporations. "These highly privileged firms," Hughes recalled, "seemed to hold in an enduring grasp the best professional opportunities and to leave little room for young aspirants outside the favored groups." Hughes was an insider who capitalized on his opportunities: within five years he and Paul D. Cravath (whom Hughes had met at Columbia) were Carter's partners and Hughes became Carter's son-in-law. Two decades in practice, interrupted by a brief hiatus on the Cornell law faculty, preceded his meteoric rise in public life after he served as counsel to the New York gas and insurance investigations. To Hughes, the lessons of his career were self-evident: "If the young lawyer sees to it that his work is of the best and if by intelligence and industry he stands well in his own

---

"Lawyers and Clients," *Harvard Law Review*, 87 (1974), 1100-11.

generation, he can afford to await his share of the privileges and responsibilities which to that generation are bound to come."

Davis followed a more circuitous path to Wall Street. He lacked Hughes' intellect; Mrs. Davis observed knowingly that her son was not brilliant but he would work as hard as anyone. Washington and Lee, where Davis attended college and law school, was a parochial institution that reinforced his orthodoxies. From his father, a prominent Clarksburg attorney, Davis had learned to misread Jefferson in support of natural law, constitutional fundamentalism, and states' rights. College refined his ability to reason from fixed principles and to deport himself as a gentleman. His legal education was no less conventional. His teachers, he reminisced without criticism, wanted their students to learn what law was, not speculate about what it ought to be. Davis was a good student. Orthodoxy did not impede success in Clarksburg, especially for the son of an established lawyer. Davis & Davis was not Carter, Hughes & Cravath but, as the elder Davis reminded his neophyte partner, no young attorney in West Virginia enjoyed more opportunities at the outset of practice. The father's clientele provided initial security; the surging prosperity of local railroads and mining companies offered subsequent opportunity. Young Davis was blunt about his ends. He conceded that he was "after every dollar in sight;" that he would "do any amount of work on the *chance* of gaining prestige by it." The strain of working and earning showed. Once he hit an attorney in court; another time he threw an inkwell.

By 1910, when Hughes was appointed to the Supreme Court, Davis had reached the pinnacle of the West Virginia bar. A reluctant candidate for the House of Representatives, he quickly won distinction in Washington as the ablest lawyer in Congress and as an outstanding Solicitor General. When he relinquished his ambassadorship in 1921 he was certified by his government experience for the professional elite. As Hughes left Wall Street for Washington, Davis arrived on Wall Street from Washington. Their careers, converging at the apex of professional life, demonstrated that success was possible for educated white Anglo-Saxon Protestant sons of professional fathers whose positions provided a boost on the mobility ladder.

But Hughes and Davis paid for their success in ways that neither their society nor their profession prepared them to comprehend. Hughes, from the age of six when he composed a "Plan of Study," was so driven by the compulsion to work, and to ascribe his work to the dictates of duty, that his professional and public life were constant sources of psychic distress. Law school exhausted him; practice left him "nervously depressed because of the steady grind." He accepted the professorship at Cornell with expectations of surcease. But Cornell also was a "hive of industry," where Hughes remained ensnared in "constant toil." Regaining his "nervous poise," he returned to practice and to periodic "fits of depression." Much of his professional life, he conceded, was "unrequited drudgery." Public service was also private torment. During the life insurance investigation he felt "worn out and utterly depressed;" as governor he was "nervously worn"; when he joined the Court he felt "tired out." Back in practice, he "almost suffered a breakdown." Only duty (he claimed) enabled him to accept the gubernatorial nomination and the Supreme Court appointment. He told President Taft that he could "withstand any personal inclination" to serve on the bench "if it were opposed to the obligations of public duty." It "reassured" Hughes, upon reflection, to discover that his duty to serve impelled him to accept what mere desire (to say nothing of ambition) never could.

What Hughes did from the spur of duty, Davis did for the love of money. He, too, was frustrated by work that consumed his energies and required stringent control over his emotions, yet left him feeling "peevish & fretful." (His absorption with work elicited the poignant lament from his daughter: "What I wanted from him was his time, and he had little to spare."). The harder he worked the more he earned; the more he earned the more he craved. He spurned a teaching offer for the "millions" he wanted from practice. Asked to run for Congress, he pleaded financial insecurity with an annual income (in 1910) of $10,000 and $83,000 in investments. In search of "congenial partners and a remunerative situation," he joined the Stetson firm (whose major client was J. P. Morgan & Co.), although only recently he had described some results of Stetson's craft as "abnormal" and "immoral." He declined a feeler for the Supreme Court because he wanted "some economic independence," provoking Chief Justice Taft to complain that "If you people in New York were not so eager for money...you might have some representatives on our bench." Davis suffered severe reversals after the crash: his average annual income declined from $400,000 to $275,000 and rising taxes made it a struggle to maintain his Long Island estate and his Fifth Avenue apartment (each with its staff of six). Too much was never enough, as Davis probably sensed when he conceded: "I feel even poorer perhaps than I am."

At critical junctures in their careers public accountability was demanded of Davis and Hughes for their personal and professional choices. As Davis edged closer to the presidential nomination in 1924, the Morgan retainer, his major economic asset, became a political liability. Davis found refuge in the duty "to serve those who call on him" without regard for the implications of service for personal popularity or political reward. "Any lawyer who surrenders this independence or shades this duty...disparages and degrades the great profession to which he should be proud to belong." Six years later, when Hughes was nominated for Chief Justice, he was "most bitterly and unjustly attacked," he claimed in his *Notes*, for his corporate counseling. Hughes, like Davis, was distressed by "prejudice arising from a misconception of the character and effect of the activities of a lawyer in active practice."

Their indignation was misplaced. Critics did not question their right to choose corporate practice for the ample financial and professional rewards it assured; they asked only that Davis and Hughes be accountable for their choices. Both lawyers evaded accountability by seeking refuge in professional duty, which was sufficiently resilient to accommodate any demand upon it. But a lawyer who was obligated to serve well those who called was hardly compelled to engage in practice which virtually eliminated noncorporate callers. It was sophistry for Davis to claim that he was asked to betray his professional independence when, in fact, he was being urged to demonstrate it. Hughes, who casually dismissed any inference that a lawyer might be judged by the clients he kept, cited Professor Zechariah Chafee, Jr. approvingly for declaring that Hughes had merely fulfilled his "duty to represent loyally the client for whom he happened to be working." But the question was not whether loyal representation was provided. It was whether the recipients of loyal representation constituted a restricted, identifiable clientele whose interests shaped a lawyer's practice, values, and politics, and thus his qualification for public office.

Hughes and Davis were momentarily embarrassed by their professional identity, but they were not impeded by it. Hughes was confirmed; Davis remained the acknowledged leader of the corporate bar. But the accumulation of prestige and dollars exposed the nagging predicament of Davis' career: he was a Jeffersonian individualist whose corporate retainers "imposed subtle restraints on his freedom of action." Unable to reconcile constitutional fundamentalism with social change, he violated in practice every precept of his Jeffersonian and professional faith. He displayed a "consuming concern for the preservation of individual liberties," but corporate counseling "slowly forced him to inure himself to the injustices wrought against individuals." He defended states' rights but "it was the national corporations on whose boards Davis sat...that set in motion the subversion of states' rights." He defended strict constructionism and limited federal power, but he demanded the broadest construction of treason and the war powers during World War I. He claimed that he would take any case that came into his office, but when Gus Hall, a Communist convicted under the Smith Act, approached him, Davis responded that he was too busy.

It is an article of professional faith that when constitutional freedoms are in jeopardy bar leaders like Hughes and Davis will rise to the responsibility of defending unpopular and beleaguered persons. Indeed, Hughes protested against the expulsion of duly elected socialist members of the New York legislature during the red scare, and Davis carried an appeal to the Supreme Court on behalf of a theologian who claimed that selective conscientious objection should not disqualify him from citizenship. Yet there lurks the suspicion that incidents like these are celebrated less because they are typical than because they are exceptional, despite Davis' insistence that it was the "supreme function" of lawyers to serve as "sleepless sentinels on the ramparts of human liberty and there to sound the alarm whenever an enemy appears"....

It is unnecessary to linger over Davis' refusal to oppose the indictment of Trotskyites under the Smith Act; to sign an amicus brief protesting the internment of Japanese Americans in concentration camps; to sign an amicus brief attacking federal loyalty programs; to argue "the 'Commie' case" before the Supreme Court; or to sign an amicus brief on behalf of the lawyers cited for contempt by Judge Medina after the conclusion of the trial of that case.... Considering Davis' volubility during the 1930's, his subsequent silence might suggest a double standard. This allegation...is "somewhat unfair" if due consideration is given to his participation in proceedings surrounding the Alger

Hiss case and the security hearing for J. Robert Oppenheimer. But the sum of his activities for Hiss was belief in his innocence, occasional correspondence with his attorney, and service as a character witness during Hiss' perjury trials. (Davis was, after all, a trustee of the Carnegie Endowment, of which Hiss was president at the time of his indictment.) His efforts for Oppenheimer were presumably circumscribed by age and infirmity (although he had reargued the school segregation case just three months earlier). He agreed to serve as chief counsel if the security hearings were held in New York; when the Atomic Energy Commission refused, he cosigned a letter protesting its procedures and reviewed Oppenheimer's brief. He was not willing to do even so little for anyone else.... Davis slumbered on the ramparts of liberty, secure in the knowledge that federal power was the enemy, and Liberty Leagues were necessary, only when New Dealers regulated corporations. Not that Davis was exceptional. Twenty-three other lawyers also refused to provide Communist Party leader Gus Hall with counsel, but no one ever accused them of devotion to professional ideals...

Admission to the professional elite requires character; elite membership testifies to its presence. No independent verification is required; like obscenity, no one can define it, but to see it is to know it. Learned Hand, for example, was so enamored of the quality of Hughes' character that "to question the sincerity and purity of his motives betrayed either that you had not understood what he was after, or that your own standards needed scrutiny." Hand also was so captivated by Davis' "eloquence and charm" that he feared he might disregard the merits of any case that Davis argued. Davis (who belonged to an intimate dinner club with Learned and Augustus Hand) was mindful of the advantages bestowed. He once said of the Second Circuit, on which both Hands sat: "Nobody can hurt me in this Court!"... Elegance, grace, style, charm—some elusive components of character—are the recurrent adjectives that lawyers used to describe Davis, in part, no doubt, because he possessed these qualities and in part, one suspects, from the desire to cover substance with manner. But Felix Frankfurter, among others, knew the underside of "character": it was one of those "high-falutin' expressions for personal likes and dislikes, or class, or color, or religious partialities or antipathies."

The Davis Polk firm, like other prestigious Wall Street firms, institutionalized these qualities of character. Not coincidentally, it also gained a reputation as "the most socially exclusive office on Wall Street." This achievement culminated a process within corporate firms that began back when Hughes and Cravath joined Carter. Mass immigration and urbanization threatened the dominant Anglo-Saxon culture. The fortunate few created sanctuaries for the preservation of their group power and status in Eastern schools, careers in business and financial bureaucracies, and corporate law-firm partnerships. Reserved for those who possessed proper Anglo-Saxon social credentials (character and ethnicity did not mix, as elite opposition to the Brandeis nomination in 1916 demonstrated), the Wall Street firm was a crucial link between corporate capitalism and social elitism.... White Anglo-Saxon Protestants dominated the partnership roster, transforming it into an appendix to the *Social Register*. Davis must have done more than "acquiesce" in this pattern; his presence (including, doubtlessly, his genteel racism and anti-Semitism) "was felt everywhere within the firm." An occasional Roman Catholic was tolerable, but blacks of course were not, nor were new immigrants. Years earlier Davis had described himself as one of those "who resent all immigration in general and that of the Russian Jew in particular." Davis Polk and its counterparts on Wall Street, State Street, and LaSalle Street, were oases for club members whose social origins and character eased their journey to elite status.

Character was necessary for club membership but insufficient for professional distinction. Craft was the *sine qua non* of elite professionalism. Only lawyers with Davis' "compulsion for technical perfection" and "dedication to the case at hand" were elevated to the highest state of professional grace. Craft required skills: mastery of facts and knowledge of law; reasoning acuity; and, as an advocate, "the ability to simplify complex matters with a few pithy Anglo-Saxon phrases devoid of adjectives and drained of all emotion." But craft also required a particular definition of the lawyer's role, which disguised volition and values under the cloak of technical proficiency. Davis was "just a law lawyer" (according to his friend, Charles C. Burlingham, a prominent New York attorney) who "adhered absolutely to the principle that the lawyer's duty was to represent his client's interest to the limit of the law, not to moralize on the social and economic implications of the client's lawful actions." As Davis reminisced: "It was my duty to find out what the law was, and to tell my client what rule of life to follow. That was my job. If the rules changed, well and good." For Davis, the lawyer was merely a technician ("He does not create. All he does is lubricate the wheels of society") wearing a surgeon's mask ("The lawyer must steel himself...to think only of the subject before him & not of the pain his knife may cause"). Such professional tunnel vision was designed to obliterate those disturbing substantive issues that Davis preferred to ignore: once the laws regulating corporate activity changed in the 1930's, he found it neither well nor good; his lubricant was selectively sold and applied; the clients whose retainers he avidly procured were immune to the pain he inflicted.

Exaltation of craft eliminated the political and social implications of a lawyer's work from consideration and sustained the illusion that law was science, not politics. Proficiency certainly matters: how well something is done is never inconsequential, but the "morality of process," to quote a recent phrase of Professor Bickel, is the highest morality only for those trained from their first day in law school to separate method from substance: It is important to know, for example, that Solicitor General Davis presented an argument in support of broad federal power over commerce and civil rights that was as technically impeccable as the argument that private attorney Davis made in opposition to both policies. But preoccupation with craft ignores the substantive differences between these policies, the social consequences of those differences, and the fact that Davis argued the Government's cases for six years and corporations' cases for half a century. The point is not that Davis was a hired gun, but that he consistently sold his craft to the highest bidder while claiming that the practice of law was "an avenue for service and not a means for private gain." If lawyers must believe this, historians are only obligated to record professional pieties, not accept them. Acceptance means tacit ratification of the politics of the professional elite in the mistaken belief that craft has eliminated politics from professionalism.

Fifty years ago when Davis ran for President, Professor Felix Frankfurter, dismayed by the "crass materialism" of his students, wrote that "it is good neither for these lads that I see passing through this School from year to year, nor for this country,...that we should reward with the Presidency one to whom big money was the big thing." Although the White House eluded Davis and Hughes, virtually nothing that their profession could offer exceeded the reach of these supremely successful practicing attorneys. Nevertheless, the professional culture exacted its toll. Its elevation of craft as the ultimate criterion of value detached process from purpose and divided the psyches of its ablest practitioners. Although it sanctified these debilitating divisions, and rewarded as lawyer's lawyers those who submerged their personal lives in their professional careers, both Davis and Hughes displayed persistent symptoms of discomfort, avoidance, and repression. They could not express their conundrum as openly as did their contemporary, W.E.B. DuBois, who described the "double-consciousness" of black Americans: "One ever feels his twoness..., two souls, two thoughts, two unreconciled strivings; two warring ideals in one...body." But they shared a variant of the experience, for the real American dilemma was not confined to race. Within the value system that Hughes and Davis embraced (which also embraced them) they excelled as lawyers of character and craft. Indeed, it is necessary to come to terms with their careers to understand the contemporary efforts of so many lawyers to integrate their personal and professional selves. Hughes and Davis personify the past from which any healthy future of the legal profession must be wrested.

3 · Lawyers in the Depression Decade

During the Great Depression decade, the American legal profession, structurally and ideologically committed to stability, underwent wrenching change. Its texture was woven from various strands—some dating from the turn of the century, others quite new: the impact of corporate capitalism on professional values and structure; the emergence of university legal education as the primary channel of access to the professional elite; social stratification that produced blocked mobility and generational conflict; and the employment crisis created by the depression in conjunction with the opportunity structure established by the Roosevelt administration. Although lawyers are functionally committed to a process of social ordering designed to mitigate abrupt or unpredictable change, the nexus between law and public life requires their profession to serve as a sensitive barometer of social change. Amid the turbulence of the thirties, the legal profession, buffeted by external pressures and rent by internal conflict, uneasily confronted both its past and its future.

The crash, Arthur Schlesinger, Jr., has written, produced "a profound shaking up of American society: it led to a general discrediting of the older ruling classes...and a sudden opening of opportunity for men and ethnic groups on the way up in the competition for position and power." The experience of the legal profession during the New Deal decade offers a striking example. A pivotal institution in that process was the university law school.... Once law schools began to serve as a training ground for public service, and once law teachers became, according to Richard Hofstadter, "the keepers of the professional conscience," the gulf between teacher and practitioner widened. The business-as-usual approach of the practitioners offended their academic brethren, whose distance from the marketplace shaped their perception of practitioners, especially corporation attorneys, as money-grubbers and lackeys of big business. Practitioners reciprocated with an image of law teachers as utopian dreamers committed to the subversive view of law as an instrument of social change. Discord and animosity accompanied their struggle for power within the legal profession. The dominant business values of the 1920s, which practicing lawyers shared, followed by the ferment of legal realism, the heady brew of law

---

"Lawyers and Social Change in the Depression Decade," *The New Deal* (1975), 133-39, 142-45, 150-57, 160-64.

professors, pushed these rivals far apart.

Teachers repeatedly complained that professional leadership was reserved for lawyers with restricted social vision. Harvard law professor Thomas Reed Powell, who heard one ABA president advise his students to go to church and join Rotary clubs, concluded that the association presidency was reserved for men of "no distinction." His colleague, Zechariah Chafee, Jr., told the members of a local bar association that professional leaders devoted their attention to "matters just as appropriate to plumbers as to lawyers." Dean Charles E. Clark of Yale Law School, speaking to members of the American Bar Association, maintained that their organization was nothing but "a social gathering of the older and financially successful lawyers." Teachers, convinced that practitioners were encumbered by self-interest and social myopia, insisted that only they possessed the necessary critical detachment and enlightened awareness to cope with social ills.

Although teachers trained eminently practical lawyers, and certified their best students for positions with Wall Street firms, elite practitioners expressed unease whenever the accelerating pace of social change quickened the reform impulses of law professors. With the Roosevelt administration turning eagerly to law faculties and to recent graduates, rather than to the practicing bar, established lawyers knew that their public influence was waning. Their knowledge accounted for the tone of irascibility that characterized so many of their observations about law teachers. John W. Davis put it bluntly when he referred to "wild men" at Yale and Harvard law schools "whose social, economic and legal principles I distrust." Publicly, lawyers were more discreet. James Beck, confessing high regard for law professors for their "philosophic detachment" and for their renunciation of high fees, found them prone to "visionary ideas" which "are not helpful in the development of sound public opinion." An ABA member, reporting extensive correspondence with practitioners regarding their evaluation of recent law-school graduates, described "a schism between the thought of the law schools and the thought of the Bar." The notions held by professors might be "scintillating in their brilliance and evince profound learning, but at the same time display an utter lack of touch with the realities of the law." It was one thing to teach law as it was; it was quite another to teach law as it ought to be, and to train men who might become critics rather than defenders of the old order.

Practitioners distorted the subversive influence of teachers, but they accurately perceived that economic collapse had undercut those patterns of deference and emulation that had placed the corporation president and his attorney in the pantheon of postwar heroes. They also knew that scattered through the world of law teaching were legal realists who repudiated law as a "brooding omnipresence," stressed its use as a flexible instrument for the resolution of social problems, and sharply challenged the prevailing wisdom regarding the nature of the judicial process. At a time when practitioners viewed the courts and the Constitution as their bulwark against revolutionary change, legal realists, who rejected the mechanical notion that judicial decision-making rested solely upon syllogistic reasoning from rules and precedents, doubtlessly sounded like the bar's bolsheviks.

Simultaneously, demographic changes were undercutting the foundations of the older professional culture. Fledgling lawyers from ethnic minority groups, who were graduating from law schools in unprecedented numbers, confronted imposing obstacles. Disqualified by their social origins in the best of times, they now entered a professional world in which restricted law firms were cutting back on new recruits and opportunities to earn a living wage in solo practice were sharply constricted. Aspiring Jewish lawyers bore the brunt of professional prejudice. They were disproportionately concentrated both at the top of their law school classes and at the bottom of the metropolitan bar. Their presence in such profusion threatened to unsettle the apex and the base of the professional structure. In this setting, the New Deal loomed as a source of salvation to them and as a menace to the established bar. Its alphabet agencies exerted a magnetic pull on professionals who, by tradition, had been drawn to public service, by training had been prepared for it, and by circumstance found curtailed opportunities in the private sector. The New Deal needed talent; lawyers needed jobs, which the New Deal provided. It also provided a program that infuriated defenders of unregulated corporate enterprise, who were predictably enraged to see young Jewish lawyers drafting and enforcing regulatory statutes. Consequently, the Roosevelt administration posed serious challenges to the dominant professional culture and to its values and symbols. It enabled a new professional elite to ascend to power, an elite drawn from different social and ethnic strata and encouraged by their teachers to seek professional fulfillment in the public sector.

Felix Frankfurter stood at the intersection of many of these trends. Back in 1911, he had rejected the "drab uniformity" of his Harvard Law School classmates by spurning private practice for government service. Practice, Frankfurter complained, meant "putting one's time to put money in other people's pockets." After working in the United States Attorney's Office and in the War Department, Frankfurter turned to law teaching as the career par excellence for involvement in public life. Inspired by the Wisconsin Idea, he carved out a role for law teachers and law schools as participants "in a great state service." During the postwar years, he often expressed his disappointment at the role models provided by bar leaders. He waited in vain for lawyers to protest against the "enveloping commercialism and general corrupting atmosphere" of the Dollar Decade. The 1924 presidential candidacy of corporation lawyer John W. Davis angered him. Dismissing Davis as "the employee of Big Business," he complained that "it is good neither for these lads that I see passing through this School from year to year, nor for this country...that we should reward with the Presidency one to whom big money was the big thing." Years later, it still pained him that "the attractions of New York"—meaning Wall Street practice—lured the best Harvard law students of that generation. Frankfurter himself was responsible for placing many of them. He virtually served as an employment broker for his old friend Emory Buckner, partner in the Root-Clark firm in New York, and he performed a similar service for the Cravath firm, for his former mentor Henry Stimson, and for others who came to rely upon his appraisal of legal talent....

These achievements were made possible by demographic and social trends that originated beyond the profession and affected university law schools, the key institutions of professional access. Samuel Lubell has written about the voting patterns of the children of the thirteen million new immigrants of 1900-1914 who came of age after 1930; concentrated in cities, they became "the chief carriers of the Roosevelt Revolution." More than voting patterns were affected by population changes. Between 1919 and 1927, there was a sharp spurt, exceeding 80 percent, in law school enrollments. And from 1920 to 1930, in a few eastern cities with a heavy concentration of immigrants, there was a substantial proportional increase in the number of foreign-born lawyers. In New York, where the number of lawyers increased by 57 percent during that decade, the number of foreign-born lawyers increased by 76 percent. In Philadelphia, the bar grew by 21 percent while the number of foreign-born lawyers increased by 76 percent. Expanding law school enrollments, and the changing ethnic structure of the bar, threatened the professional elite ensconced in law firms and dominant in professional associations. Although it could, and did, easily defend these redoubts against intruders, it could not protect what it did not control. New Deal agencies were enemy country. They attracted younger lawyers who came disproportionately from ethnic minority groups; lawyers with relatively weak commitments to private practice in corporate law firms; lawyers trained in administrative law, skilled in legislative draftsmanship, exposed to the stimulating currents of legal realism, and eager to apply their expertise; and lawyers who responded with alacrity to a call for public service once a liberal reform administration came to power.

The establishment of a New Deal counter-elite among lawyers had nothing of an underclass rebellion about it. Lawyers who occupied responsible positions within the administration possessed impeccable professional credentials and were committed to quite traditional professional and social goals: opportunity, success, money, and power. Many of them had successfully carved out niches in the private sector. Others, especially from depression years graduating classes, could not do so. Circumstance, rather than choice, may have deflected them from private firms. Excluded from Wall Street and welcomed in Washington, they fused personal ambition, social mobility, and liberal reform in government service. Few of them, however, became career lawyers for the government. In time, with the expertise provided by their service in New Deal agencies, many entered corporation law firms. Professional democratization, never an articulated goal, was indefinitely deferred. The New Deal offered new positions of power to ethnically, not professionally, disadvantaged lawyers. It restricted mobility opportunities to those already designated as the most talented graduates of the best schools. The remainder of the profession was left to fend for itself; marginal lawyers remained forgotten professional men, and marginal clients were still without the legal services that corporations, and now the federal government, could command.

For lawyers, the newness of the New Deal resided in the multiple possibilities it afforded for personal and professional opportunity. Like a freshly cut diamond, it displayed many facets and attracted a variegated band of admiring attorneys. It could simultaneously appeal to an independent country lawyer whose model was nineteenth-century practice (Robert H. Jackson); to a legal realist who made intellectual leaps beyond most of his twentieth-century counterparts (Jerome N. Frank); to a craftsman who saw nothing incongruous in voting for Hoover and then committing his energy to the Roosevelt administration (Charles E. Wyzanski, Jr.); and to young, upwardly mobile, minority group lawyers. Notwithstanding the variety and the inevitable exceptions, a common thread wound through many of their careers. Lawyers who felt displaced, and those who sought a place, turned to the Roosevelt administration. A drop of nostalgia blended with a torrent of anticipation to produce the characteristic New Deal tang.

Robert H. Jackson was an unlikely New Deal lawyer. The prototypical New Dealer was an upwardly mobile urbanite, a second-generation member of an ethnic minority group with superior academic credentials and, perhaps, some Wall Street experience. Jackson was the obverse: an upstate Protestant New Yorker who never attended college, never graduated from Albany Law School, served an apprenticeship in a Jamestown law office, and incessantly preached the nineteenth-century virtues of the small-town practitioner: "hard work, long hours, and thrift." The son of a Pennsylvania farmer, he would aptly be described as a lawyer whose "bent was to plow old pastures in a new way, not to leap fences and attack virgin soil....It was his job to defend, not to formulate, policies." The consummate advocate, he defended the New Deal as special counsel for the Securities and Exchange Commission, as assistant attorney general in the Tax and Antitrust Divisions of the Justice Department, and as solicitor general and attorney general. Regardless of office, Jackson remained the nineteenth-century liberal in the twentieth century. His anachronistic liberalism was apparent, even conspicuous. Yet as a New Dealer Jackson seemed to march in step with the times. This was less paradoxical than it appeared. His critique of the legal profession, a recurring theme in his public addresses, focused on the corporation lawyer as the personification of wrongdoing. His was the animus of Main Street, displaced professionally by Wall Street. Jackson's New Deal colleagues, who voiced similar complaints, fired at the same target for different reasons. Theirs was the cry of contemporary experience; his was the voice of nostalgic betrayal....

Speaking to law teachers in 1934, Jackson acknowledged the benchmarks of change, especially the concentration of legal business and talent in large metropolitan firms and the consequent malaise of the middle-class bar, once the backbone of the profession. But he refused to retreat to the storm cellar of the nineteenth century; rather, he sought to transplant its virtues to a different era. He spoke of the government's need for lawyers who possessed education and experience, but were devoid of "mental ossification." Legalism "has a place in shaping any new deal. Why should the bar so largely renounce its function of shaping it to oppose it?" At present, he concluded, the bar "is one of the most stubborn, reactionary and shortsighted groups in our national life." But, he added with revealing ambivalence, "I should be sadly disappointed if my son should fail to join it." Jackson, like the country lawyers he constantly praised, viewed law more as a religion than as a means of remuneration. "He embodied a significant part of the American dream," one of his admirers has written—"the storybook American boy who by dint of brains and work and pluck drives himself from an unpromising start to a glorious finish." For this very reason, he was, in the words of a less-unabashed analyst, the "Everyman of the law." He won the highest legal prizes the Roosevelt administration could bestow, yet he was an incongruous New Deal lawyer. Misplaced in time, he seemed most contemporary when he spoke for the bygone liberal professionalism of an earlier era.

If Jackson carefully tilled old soil, Jerome Frank preferred to leap fences. A precocious graduate of the University of Chicago at nineteen, he hoped to become a novelist, unwillingly became a lawyer at his father's insistence, and developed a lucrative corporate law practice, first in Chicago and then in New York, which he never enjoyed. After the crash, when the concerns of his clients preoccupied him, he became increasingly restless. From psychoanalysis, he learned that lawyers chose "childish thoughtways in meeting adult problems." He wrote *Law and the Modern Mind*, an exciting venture into the psychology of jurisprudence, out of the desire "to see and have others see and help me see more clearly just what we lawyers are doing daily." Why, he asked Roscoe Pound, was "absolutistic thinking so difficult to surmount in cerebration about law? Why is certainty-hunger peculiarly vigorous in lawyerdom?... How make [lawyers] eager to think pragmatically, to use concepts operationally, instrumentally?" Frank, who delighted in tilting against "illusions about legal certainty [that] get the lawyers in bad with the public," rebelled against what he perceived as legal authoritarianism. Most lawyers and judges, he wrote in his book, insisted upon the certainty of law when it was, in fact, "largely vague and variable." They did so because they had "not yet relinquished the childish need for an authoritative father and unconsciously have tried to find in the law a substitute for those attributes of firmness, sureness, certainty and infallibility ascribed in childhood to the father." Frank demanded (and perceived in his fellow realists) "a skepticism stimulated by a zeal to reform, in the interest of justice, some court-house ways." He tried, in the words of his close friend Thurman Arnold, "to free the law from its frustrating obsessions. His jurisprudence was the jurisprudence of therapy."

The more clearly that Frank perceived his daily activities, the more frustrated he became. Although he managed to write his book, maintain a voluminous correspondence, and engage in a busy practice, he complained, "Its hell how practicing law interferes with decent intellection." Shortly before the 1932 election, he confessed to being "so fed up with the tawdry aspects of practice" that he would welcome an academic appointment. Roosevelt's victory opened tempting possibilities. He offered his services to Adolf Berle; he suggested to Thurman Arnold that Yale, where Frank lectured, organize its own brain-trusters; and he accepted with alacrity an invitation, extended at Frankfurter's behest, to draft farm legislation and then to become general counsel of the Agricultural Adjustment Administration. "Financially, it is a somewhat risky adventure for me," he conceded, "but I couldn't resist the opportunity."

Frank personified the affinity between legal realism and the New Deal. Realists, he declared in a thinly veiled autobiographical statement, could easily become New Dealers because they were "less Procrustean and more flexible in their techniques" and because they judged legal institutions by their human consequences rather than by their Platonic essences. As experimentalists, they were skeptical of their own notions but not paralyzed by inaction. The lawyer who believed in "undeviating fixed legal principles," Frank's "Mr. Absolute," would be repelled by the New Deal. His adversary, "Mr. Try-it," could run social experiments for sixteen hours each day without strain or fatigue.

Yet those very social experiments, as Frank conceded, were designed merely to harness private financial gain to social welfare. This presumably rash, brash experimentalist, freed from authoritarian dogma, only wanted *"the profit system to be tried, for the first time, as a consciously directed means of promoting the general good."* Therein lay the outer limits of his experimentalism—a point never perceived by those who criticized him as the New Deal's Robespierre. Frank suffered from a reputation exceeded only by Frankfurter's as the radical lawyer-ogre of the administration. Once the Agricultural Adjustment Administration became the battleground for a clash between southern tenant farmers and their landlords, Frank and his group of talented, socially committed young associates, sympathetic to the plight of the sharecroppers and eager to secure their legal rights, were suspect, vulnerable, and finally expendable, But Frank, who wrestled self-consciously with the boundary between policy preferences and legal judgments, demonstrated considerably greater restraint than his public reputation suggested. Policy considerations must affect a lawyer's opinion, he wrote, but they "should not play at all a dominant role in a lawyer's thinking." Frank insisted that his own advocacy was usually directed toward inducing his colleagues "to narrow the issues so as to confine the argument as far as possible to controversy *on traditional lines.*" As he told Frankfurter: "I do not believe in trying to vindicate abstract principles...and to me the important thing is to win *particular* cases." Frankfurter knew that Frank wanted to win cases; he also saw that Frank was "a damned romantic intellectual." Frank conceded, yet denigrated, the romance. He described his work as general counsel as "heartbreaking days and nights spent with almost reckless financial sacrifice in aid of public causes [I] deem desirable." Yet, he hastened to add, one of his major aims was "to have our job done with legal accuracy—so that it would stand up in court."

Therein lay the tension that tormented Frank as long as he remained in Washington. His commitment to realism and to experimentalism impelled him toward policy-making; his lawyer's commitments to process and precedent restrained him. More venturesome than most of his colleagues, he suffered from the knowledge of his radical reputation. Critical of lawyers' absolutes, he nonetheless was inhibited by the restraints of professionalism. An experimentalist about means, he unquestioningly accepted ends. Standing at the cutting edge of legal thought and of the New Deal, he demonstrated their compatibility and the strength that each derived from the other. Liberated by both, he was nonetheless bound by his commitments to professionalism and to capitalism. By 1935, he felt "functionless." He sensed that his effectiveness in Washington was at an end; but he dreaded returning to private practice, and he anticipated a hostile reception should he attempt to do so. "I'm badly bewildered," he told Frankfurter, "—and not a little frightened." Frank, like the administration he served with such passionate distinction, was simultaneously liberated by lawyers' skills and inhibited by lawyers' values.

If the New Deal appealed to nostalgic liberals and to bold realists, it also attracted able legal technicians who found matchless opportunities for honing their skills and practicing their craft. Charles E. Wyzanski, Jr., grandson of a successful immigrant peddler and a product of Exeter, Harvard College, and Harvard Law School, was one of these. Drawn to law study after reading Zechariah Chafee's *Freedom of Speech*, he was a law review editor, clerked for both Learned and Augustus Hand, and practiced for three years in Boston's prestigious Ropes, Gray firm. When the Roosevelt administration came to power, Wyzanski's career was still in its formative stages. New Deal opportunities set Wyzanski's course. As solicitor for the Labor Department, he nearly tripled his salary and enjoyed immeasurable freedom to exercise his lawyer's craft. Wyzanski, who had voted for Hoover in 1932, did not go to Washington as a crusading reformer. But he took pride in the fact that "we were a level of employees that Washington hadn't previously seen." And the considerable demands upon his skills were exhilarating. Given twenty-four hours to draft the public works title of the National Industrial Recovery bill, he compared the travail to "plunging into the furnace."

Wyzanski's instinct for craftsmanship made him eager for "more law work, and less administration." By 1935, he concluded that the solicitorship offered "less play to legal than to political and administrative currents." Moving over to the Justice Department, he compared his earlier government work, which taught him "to analyze quickly, to assume responsibility and to act courageously," with the greater fulfillment provided by "the intellectual satisfaction which comes from a chance to turn problems around so that every angle is displayed." He subsequently referred to the *process* of drafting the Wagner Act brief as the consummate experience of his Washington service: "We would talk back and forth at each sentence.... We were just a crowd hard at work...doing our best to understand the kernel of the thought, and then reducing it to the narrowest possible statement." This was the distillation of his law school training under Reed Powell, who, Wyzanski recalled years later, could "make you think twenty times before you write that sentence quite that way." Wyzanski knew, in addition, that he was participating in the lawyer's resumption of his role as social mediator, a role weakened by lawyers for corporations who were "too loyal to a *part* of a community to see the new problems in the light of the *whole* community." New Deal social legislation represented an attempt to restore the equilibrium between public and private right. Thus, Wyzanski could fulfill the lawyer's historic mission in the process of maximizing his professional satisfactions. He could also set a valued precedent, for he treasured nothing more about his Washington experience "than the feeling that I have been part of a practice (which I hope will become a tradition), under which young men give part of their early manhood to public service."

Although scores of young lawyers, and a sprinkling of older ones, went to Washington during the thirties, it is impossible to know how many responded to "public service," or how many would have agreed with Wyzanski's definition of it. "Public service" had complex meanings to lawyers from various backgrounds who reached Washington at different stages of their careers. A special fillip of excitement aroused successful, established lawyers who were secure and prosperous in private practice. Francis Biddle renounced his family firm in Philadelphia for "the sense of freedom, the feeling of power, and the experience of the enlarging horizons of public work." Lloyd Landau, president of the *Harvard Law Review* during World War I and subsequently clerk to Justice Holmes, was prepared to abandon a substantial private practice with a large annual income for the opportunity to serve under Frankfurter if his old mentor became Roosevelt's solicitor general. A New York attorney, who had served in Washington during the war, wanted to return because he sensed that a position with the New Deal "might be even more of a thrill." Established law teachers found special gratifications. James Landis, who temporarily vacated his Harvard professorship, quickly discovered that he could enjoy "a larger share in the handling of government than I ever had after years in the handling of the Harvard Law School." Landis had dreaded interviews with Dean Pound; he never enjoyed the privilege of an interview with President Lowell; but he anticipated conferences with Roosevelt "with pleasure, knowing that there will be an exchange of views.... It is things like this that make life fun."

Young men who went to Washington were exhilarated, edified, and often exhausted by the demands upon them, especially in the newer agencies. Abe Fortas, who worked under Frank in the Agricultural Adjustment Administration, "could see the new world and feel it taking form under our hands." A young lawyer for the National Labor Relations Board described his experience as "helpful to me as a lawyer and as one who is trying to understand some of the social forces at work.... I think my concepts are more direct and real than they were." Another NLRB attorney recounted a year "crowded with action and providing many opportunities for intensive labor." For these lawyers, the opportunity to function provided the paramount satisfaction.

Other attorneys found the New Deal ideologically compatible—or sufficiently flexible to permit them to implement their own political and social commitments. Nathan Witt, galvanized by the Sacco-Vanzetti case, drove a taxi for two years to earn enough money to afford Harvard Law School. His greatest ambition, he told Frankfurter, was to devote his energies to "the public service of the law." This meant to work for minority groups, who were most likely to complain of the failure to be accorded evenhanded justice. Witt battled for sharecroppers in the AAA and for workers as general counsel for the National Labor Relations Board. Lee Pressman, his classmate and friend, followed a parallel path. Pressman received his decisive intellectual push from a course on labor unionism at Cornell. Unable to find work in labor law, because no firms specialized in the field, he did corporate receivership and reorganization work with Frank, until he eagerly escaped the "yoke" of private practice after Frank went to Washington. Pressman, like Witt, joined Frank in the AAA; like Witt, he moved over to the labor movement; like Witt, he flirted with the Communist party....

The Jewish lawyer from an immigrant family who managed to secure a New Deal position recognized his own coming of age as an American. Malcolm A. Hoffmann, a Harvard graduate, described himself at the outset of his governmental service with the NLRB as "a young neophyte at the bar, a member of a minority religious group, a boy who had never seen the inside of a political club nor had power nor status in our huge egalitarian society." Governmental employment provided just that sense of power and status. It legitimized the aspirations of minority-group members and assuaged the disappointment that they encountered in the private sector. Roosevelt, cognizant of the social implications of government service, tried to tap that supply. "Dig me up fifteen or twenty youthful Abraham Lincolns from Manhattan and the Bronx to choose from," he told Charles C. Burlingham. "They must be liberal from belief and not by lip service. They must have an inherent contempt both for the John W. Davises and the Max Steuers. They must know what life in a tenement means. They must have no social ambition."

Except for the absence of social ambition, Roosevelt procured the type of lawyer he sought. Indeed, in Washington the problem was too many Jews, not too few. Nathan Margold, solicitor for the Interior Department, and Jerome Frank, in the AAA, had numerous legal jobs to fill; both, however, were troubled by the overabundance of qualified Jewish lawyers and by the political liabilities inherent in placing too many of them on their staffs. The poignancy of the problem was compounded by the flood of requests from young, highly qualified Jewish lawyers who pleaded, usually with Frankfurter, for New Deal employment. Other minority-group members were, if anything, at an even greater disadvantage. An Armenian-born female law review editor from Wisconsin Law School, suffering from the double professional handicap of social origins and sex, asked in vain for help. Black lawyers not only were barred from white firms; they also suffered discrimination at the administration's own hands. One black attorney, seeking an NRA position, was kept waiting for three hours while every white applicant was interviewed; finally he was told that the position was reserved for whites only. Angrily, he confronted his painful dilemma: "One is driven either to hate his color or his country." The New Deal opened the door to professional mobility—especially for Jews and, to a lesser extent, for Irish Catholic lawyers like Corcoran, Frank Murphy, and Charles Fahy, and, on rare occasion, for a black lawyer like William Hastie. But the great wall of exclusion, made more imposing by depression conditions, still surrounded the legal profession.

Driven to desperation, young lawyers in private practice began to consider structural reforms in the profession that would alleviate their own plight by extending the provision of legal services to neglected constituencies. The major theoretical impulse to their effort was provided by Columbia professor Karl Llewellyn, who was dismayed by the individualism of the bar and the corporate orientation of its professional associations. Early in the life of the New Deal he suggested government action. Between legal aid, available only to the most impoverished, and specialized corporate counseling, reserved for the most privileged, a vast area existed for "legal hygiene" that would inform middle-class people of their legal needs and rights and provide the services required to alleviate or secure them. In an article published in *Law and Contemporary Problems* in 1938, Llewellyn indicted the bar for its anachronisms and deceptions. Complaints about overcrowding masked low professional incomes. Complaints about ambulance-chasing diverted attention from inadequate legal services. Complaints about unauthorized practice by title companies or banks emphasized the danger "to the Bar's needed service being rendered" by camouflaging the danger "to the Bar's needed living being earned." Ethical canons prohibiting solicitation, suited for small-town life, victimized urban dwellers and city lawyers. Two-thirds of the bar and 80 percent of the public, Llewellyn estimated, needed each other but lacked both the contact and the means of making contact. Llewellyn closed with a vigorous plea for the establishment of legal service bureaus that would serve these unmet needs.

Young urban lawyers responded with alacrity to Llewellyn's call. Writing from Chicago, Atlanta, Denver, and Philadelphia, they expressed interest in establishing low-cost legal service bureaus in urban neighborhoods far from downtown clusters of exclusive law firms. These struggling attorneys, prepared to seek out clients with legal problems, knew that expanded legal services would simultaneously serve clients' interests while enlarging their own opportunities. In this way, professional reform and self-interest dovetailed. One law student told Llewellyn that law clinics would provide "a wonderful chance for both the young lawyer and also the people who can't afford to pay large legal fees." And a Chicago attorney, eager to serve needy clients, conceded that clinics would also be "an excellent training ground for the young lawyer as well as a basis for a fair income."

These various streams—restricted professional opportunities, an obsolete bar structure, the precarious status of minority-group lawyers, generational turmoil, and reform agitation—converged in the National Lawyers Guild, the first professional association to challenge the hegemony of the American Bar Association. Its membership was drawn primarily from those groups—especially Jews, Catholics, and Negroes—who were disproportionately confined to the lower levels of professional life. But its leaders, from the same groups, were men from the most progressive professional circles who, attainments notwithstanding, found the American Bar Association professionally and politically objectionable: labor lawyer Frank Walsh; civil liberties lawyer Morris Ernst; New Dealers Jerome Frank, Abe Fortas, and Thomas Emerson; and black civil rights lawyer Charles Houston. These men, together with other New Dealers and law teachers, exemplified the rising elite within the profession—an elite distinguished by its youth, ethnicity, and sensitivity to jurisprudential and doctrinal innovation. For too long, Guild leaders proclaimed in their "Call to American Lawyers," the profession's concern for liberty had been secondary to its concern for property. The Guild's constitutional preamble addressed itself to lawyers who regard adjustments to new conditions as more important than the veneration of precedent, who recognize the importance of safeguarding and extending the rights of workers and farmers...of maintaining our civil rights and liberties...and who look upon the law as a living and flexible instrument which must be adapted to the needs of the people." Rank-and-file membership was drawn from those groups that scrambled for position during the depression years and identified their struggle with the cause of liberal reform. A 29-year-old Catholic lawyer of "good but humble birth" eagerly responded to the Guild's appeal. So did Negro lawyers, especially once the Guild banished color as an informal qualification for membership—in sharp contrast to the American Bar Association, which, in 1937, had only two Negro members. Jewish lawyers, especially from New York City, enthusiastically enrolled as Guild members. Within five months, 2,600 lawyers had joined; an overwhelming majority came from the lower economic strata of the profession.

In 1939, the Philadelphia chapter of the Guild implemented a neighborhood law office plan to provide middle-income groups with competent legal assistance and preventive legal services. The thirteen-member executive committee of the Philadelphia Guild chapter consisted, revealingly, of eight Jews, three Catholics, and one Negro. Here was the operative reality of law and social change during the 1930s. An insurgent professional association confronted the ethnic and social structure of the professional elite with a reform proposal that challenged traditional assumptions regarding the provision and adequacy of legal services. With stark clarity the lines were drawn: between American Bar Association and National Lawyers Guild; between age and youth; between the established Protestant elite and the aspiring ethnic outsiders; between service to wealth and service to needy urban masses; and between professional values suitable to a bygone golden era and those required in a heterogeneous, urban, industrial society. A single neighborhood project hardly affected an entire profession—but it did indicate the direction from which the future winds of social change would blow. The Guild, Thomas Emerson would claim in retrospect, "was born in revolt—a revolt that embraced the entire intellectual life of the times."

In significant respects, the New Deal was a lawyer's deal. The virtues and vices of the legal approach to problem-solving were readily apparent. A commitment to flexibility, to instrumentalism, to skeptical realism, and to administrative discretion, applied by lawyers who were (in James Landis's words) "bred to the facts," freed the New Deal from the debilitating paralysis so characteristic of the Hoover years. Yet no result was permitted to assume such transcendent importance as to rule out compromise. The lawyer's obsession with process may liberate his skills, but it also dominates his values and inhibits his social goals. Lawyers guided New Deal solutions between the bargaining extremes but toward the existing balance of power between competing interest groups. This trait gave the New Deal its opportunistic, shallow side and made it all too willing to capitulate to its opponents. The prototypical New Dealer may well have been "a freewheeler and an activist" with considerable discretion and responsibility, who played a "pervasive role" in the policy-making process. Yet there were clear limits, and indeed narrow boundaries, to that process. At most, the lawyer controlled the pace of change, not its direction—for the lawyer's characteristic function, even during the turbulent New Deal years, has always been to mediate and adjust those social forces set in motion by others.

New Deal lawyers did not make the world over; they were neither empowered nor inclined to do so. Their profession was, however, profoundly affected by patterns of social change that reached fruition during the New Deal years. As new areas of law emerged with new arenas in which to practice them, and as new careers opened, new groups of lawyers jostled for power and elite status. Although the strength of an elite usually is measured by its ability to set the terms of admission into its circle of influence, its survival may depend upon its ability to adjust to outside pressures and admit challengers. During the 1930s, the traditional professional elite retained its privileged bastions in corporation law firms, in bar associations, and in pressure groups like the Liberty League's lawyers' committee. But it could not halt the growth of parallel professional institutions that trained and certified a newer elite drawn from different ethnic groups and social classes. These rival elites—one private, the other public—coexisted in uneasy equilibrium during the New Deal years. Just as many members of new immigrant groups "made it" in the business world by developing their own areas of marginal entrepreneurial activity—Hollywood, for example, and organized crime—so many minority group lawyers, excluded from Wall Street firms, served the administrative needs of the New Deal, practiced labor law, or litigated civil rights and civil liberties causes. Not until after World War II, when corporate firms perceived the utility for their own practice of the expertise developed by lawyers in New Deal agencies, could minority group lawyers gain access to the Protestant professional establishment. The New Deal certified its own lawyers for their eventual careers on Wall Street or on law faculties.

The growth of a parallel elite, followed by its assimilation into the traditional structure, had dual significance. First, it made possible a necessary degree of social mobility within the legal profession; exclusionary patterns of access were weakened, although hardly destroyed. But the traditional professional structure, which defined elite positions as those in the service of business corporations, was retained. The New Deal created new elite positions, while leaving that structure, and the values that sustained it, relatively untouched. Elite circulation was achieved at the expense of professional democratization.

At the base of the professional pyramid, nothing had changed. The battleground was reserved for the apex, where old and new elites clashed. When the dust kicked up by their professional rivalry had settled, the old structure—altered but not replaced—was greatly strengthened by its newest inhabitants, who were, by their presence, its newest defenders.

4 · Law and Acculturation

Jews were a people whose religion was law; they clung to the Torah to preserve their identity as a people during two millennia in dispersion, while they were suspended in exile, at least spiritually, between their temporary residence and their once and future home. (In the most literal respects, the Torah was their living law: Jews danced with their holy scrolls in celebration; the Torah, if profaned, was buried in a cemetery.) Yet necessity constantly imposed the burden of adaptation. As Jews were reminded all too frequently and tragically, they dwelled in other nations at the sufferance of their Gentile hosts. Reverence for their own law always involved sufficient flexibility to permit survival in the threatening environment of Jewish dispersion.

According to Talmudic doctrine, the law of the state was the law that governed Jews. This principle of accommodation co-existed uneasily with the autonomy necessary for Judaism to endure; conflict between Jewish law and the law of the state was inevitable. (Indeed, it was doubtless such conflict that had generated the Talmudic principle.) Jews had struggled with this problem at least as far back as the second century, when the Romans abolished Jewish courts and Jews developed their own informal dispute-settlement procedures as an alternative to litigation in Roman tribunals. Disputants selected their own arbitrators; communal pressure encouraged compliance with their decisions. By the Middle Ages Jews had centuries-old admonitions against bringing their disputes before "heathens," even if a non-Jewish court would have decided a case consistently with Jewish principles. According to Maimonides, Jews who submitted disputes to Gentile judges "cause the walls of the Law to fall." Jews who resorted to Christian courts might be treated as informers, guilty of treason against divine and Mosaic law. External hostility reinforced internal constraints. Often Jews were not permitted to testify in court; special oaths were required of them when the plaintiff or defendant was Christian.

The retention of disputes within the Jewish community was not merely a defensive response to external hostility. It expressed deep desires for religious and cultural autonomy in exile. To sustain their distinctiveness as a people within a state, Jews relied upon the synagogue, their house of prayer, and the Bet Din, their house of judgment. The Bet Din, or rabbinical court, was in theory restricted to religious issues. But in practice, Judaism made no clear demarca-

---

Justice Without Law? Resolving Disputes Without Lawyers (1983), 76-89, 93-94.

tion between religious and secular spheres. By the Middle Ages, only serious crimes involving capital punishment were explicitly beyond Bet Din jurisdiction. Disputes were judged by rabbis, before whom parties pleaded without the assistance of counsel. (Lawyers were feared for their ability to manipulate and distort, and especially for their willingness to rely upon the law of the state, instead of Jewish law, when state law might better serve their client.) Amid procedural informality there was considerable substantive formality: decisions were based not only upon written Jewish law but upon the known precedents of other Jewish courts. In virtually all religious and civil matters, including family and commercial disputes, the decisions of the Bet Din were binding. But Bet Din legalism was softened by other considerations. Justice required reconciliation, not victory. According to Maimonides, "a court which always settles cases by *pesharah* [compromise] is praiseworthy." So the Bet Din combined the forms and substance of law with the informalities of community arbitration. It provided an internal, legalistic alternative to Christian regulation of Jewish affairs.

The complexities for Jews of a dual legal system were intensified in the nineteenth century by the Enlightenment and emancipation. Jews were promised legal equality and citizenship; in return, they were expected to compress Judaism into a religion. As the traditional wholeness of Jewish life was sharply bifurcated into sacred and secular spheres, the jurisdictional role of Jewish courts was reduced. Milder penalties were now imposed for diverting disputes from Jewish courts, suggesting that such defections were more frequent. Offenders were still punished with banishment from the community, but their removal was more symbolic (exclusion from Torah readings) than actual (excommunication). The authority of the Bet Din was confined to "religious" questions—in the modern world the questions that held the least significance for the most people.

The mass exodus of Eastern European Jewry around the turn of the twentieth century further devastated Jewish community life. Institutions already weakened by more than a century of turbulent change in Europe were not easily transplanted to America, especially when the most secular Jews displayed the greatest eagerness for the opportunities emigration afforded. They, of course, were the uneasiest carriers of tradition. Breaking with the past, they confronted the peril and the challenge of building new lives and new communities in their adopted land. But the centrality of law in Jewish history was, with intriguing variations, replicated in the American Jewish experience.

American Jews transformed old institutions into forms appropriate to their new setting. The difficulties of the task were compounded by the suspicious encounter of sharply clashing Jewish cultures, especially in New York, the center of American Jewish life. Established German Jews viewed the ragged, impoverished newcomers with a mixture of sympathy, condescension, and disdain. The immigrants responded with respect, mistrust, and apprehension. They needed assistance, which German Jewish philanthropists and social workers provided. But the price was high: immigrants were expected to Americanize rapidly lest their conspicuous poverty and distinctive manners cast aspersions upon even the most assimilated German Jews, who worried that their own successful absorption and comfortable status were in jeopardy.

The search for coherence and order within a communal framework prompted the revival of a venerable European institution, the *Kehillah* (Hebrew for "community"), to coordinate communal activities and, if possible, to speak for New York Jewry with a single voice. The *Kehillah*, an inclusive organization designed to represent the interests of New York Jews, forged a tenuous alliance among socialists and Zionists, assimilated German-Americans and Yiddish-speaking newcomers, philanthropists and factory workers, Reform and Orthodox rabbis. For religious and secular reasons, dispute settlement figured prominently in *Kehillah* activities. The dispute-settlement functions of rabbis were virtually moribund in the United States. The rabbinate was in disarray, ripped from its Old World foundation. *Kehillah* leader Judah L. Magnes developed a plan for neighborhood rabbinical judges to answer questions of ritual and to mediate minor disputes. Their participation in dispute settlement was intended to restore a traditional rabbinical function, but it could not restore the rabbinate to its traditional place in the Jewish community. The rabbis resolved a restricted sphere of ritual issues for a dwindling constituency.

For the overwhelming majority of immigrants, earning a living was more urgent than ritual purity. In the teeming commercial world of the Lower East Side, labor-management conflict, spiced by European socialism and militant feminism, cleaved the community. A series of strikes in the clothing industry during 1909-10 stirred forebodings of class warfare in the absence of a conciliatory framework. Julius Henry Cohen, counsel to the manufacturers (and subsequently a prominent advocate of commercial arbitration), cited the European Jewish experience as a model for successful dispute settlement through mediation. In response, the *Kehillah* established a Bureau of Industry, staffed by full-time mediators, whose efforts in the clothing, fur, and millinery industries brought a measure of harmony to industrial relations in the sweatshops and factories where Jewish immigrants worked.

Kehillah leaders then looked beyond industrial mediation to a more inclusive pattern of dispute settlement for the full range of conflict in the Lower East Side. An experiment in Baltimore sparked their interest. There Jewish lawyers, distressed by corrupt justices of the peace, had established a lay arbitration tribunal for the resolution of commercial (and also religious) disputes among Jews. But New York law, which encouraged the easy revocation of arbitration agreements, was an impediment. While Magnes lobbied diligently (and successfully) for legislative reform, his associates developed a plan for *Kehillah* arbitration. By 1914 a Court of Arbitration and a network of neighborhood arbitration boards functioned within the Jewish community of New York.

The theme of harmony resounded through *Kehillah* arbitration literature. Community leaders, concerned with the intensity and potential disruptiveness of conflict among their own constituents, looked to arbitration to restore "peaceful relationships" among friends and neighbors. There was, additionally, a defensive side to *Kehillah* arbitration, consistent with the traditional Jewish preference not to display dirty linen before a hostile Christian public. Squabbles must be contained within the community lest outsiders suspect division and weakness, or draw unsavory conclusions that might fuel anti-Semitism. Disagreements between Jews were regarded by arbitration proponents as "family differences...in which the public is not interested." Public attention, according to a *Kehillah* executive committee member, "would be unfortunate and militate against the good name of the Jewish community." If a dispute went to court one party would win, but "the Jews as a body" surely would "suffer much more in reputation."

The arbitration tribunals straddled the secular and religious worlds, blended informality and legality in their composition and procedures, and spoke in the various tongues of their constituency. The official language was English, but opinions were also announced in Yiddish, the language of the Lower East Side. (The contrast with Chinese tribunals is instructive: Chinese immigrants, intending to return to China, retained their native language.) In disputes over ritual issues that were enforceable by "religious or moral suasion" the parties were urged to select a rabbi as arbitrator; his decisions were expected to be "as free as possible" from "the strict rules of technical legal evidence." (In at least one *Kehillah* district, a Bet Din functioned in conjunction with the local arbitration court to provide disputants with their choice of forum.) When rabbis were not conspicuous, lawyers were. Legal representation of the parties was prohibited, but lawyers usually sifted the complaints, dismissed those without merit, advised the parties, and guided the selection of arbitrators. Gradually community power drifted from the rabbinate, and dispute settlement began to function as an instrument of immigrant acculturation rather than as a shield to protect religious isolation.

The *Kehillah* faded away after World War I, its fragile cohesion shattered by the fractiousness of New York Jewry and its concerns overwhelmed by a new agenda of international issues relating to Zionism and statehood. But there was still a compelling need to preserve Jewish religious and communal values. During the war, the Jewish Ministers' Association of America was organized to unite Orthodox congregations against "flagrant desecration of the Sabbath," the "ruined Jewish home," and the "lamentable state of Jewish education." Among its contributions was a Jewish arbitration court, designed to provide "Jewish justice" and to preserve Jewish values against secular erosion. The arbitration principle expressed a "more modest" communal vision than the *Kehillah* had pursued, but it lingered long after the *Kehillah* had expired.

In the post-war decade the New York Jewish community generated a variety of arbitration tribunals whose presiding rabbis, despite divergent religious persuasions, shared a common vision of acculturation. Samuel Buchler, an Orthodox member of the Ministers' Association, described his arbitration court as "a medium of assimilation into cosmopolitan life." It did not, he emphasized, contribute "to isolation from the life of the citizenry. On the contrary, it has served to enhance appreciation of the nature of religious liberty, and encourage respect for the authority of the civil courts." Similarly, Israel Goldstein, a prominent New York Conservative rabbi, defended his Jewish Conciliation Court for its vital role "in the Americanization process of many Jewish immigrant families." Americanization required a delicate balance between secular and religious interests and between Jewish and American values. So the tribunals invariably included a rabbi, a lawyer, and a layman (usually a businessman). The rabbi symbolized continuity with religious tradition; the lawyer offered reassurance that the law of the state would not be contravened; the businessman provided access to the practical values of commerce. Like carefully balanced political tickets, the postwar arbitration tribunals stitched together the various constituencies of the New York Jewish community.

The range of disputes that came to these tribunals was as varied as the tribulations of their Jewish working-class clientele: a disgruntled widow refused to pay the rabbi for his uninspired eulogy; a disenchanted spouse felt cheated by the marriage-broker's assurance of an "everlasting" marriage; an observant husband and his assimilated wife disagreed over the retention of a *mezzuzah* on their door-post after they moved from the Lower East Side to a more respectable address (the woman was apprehensive lest the religious symbol cost her daughters prospective secular suitors). The arbitration process was always casual, inhibited neither by procedure nor by precedent. The parties agreed to be bound by the arbitrators' decision. (Occasionally challenged, it was invariably affirmed by the state supreme court.) No matter how bitter the disagreement, the choice of arbitration reflected a preference for dispute resolution within the framework provided by Jewish values and Yiddish immigrant culture.

Nevertheless, the pursuit of Jewish justice was occasionally elusive among the discordant babble of Jewish voices. The competing claims of traditional Judaism and American modernity, of elite control and popular preference, were difficult to reconcile, and the various tribunals had their own conflicts involving power, respectability, and status. These quarrels suggest that protecting the reputation of the Jewish community, their ostensible common purpose, was uncommonly difficult at a time of wrenching transition from the Old World to the New.

The Jewish Arbitration Court, launched under Orthodox auspices by lawyer-rabbi Samuel Buchler, secured a base of philanthropic and professional support during the twenties. It resolved thousands of disputes, and was sufficiently active to justify the establishment of branch offices in scattered Jewish neighborhoods throughout the city. There is a hint, however, that lawyers who organized the court (nobly dedicated to the pursuit of "Truth, Law and Peace") may have capitalized upon its more lucrative disputes to enrich their private practices. By the end of the decade, the avid pursuit of clients, especially by immigrant lawyers, was viewed unkindly by the legal establishment in New York. A publicized investigation of "ambulance-chasing" produced a spate of disbarments and considerable righteous condemnation (especially from lawyers whose family connections, law-firm partnerships, and social clubs provided more discreet advertisements for themselves). The Arbitration Court, evidently unsettled by these developments, invited Israel Goldstein, a young rabbi from one of the oldest Conservative congregations in New York, to repair the damage to its reputation. Within a year, however, a new tribunal emerged; the Jewish Conciliation Court of America was incorporated "to advance the cause of the amicable adjustment of disputes...affecting the good name and reputation of Jewry."

Goldstein had a shrewd understanding of the politics of institutional success, a firm conception of Jewish honor to protect, and extensive contacts among prominent Jews whose vision of purpose (and power) he shared. He obtained their support for the efforts of the Conciliation Court to preserve harmony, achieve respectability, and prod immigrants along the road to Americanization. The court, like other Jewish philanthropic and social-service ventures, combined some of the strongest desires and deepest anxieties of American Jews, who were apprehensive lest the tide of Eastern European Jewish immigrants obliterate their own precarious beachhead of decorum and success. They wanted to Americanize the newcomers by scrubbing away their Orthodoxy and *Yiddishkeit* with Reform, patriotism, and the King's English. Dispute settlement (removed from Bet Din Orthodoxy but not yet consigned to the scrutiny of Christian judges) moderated intratribal Jewish conflict and cleansed it for public scrutiny.

Jews who brought their disputes to the Conciliation Court were, in Goldstein's words, "my humble, often underprivileged brothers and sisters, who were in need of help, sympathetic understanding, and guidance." Resolving their disagreements was the primary task of the court, but not its exclusive purpose. The preservation of Jewish dignity and honor depended upon the resolution of conflict between Jews by Jews. Not only was it unreasonable to expect Christian judges to penetrate the intricacies of Jewish ritual or custom; it was dangerous to give them the opportunity. (Occasionally, a state court judge perceived his own disability: in one dispute involving conflict between a congregation and a school over possession of a Torah the judge told the parties, "You have come to Rome. I will show you the way to Jerusalem," and referred them to Jewish arbitration). Once a dispute entered the public domain it might desecrate the Jewish name and invite anti-Semitic retribution. Unassimilated immigrants must be protected from the hostility that their Old World manners and mores would elicit.

The pursuit of dignity was complicated and frustrated, however, by the tormenting persistence of Rabbi Buchler's Arbitration Court. The Buchler court (perhaps too Orthodox and obtrusive for its Conservative rival) was treated like a nagging Old World uncle, whose mere presence (to say nothing of his uncouth behavior) constantly embarrassed assimilated family members. They were still sufficiently insecure in their new home to worry about what the neighbors might think of them, especially for having such an offensive relative. Goldstein invested Buchler and his court with enormous power to inflict harm on the Jewish community, which only magnified the responsibility of Goldstein's court to preserve the good name of Jewry.

The bad feelings between the tribunals surfaced when the Arbitration

Court began to broadcast its proceedings. The practice infuriated Goldstein and his associates, who denounced it as a degradation of Jewish honor. "Radio courts," they insisted, were nothing but "cheap sensationalism," exposing conflict merely for audience amusement. But the allegations (even if true) missed an important point: radio broadcasts invited the Jewish masses to participate vicariously in a compelling drama of conflict and catharsis. The radio, a new medium of direct communication, instantly transformed an individual dispute into a communal concern, thereby stimulating communal participation in the disputing process. The Conciliation Court, which tried to stifle the broadcasts, was itself a competitor in the marketplace of disputes. As one official posed the dilemma: "While we must be both proper and dignified, we must, in some way, overcome the competition" from rival courts. Thus, the Conciliation Court cultivated good relations with the Jewish and secular press; it encouraged the *Forward*, the popular Yiddish newspaper, to cover its proceedings; and its definition of propriety permitted newspaper advertisements. (But the printed word was carefully monitored: in an early decision about publicity pamphlets Goldstein rejected "Semitic" typeface for a more dignified alternative.)

The tribunals, as voluntary institutions that depended upon disputes for their survival, competed vigorously for a share of the Jewish audience. Some spoke from the Lower East Side (the Jewish Board for Justice and Peace, conducted by a radio station, was located adjacent to a Loew's theater to capture departing movie-goers in search of more entertainment). Goldstein's Conciliation Court, reflecting his elitist preferences, prodded disputants to be good Jews, and to become good Americans. To do this, he relied upon "the very best element in this community…a selective gathering." Not only as donors but as judges, their participation was vital to the acculturation process. Among the leaders of New York Jewry, they provided a model of respectability and decorum for disputants. The Conciliation Court convened its sessions on the Lower East Side, but its judges traveled to East Broadway from the Upper West Side, where the "best" Jews lived. It was a short subway ride, but it represented a journey of cultural refinement that usually took at least a generation to achieve. The Conciliation Court proudly touted its roster, which included philanthropist Jacob R. Schiff, David Sarnoff of RCA, and a cross-section of prominent judges, rabbis, and lawyers. But between these successful acculturated Jews and the struggling new immigrants whose disputes they resolved (the relation was never reversed) existed a cultural gap as wide as the ocean that separated Europe from America.

If shared communal experience was the measure of empathy, however, there were deficiencies in the principle of selection. One self-critical judge wondered whether three imported listeners, hearing a dispute without any specialized knowledge or preparation, could render qualified judgment. Once, when Goldstein tried to arrange interesting sessions for favored English visitors to preside over, he had to be cautioned to seat them on the same panel with Americans, who would be more familiar with the culture of the disputants. And the occasional trading of a judgeship for a donation, to secure necessary income, hardly strengthened the process of dispute settlement. In the end, the beneficiaries of that process were not only the disputants but the dispute resolvers, whose good name was protected as they spread their influence in the Jewish community. A photograph taken in 1954 provides vivid testimony of the distance between judges and judged: arrayed behind Supreme Court Justice William O. Douglas, speaking at the twenty-fifth anniversary celebration of Goldstein's presidency, are well-dressed, clean-shaven men (and one trim woman) identified as guests of honor by their various titles—Doctor, Judge, General. Closest to the camera is an elderly couple, identified merely as "two clients." The full-bearded man wears a black hat that signals his religious orthodoxy; the woman wears a babushka, a loose-fitting peasant dress, and a shawl. They are evidently uncomfortable; unlike the other guests, their eyes are carefully averted—from both speaker and camera. In the Conciliation Court, the Jews of modernity sat in judgment upon the Jews of tradition.

For the Jewish Conciliation Court, the final stage in its own acculturation process, appropriately, involved a name change. In 1939, in a modest alteration of symbolic significance, the court became the Jewish Conciliation Board. The change had been suggested two years earlier by a lawyer who anticipated state legislation prohibiting any private group from using "court" in its title. Goldstein, supported by the board of directors, had resisted the proposal as an implied demotion that would diminish the stature of his court. But the proliferation of ethnic and religious tribunals remained troublesome to bench and bar, who wanted to protect the legitimacy of courts by confining the name to government institutions. Renewed pressure from established Jewish lawyers was brought on the Conciliation Court to consult with "the right people"—prominent Jewish judges and bar leaders—and reach "a correct conclusion." The executive secretary was instantly persuaded: "We should have the complete approval of the Judiciary and the Bar Associations and if by changing our name we would have such approval, we ought to do so." Goldstein and the directors concurred.

The name change symbolized a subtle shift in the court's evolving identity. At first, Goldstein had resisted the change as an affront to the Jewish community it served; then he acceded to retain the approval of bench and bar, an entirely different constituency. The word of lawyers was now the law. As the Conciliation Court became the Jewish Conciliation Board, its transformation into an American institution was complete. The first step had been the decisive rejection of Rabbi Buchler's court as an embarrassing symbol of parochial orthodoxy. Then came the imposition of propriety, decorum, and honor as primary norms of acculturation, encouraging the immigrants to adjust to their American environment. The name change was the final gesture: under pressure from the formal legal system the court proclaimed its American identity.

Despite immense pressure for acculturation, remnants of the immigrant culture survived. Elderly Jews, enclosed in tradition, remained isolated from the dominant patterns of American society. Decades after the era of mass immigration had ended, and long after their upwardly mobile children had departed for the suburbs (where there were no Jewish courts), their preference for "Jewish justice" over law reflected not only their continuing marginal status in America but the strength of their bonds to the Old World culture that they had never entirely abandoned. Jewish tribunals still provided a reassuring framework. Whether it was the substantive principles that guided a decision, the presence of a rabbi (and the exclusion of Christians), or the neighborhood proximity of the proceedings and the comforting knowledge that Yiddish could be spoken there, disputants who selected that forum still preferred to insulate their Jewishness from American society....

For most American Jews, however, emigration and acculturation decisively rearranged their commitment to law. As Jews capitalized upon their unprecedented opportunities in the United States they developed a boundless love affair with American law. Traditionally, religious law had preserved the Jewish community; in the United States, secular law provided an escape from it. Jews arrived in America with important middle-class values already internalized, at a propitious historical moment of rapid urbanization, industrialization, and professionalization. They capitalized upon their opportunities to rise rapidly in occupational status and affluence. The legal profession attracted droves of ambitious Jews who thirsted for personal fulfillment. Law, like medicine and education, drew them in numbers vastly disproportionate to their distribution in the national population. Jews had an abiding faith in law as their only reliable safeguard against the reversions to violence that had victimized them throughout their history. By the second generation (occasionally in the first), they were far along the professional road from rags to robes, from shyster to Wall Street—and even to the Supreme Court....

All immigrant groups struggled with similar conflicts of autonomy and absorption. Their alternatives to the formal state legal system enabled them, at least for a time, to retain (or even develop) protective cohesion against threatening forces of acculturation. But as time eroded resistance to accommodation, alternative institutions were no longer necessary, or possible. Other affiliations—unions and professions—cut across ethnic lines, creating new loyalties and providing their own grievance procedures. The Americanization process, with its overriding emphasis on individual achievement, encouraged adversarial competitiveness and communal fragmentation.

For a time, however, immigrants, like seventeenth-century colonists and nineteenth-century utopians, retained an alternative vision of social organization: not merely an aggregation of individuals but a community with shared values and commitments. Inevitably its members would quarrel among themselves, but when they did they turned toward each other, looking to restore group unity. Conflict was predictable; deviance lay in the pursuit of individual advantage against another group member beyond group boundaries. So Scandinavians replicated an earlier model of village serenity, secure from litigious warfare. The Chinese preserved the power of the patriarchal headman and the strength of associational life. (No other voluntary immigrant group used internal dispute settlement in such tenacious protection of a traditional structure of authority; in part, surely, because none was as blatantly mistreated in America as the Chinese.) Jews, consistent with their entire history in exile, reshaped traditional institutions to ease their transition as Americans. For all of them, and doubtless for others, litigiousness was intolerable as long as a community of common interest transcended individual self-interest. Once that community dissolved amid the promise of individual opportunity, the immigrants were Americans.

5 · A Plague of Lawyers

Not frogs or gnats, flies or boils, hail or locusts, persuaded Pharaoh to let the children of Israel go. It is foolhardy to question divine wisdom, but it is at least arguable that somewhere between gnats and locusts, and surely before the death of the firstborn shattered Pharaoh's stubborn resolve, a plague of lawyers would have been enough.

What God spared Egypt Americans inflict upon themselves. At the beginning of this century there was approximately one lawyer to every 1,100 Americans. Twenty-five years ago the ratio was 1:700. Now it is 1:530. Since 1970 the population has grown by 6 percent, but there has been a 14 percent spurt in the size of the legal profession. A steady stream of law students (53,000 in 1950) swelled by 1968 (68,000) to become a flood (97,000) just three years ago. By the time we celebrate our tricentennial, at these rates, we will be fortunate indeed if any Americans but lawyers are alive to see it.

No other country in history, or in the world today, has shared our obsession with lawyers. Israel (1:670) comes closest; Finland, Greece, Spain, and some South American countries follow; Canada and England round out the top ten. Other Western industrial nations—France, West Germany, Denmark, the Netherlands—are well down the list. At the bottom are the Asian, Muslim, and African nations. This suggests a pattern to which modernization provides one important clue. Thus Lebanon (like Israel, an anomaly beside its Arab neighbors) has had a substantially higher proportion of lawyers than the Muslim nations. Yet it is not modernization alone that breeds lawyers. Urban industrial Japan has quite a low ratio (1:10,300), higher only than the new nations of Africa and the People's Republic of China. Modernization seems to generate lawyers only if, as in Israel and Lebanon, it is infused with Western expertise, capital, and personnel. The modern Western nations that most closely resemble the United States, however, have managed to survive with substantially fewer lawyers. Even England, from which Magna Carta, trial by jury, Jarndyce v. Jarndyce, and other Anglo-Saxon legal blessings flow, has a ratio only one-third as high as ours.

It comes as no surprise to discover still another example of American uniqueness. The belief (or conceit) that we are, and ought to be, special is deeply embedded in our national character. Partial as we also are to size, growth, and

---

"A Plague of Lawyers," *Harper's* (October 1976), 37-40, 42-44.

quantity, it follows that more of anything is better. Therefore, more lawyers are as commendable as more automobiles, even if we pollute our public life (and private lives) in the process by encouraging people to act as if every human problem had a legal solution. This may suggest that, as lawyers multiply, civilization crumbles. But our bloated legal profession is merely a symptom, not a disease. Unlike the biblical plagues, it is self-inflicted, not superimposed. It does not mold our culture so much as it reflects basic American values. If we hold it up to ourselves as a mirror, we can (if we can stand the sight) easily discern our consuming individualism, unrelenting contentiousness, and discordant heterogeneity. We can, in short, see one divided nation, under lawyers, with liberty and justice for some.

Five hundred years from now, when historians sift through twentieth-century artifacts, they doubtlessly will be as uncomprehending of our legal piety as we are of medieval religious piety. In fact, there is more than a slight resemblance between the pre-Reformation medieval church and the contemporary American bench and bar. Law is our national religion; lawyers constitute our priesthood. Legal ritual now, like religious ritual in the fifteenth century, provides coherence and form within a disorderly, chaotic universe. A trial, with its controlled forms of address, cross-examination, and procedural orderliness, offers a comforting framework to dispel feelings of helplessness and fears of randomness. The bar, like the church, relies upon mysterious language and procedures to instill reverence and to remove itself from the people. As Latin was the language of the Mass, so it remains embedded in the language of the law, serving as a reminder to the uninitiated that what may be gibberish to them is *res ipsa loquitur* to a lawyer. The black robes of bishop and judge clothe mere mortals with the power of the Lord or the law. The courtroom is our cathedral, where contemporary passion plays are enacted. In both buildings silence, awe, and deference—if not subservience—placate the authorities. Solemnity is most characteristic of the Supreme Court, where government lawyers traditionally appeared in cutaways and striped pants to present their arguments. Because priests and lawyers constitute classes of certified experts who monopolize access to pivotal social institutions, they are both respected and mistrusted. As the priest mediated between man and God for the salvation of souls, so the lawyer manipulates a different form of life after death (through trusts and wills). The lawyer may even have an edge, purgatory constituting a slightly better fate than dying intestate. Purgatory, after all, is for the sinner alone, but the omission of a will dooms generations of descendants.

If history repeats itself, as it occasionally does, there may be an instructive parable for our own time in the medieval experience. As the church grew in size and complexity, redoubling its acquisitive energies as it lost sight of its pietistic purpose, it became crippled by inertia and riddled with corruption. Priests capitalized upon their monopoly of salvation to sell forgiveness. They charged fees, or indulgences, for burials, probate of wills, and the administration of the sacraments. Obviously, the larger a believer's purse, the more direct his journey to heaven. The situation bears an uncanny resemblance to the cartoon in which an attorney reassures his anxious client about the substantial merits of his case, and inquires, "How much justice can you afford?"

As ceremonial mystery deteriorated into corrupt authority Martin Luther broke through forms to substance—always a dangerous threat to any priestly class. Luther demanded direct communication between God and man, without church intervention. In perhaps his unkindest cut he declared that all believers were priests. Luther's reforms brought substantial benefits: simplified services and translation of the Bible from Latin to the more widely comprehensible French, German, and English. Theology was demystified and transferred into the public realm, where not only the privileged priesthood but mere mortals could participate in salvation.

A Luther of the law would discover an equally encrusted institution, no less certain of its rectitude and no less committed to the preservation of privilege and power. In the twentieth century, as in the fifteenth, form has superseded substance. Now it is justice, the secular equivalent of salvation, which is sold for a fee. Now it is lawyers who corrupt the temple. The long roster of Watergate lawyers convicted for obstruction of justice or perjury does not even include Richard Nixon, who although pardoned by an alumnus of Yale Law School, was recently disbarred in New York. Assertions of lay competence (how to avoid probate without retaining a lawyer) elicit howls of outrage from our contemporary salesmen of indulgences. Efforts to simplify procedure and ease recovery of damages (no fault insurance) rally lawyers to do battle for their fees. Imagine someone intrepid enough to suggest that the language of a contract be subjected to the test of lay comprehension, or that good moral character (a popular nineteenth-century standard) suffice as a qualification to practice law. He would surely be committed, with a lawyer at his side to protect his rights (if not his soul).

It is astonishing that lawyers anywhere, no less in the United States, should ascend to eminence, or even to conspicuousness. Hostility to the legal profession is as old as the profession itself. The ancients believed that lawyers had a vested interest (their fees) in manipulating or misinterpreting tribal custom and prophetic teaching. In early Greece, republican Rome, and dynastic China there were rules against the provision of paid legal advice. The rebel Jack Cade, in Shakespeare's *Henry VI, Part Two*, asked: "Is not this a lamentable thing, that of the skin of an innocent lamb should be made parchment? that parchment, being scribbled o'er, should undo a man?" However lamentable, lawyers continued to fleece innocent lambs. Modern revolutionary movements—often led by lawyers, such as Robespierre and Lenin, who understood professional conservatism—have sought to destroy the legal profession: the French abolished the Order of Advocates and the Bolsheviks destroyed the Russian Advokatura.

Mistrust crossed the Atlantic with the earliest settlers in America, whose Edenic vision consigned lawyers to a role slightly above the biblical serpent. The *Fundamental Constitutions* of Carolina declared it "a base and vile thing to plead for money or reward." In Massachusetts the *Body of Liberties* permitted anyone who could not plead his own cause to retain someone else for assistance, "Provided he give him noe fee or reward for his paines." Both Massachusetts and Rhode Island prohibited lawyers from serving in their colonial assemblies. Benjamin Franklin's *Poor Richard* echoed the popular complaint: " 'Tis the Fee directs the Sense to make out either side's Pretense." Colonists referred to a lawyer-bird, with its long bill, and a lawyer-fish, which was slippery. Yet suspicion was no deterrent to the expansion of the colonial bar. Not long after independence, the Frenchman Crèvecoeur described American lawyers as weeds "that will grow in any soil that is cultivated by the hands of others; and when once they have taken root, they will extinguish every other vegetable that grows around them."

A democratic society, Tocqueville wisely observed nearly half a century later, nurtured the political power of lawyers. Once aristocracy, nobility, and royalty were excluded from politics, lawyers were "the only men of information and sagacity, beyond the sphere of the people," who might be chosen for public office. Tocqueville appreciated the ability of lawyers "to neutralize the vices inherent in popular government." Their sobriety and conservatism provided ballast amid democratic turbulence.

It was not merely the absence of aristocracy that thrust American lawyers into prominence. In traditional societies roles were defined, stable relationships were encouraged, and mutual responsibility was valued. In the United States people stood apart, separated from ancestors, contemporaries, and descendants. Individualism meant freedom, but it also meant solitariness, even loneliness. Here, Tocqueville wrote, people "acquire the habit of always considering themselves as standing alone and they are apt to imagine that their whole destiny is in their own hands."

Destiny might have been there in the open, mobile, simple society of our first century. With the concentration of institutional and economic power in the modern era, however, individuals often could not stand alone, and individualism became the mask for the privileged few who got there first rather than the assurance of opportunity for all. By the end of the nineteenth century American society was diverse, contentious, and unstable. Success, measured by money, was the tangible sign of God's favor—reserved, appropriately, for respectable young men with white skin, middle-class fathers, and Anglo-Saxon origins. As social discord increased, old elites zealously guarded their privileged enclaves against immigrant newcomers, with their unfamiliar names, faces, accents, and manners. Class conflict erupted spasmodically, although Americans were uncomfortable with the label, which contradicted their ideology if not their experience. The only social ethic, ironically, was competitive individualism, upheld in accordance with the loose ground rules of the Darwinian struggle. This restless movement and relentless grasping were directed toward one overriding purpose: money. A democratic nation could stratify its members only according to wealth and poverty.

In this setting lawyers were sucked even deeper into the power vacuum. When everyone was encouraged to make his own way at the expense of everyone else, the rich and powerful did not have to rely on their own six-shooters; they had the advantage of the hired gun. Lawyers were perfectly suited to play this role, which American society was uniquely endowed to provide for them. The rule of law provided the only social cement to hold a fearful and fractured society together—as long as no one bothered to inquire why, in the land of equal justice, some were more equal than others.

Modern professional training has been sensitively attuned to the rule of law and to the myth of equal justice. Resting precariously on the false (but reassuring) metaphor of law as science, legal education for more than a century has strengthened inequity under the guise of neutrality. It elevates process over result; competence over conscience; form over substance. These choices, disguised as value-free, ratify a delicate quid pro quo between lawyers and society, which provides that the size and power of the legal profession may grow, in return for assurances that lawyers are merely craftsmen, professionally competent but politically uncommitted.

Each year almost 100,000 students are taught to think like lawyers. Teaching someone who for twenty-one years has thought like a person to think like a lawyer is no mean achievement. The lesson requires suspension of belief that right and wrong have any meaning beyond what the adversary process and legal system decide. (As Johnson told Boswell: "A cause is neither good nor bad 'til the Judge determines it.") It insists that no result can be more important than the legal processes by which all results must be reached. It rests on the proposition that the social good has no content beyond the assertion of individual rights, funneled laboriously through labyrinthine channels of procedure which only lawyers can navigate. In this curious vacuum society exists without groups; thoughts are independent of theory; events occur without pattern. The legal mind must be trained to comprehend no more than the individual client and the concrete case. (That mind, a law teacher once explained, can think of something that is inextricably connected to something else without thinking about what it is connected to.) In medical school, this operation is called a lobotomy; in law school, recovery is rewarded with a JD degree.

There is a diabolical circularity to it all. A society in which individual rights are paramount requires an abundance of lawyers to defend and process them. In a society where lawyers abound, contentious individualism flourishes. Americans are as hooked on lawyers as are lawyers on clients. This arrangement is functional in much the same, self-destructive way that a neurosis is functional: as individual rights are protected, social fragmentation accelerates. It is also filled with contradictions. An individualistic society emphasizes rights, yet reserves them for citizens who assert them and can afford to pay for them. So lawyers, who belong to a public profession with broad social responsibilities, proclaim client loyalty as their highest obligation (when they really cherish loyalty to a client's fee). Similarly, the adversary system, with two combatants in every legal ring, is ill equipped to consider the social good, beyond the implicit assumption that every fight and any winner is good for society. But in any system where the wealthy and powerful have overwhelming advantages, the social good, in the end, usually means no more than what is good for General Motors. (Or its counterparts: in 1971 the First National City Corporation paid $2 million in legal fees to its New York law firm, and twenty-five other companies paid more than $500,000 to theirs. Occasionally individuals hire the biggest guns: Jacqueline Onassis was billed $400,000 by her firm, whose senior partner, according to some accounts, bills at $250 per hour; when she refused to pay, the firm—of course—sued.) Additionally, the particularism of legal inquiry, directed from the general to the specific and from society to client, obliterates critical scrutiny of social institutions. That, of course, is precisely what any wealthy client, abetted by his lawyer's mastery of the tax code, fervently desires.

Once client loyalty, the adversary system, and professional tunnel vision merge, the primary beneficiary is the status quo of maldistributed opportunity, benefits, wealth, and power. That is no accident. A legal system inevitably absorbs the values of the society that nurtures it. With consummate skill ours combines the expansive promise of equal justice with the constricted reality of justice for a fee. To conceal the disparity, the fairness of the adversary system and the neutrality of lawyers must be accepted as articles of faith. For the most part, they are. The victims are relatively silent because they are relatively powerless. They are isolated from each other, from any sense of common identity, and from access to those who control the levers of legal redress, whose services they cannot afford in any case. On rare occasions when an innovation such as the class-action suit emerges, enabling an entire group of aggrieved persons to pool their meager individual resources and exert leverage, the courts quickly step in to impede the effort. One decision required litigants, at their own considerable expense, to notify all class members that legal action was pending. Other suits were dismissed because they were "unmanageable," i.e., they threatened corporations with liability to millions of consumer victims.

So the plague spreads, and is perceived as a blessing in disguise. More Americans than ever before rush to become lawyers; the new career of paraprofessional is created to absorb the overflow; the few remaining lay deviants hasten to retain lawyers. Litigation is the characteristic remedy provided by our society to its aggrieved members. Few Americans, it seems, can tolerate more than five minutes of frustration without submitting to the temptation to sue. (Last season, for example, Washington football fans sued a referee after his disputed call on a touchdown pass.) With no grievance too insignificant, it is little wonder that despairing reformers since the turn of the century have wrestled with, and been defeated by, the problem of overcrowded dockets and the consequent delays that deny justice to those who cannot afford to wait.

Every problem seems to have the identical solution. If a doctor does not heal, the patient brings a malpractice suit. If a financially beleaguered university dismisses faculty, its chief administrator declares: "The university will be in litigation for decades over this. It will be a lawyers' paradise." If the President commits high crimes and misdemeanors, sue him for his tapes. If the legal profession refuses to permit advertising, sue the American Bar Association for violating the Sherman Anti-Trust Act. (In an appropriate twist of irony, the Department of Justice has done just that.)

The United States is a lawyers' paradise. So much of our institutional thought and language is legalistic that it is accepted without question. Legalese, aided and abetted by bureaucratic circumlocution, fills our vocabulary with what Yale Law Prof. Fred Rodell long ago labeled "fuzzy-wuzzy words." We give full faith and credit to the terminology of lawyers; only if they were to cease and desist would we deem it fit and proper to take notice. Elsewhere legal language may run the risk of losing contact with ordinary language, but in the United States it is the ordinary language, imprisoning all of us in its archaisms, redundancies, and seductive evasiveness, while channeling thought into the limited choices that law provides.

Precisely because law so pervades American culture, legal careers have served as the surest passports to success, except for inherited wealth. Students who flock to law school have only the vaguest notions about law practice, but they do have an accurate appreciation that a law degree will certify them as instant experts in the art of problem-solving. At the very least, they can always go to work for problem-solving government agencies created by the previous generation of problem-solving lawyers. For ambitious students, there is always the hope of a career in politics. With nearly two-thirds of our Presidents, a majority of Congressmen, and all Supreme Court justices lawyers, absence of a law degree is almost as effective a disqualifier for high office as being nonwhite or female. Much of the early distrust of Jimmy Carter may be attributable to his lack of legal credentials. Americans can tolerate lawyers as priests, but they distrust evangelical politicians. A legalistic culture becomes suspicious when love and religion intrude.

If it is odd that a low estimate of lawyers should yield a consistently high proportion of them in public office, it seems even stranger that a law-obsessed society should be so lawless. The essence of legalism is obedience to rules, yet American history is so replete with episodes of lawlessness in defense of law that it is difficult to discern any line separating them. Appropriately, the only American frontier figure with more luster than the sheriff was the outlaw, condemned at the time and adored by everyone since. From the James brothers, through Bonnie and Clyde, to Patty Hearst, the outlaw as hero or heroine has remained a riveting figure in American popular culture. Back when lynching bees were almost as popular as spelling bees, vigilantism—the favorite extralegal device for preserving law and order—was enthusiastically praised by community leaders, occasionally including Presidents, judges, and lawyers....

There is an inescapable relationship between our legalism and our lawlessness. Neither vanishes because both tap a common source in our culture: the compulsive individualism, reinforced by materialism, that is the glory and bane of our national existence. As long as Americans remain a fragmented people, they will search for the elusive binding cohesion of the rule of law (with sprinklings of patriotism and anti-Communism reserved for critical moments). But just so long will substantial numbers of them break laws which thwart their individualistic yearnings. To offset disobedience we will enact more laws. To protect rights we will need more lawyers. Since more rules mean a greater probability of rule violation, the more strident will be the claim that with just a few more laws, and lawyers for those who cannot now afford them, all will be well. But all will not be well. The vicious cycle will merely have been accelerated.

If there is any solace in this dismal diagnosis it is that there may be no preferable alternative—or so, at least, we would like to believe. Throughout this century social theorists have taught us that a formal legal system, with a trained professional class, offers distinct advantages over its competitors. Submission to the authority of "law prophets" (Moses or Mohammed), or "charismatic law creators" (Lenin or Hitler), has limited appeal. The transition from unchecked theocratic or secular authority to the administration of a legal elite is counted as one of the undisputed blessings in the evolution of modern Western civilization. It marked the triumph of formal justice, with its rationality, consistency, impersonality, and predictability, over arbitrariness and instability. These virtues were crucial to the development of a modern capitalist economy, which needed to exclude personal and irrational calculations from its cost-benefit calculations. Yet the price of progress is high....

It is not surprising that utopian visionaries expel lawyers from their paradise. There is little use for their services, or tolerance for their arts and craft, in cohesive, cooperative communities. On an Israeli kibbutz, for example, the sanctions of community opinion replace police, lawyers, and prisons. All the problems of human intercourse remain, but the procedures for resolving them reflect the mores of cooperation and common purpose. Disputes are mediated by a respected community member; neither party feels aggrieved without counsel. The lay members of the kibbutz welfare committee make final decisions, from which there is no judicial review. Expulsion is the ultimate sanction—precisely as it was in seventeenth-century Massachusetts, when deviants such as Roger Williams became obstreperous to Puritan wanderers in the New World wilderness.

Modern America could not easily survive the absence of lawyers. They not only sustain and profit from its rapacious individualism; simultaneously, they commit the society to legalistic values, which offer the only thin veneer of unity that Americans can tolerate. As Jack Cade's fellow rebel suggested: "The first thing we do, let's kill all the lawyers." The problem, for Americans, is what to do next.

II · Promised Lands

The turn of the 20th century marked a watershed in American Jewish history. Millions of new immigrants from southern and eastern Europe transformed Jewish demography in the United States, creating new problems and possibilities of identity and loyalty. After World War I the nascent Zionist movement in Palestine compounded the American Jewish dilemma: could a Jew be a loyal American citizen yet support Jewish statehood?

To undermine insinuations of divided loyalty Louis D. Brandeis, the assimilated American Jewish lawyer with little Jewish knowledge or identification, was lauded—then and since—for defining the terms of compatibility between Judaism, Americanism, and Zionism. American Jews eagerly embraced liberalism as an updated version of the teachings of the ancient Hebrew prophets. By World War II, with their fervent pledge of allegiance to Franklin D. Roosevelt, Jewish and American identities seemed to have seamlessly converged. That may help to explain why, inside and outside the White House, the Holocaust was all but ignored.

No sooner had American Jews resolved their loyalty issues through assimilation than the birth of the State of Israel confronted them with a new challenge. Asserting the compatibility of their American loyalty and Jewish identity, they proudly proclaimed "We Are One!"—if from a distance—with the Jewish state. But as Israel tilted to the political right in the 1970s, straining its relations with the American government, the identification of American Jews with the Jewish state began to waver. Their commitment to American liberalism remained unshakable.

Jewish identity has been no less problematic, if for different reasons, in Israel. The meaning of Zionism, and its relationship to Judaism, was contested even before independence. Then, after nineteen years of secular ascendancy, the Six-Day War returned Israel to the ancient homeland of the Jewish people. The spread of Jewish settlements in biblical Judea and Samaria following the election of Menachem Begin as Prime Minister posed a religious Zionist challenge to secular Israeli values. While American Jews navigate their passage through the shoals of Jewish identity and the hazards of dual loyalties, secular Israelis yearn for Zionism to strengthen their identification with contemporary Western values and rewards.

My own meanderings between the United States and Israel during the past forty years (an appropriate time span for a Jew wandering in the wilderness) confronted me with the dilemmas inherent in modern Jewish life. Like the biblical Jacob (my namesake), I have wrestled with the competing claims on my identity and loyalty that Israel has incessantly provoked. Ever since my first visit in 1972, it has always been the Jewish content of Israeli society that riveted my attention, restored lapsed Jewish memory, and entwined me in Jewish history. As these selections indicate, I was drawn to Israelis who have found ways to fuse Judaism and Zionism, modern history with ancient memory.

6 · Liberalism and the Hebrew Prophets

It has long been an article of faith among American Jews that their political liberalism expresses traditional Jewish values. A commitment to the rule of law (the legacy of Torah), reinforced by a passion for social justice (inherited from the Hebrew Prophets), defines "the biblical heritage of American democracy."

Liberalism, however, is not an expression of the biblical tradition, but an alternative to it. Jews who rejected the authority of Torah, but wanted to remain attached to Judaism, reformulated the biblical heritage to assure its compatibility with Enlightenment values and liberal politics. Enter the Prophets.

Hebrew prophecy was rediscovered in the 19th century by Christian Bible scholars and Reform rabbis who, for their own doctrinal purposes, moderated Jewish "legalism" with prophetic "justice." Liberated from the constraints of tribe, cult, and sacred law, the Prophets were hailed as the founders of a universal religion of moral idealism and ethical monotheism (which bore a remarkable resemblance to liberal Protestantism and Reform Judaism). Julius Wellhausen, whose religious history of ancient Israel was the inspirational source of modern biblical scholarship, described with unrestrained admiration the volcanic force of prophecy as it burst through encrusted religious institutions that were "fixed and dead." The Prophets conveyed an ethical message that "destroyed the national character of the old religion" of Israel (and culminated in the religious truth of Christianity). For that "progressive step" in religious evolution, Wellhausen lavished upon them the highest praise that the son of a Lutheran minister could bestow: they had launched "the Prophetic Reformation."

American Reform rabbis of the late 19th century had a different agenda. Their rejection of Mosaic law enabled them to frame "a Judaism congenial to the free soil of America." In the "Holy Land of Freedom and Human Rights," explained Rabbi Kaufmann Kohler, the intellectual leader of Reform, "it will not do for us...to remain Hebrews in garb and custom, in views and language." As appropriate as Mosaic law might have been for "a childish and semi-barbarous nation," it was deficient by the only standard that Reform acknowledged: "modern enlightenment and progress." For Judaism to blend with freedom it must relinquish "the yoke of mere *legality*" and embrace the universal truths

---

"Liberalism and the Hebrew Prophets," *Commentary*, 84 (August 1987), 58-60.

of prophecy. These, paradoxically, enabled Jews to become "truly American."

By the turn of this century prophecy, wrenched from historical context and stripped of Jewish content, defined the appropriate faith for a secular age. Since then, the prophetic voice, once the conscience of biblical Israel, has been heard on behalf of "progressive" political causes ranging from Marxian socialism to democratic liberalism. The most conspicuous spokesmen for American liberal reform, Jews and Christians alike, have cited the Hebrew Prophets to frame their indictments of social ills. From Louis Brandeis to Lyndon Johnson, from Rabbi Stephen S. Wise to the Reverend Martin Luther King, Jr., the words of Isaiah and Jeremiah have resounded in an American vernacular. We are told that Jews especially have learned from the Prophets that it is "un-Jewish not to be preoccupied with freedom and justice for everyone." Liberalism is still good for the Jews, according to the conventional wisdom, because liberal values express fidelity to prophetic ideals.

As tempting as it has been to transform the Hebrew Prophets into Reform rabbis (or Protestant ministers), radical socialists, New Deal liberals, or social democrats, such retrospective projections should be resisted. Jewish sources and texts locate prophecy precisely within the sacred-law tradition. At a time of supreme national crisis in the life of the First Commonwealth, the Prophets passionately proclaimed themselves God's messengers to Israel, bringing the divine word to remind Israel of its covenantal obligations. They fervently defended the national religion and the sacred legal foundation upon which it rested.

The Bible makes explicit the normative Jewish understanding of prophecy. We learn in 2 Kings that late in the 8th century B.C.E., during Hoshea's rule over the Northern Kingdom, the monarch "did evil in the sight of the Lord," and the people "feared other gods, and walked in the statutes of the nations." So God sent prophets to warn them, saying: "Turn from your evil ways, and keep My commandments and My statutes, according to all the Torah which I commanded your fathers, and which I sent to you by My servants the prophets" (2 Kings 17:2,8,13-14). The book of Deuteronomy draws precise distinctions between true and false prophecy based solely upon the fidelity of the prophetic message to divine law. The true prophet was like Moses, conveying God's word to Israel.

The rabbis of the Talmud reiterated and strengthened biblical teachings. The opening sentence of the tractate *Aboth* securely linked the Prophets to the sacred-law tradition: the Torah received by Moses was transmitted by him to Joshua, then to the Elders, to the Prophets, to the Men of the Great Synagogue, and, ultimately, to the rabbis. Biblical prophecy, concluding with Malachi's admonition to remember the statutes and judgments of Torah, was rabbinically interpreted as a reminder that his prophetic predecessors had come to strengthen the Torah, not to change it.

Given Christian claims that the Prophets, anticipating Jesus, had preached a new faith that culminated in Christianity, it was all the more imperative for the rabbis to blunt any innovative potential in prophecy. (And, to be sure, anyone claiming to bear a special message from God posed a direct challenge to rabbinical authority.) But prophetic morality, as the rabbis well knew, was inseparable from Torah morality. For precisely that reason the unity of law and prophecy retains its centrality in the synagogue service today. The link between them is not the attraction of opposites. Rather, it is an associative connection demonstrating the unity of God's word to Israel: two voices conveying the single message of covenantal obligation.

Prophetic demands for justice must be located within the covenantal faith. God's children "rebelled against me," lamented Isaiah, whose prophecy concluded with a demand for covenantal loyalty and obedience (Isaiah 1:2). God wanted "loyal love" from Israel, Hosea pleaded; instead, Israel had "transgressed" the covenant (Hosea 6:6, 8:2). Jeremiah cried out in the streets of Jerusalem: "Hear the words of this covenant, and do them" (Jeremiah 11:6). Ezekiel, foretelling the return from Babylonian exile, relayed God's intention "to put My spirit within you, and cause you to follow My statutes" (Ezekiel 36:27-8).

These admonitions hardly were novel obligations thrust upon Israel. They conveyed some of its most ancient sanctions against oppression of the poor, mistreatment of the disadvantaged, and perversions of justice. They can be found, repeatedly, in Exodus, Leviticus, and Deuteronomy. Indeed, it is extremely difficult (if at all possible) to locate *any* prophetic accusation that is independent of Mosaic legislation. The Prophets knew the sacred law, cited it, and demanded obedience to it. With covenantal fidelity as their standard, they infused their indictments with legal metaphors. Isaiah, Micah, Jeremiah, and Hosea all proclaimed God's "controversy" with Israel. Appropriately, God took His people to court for breach of covenant. In these divine lawsuits, the Prophets acted as God's prosecuting attorneys. They indicted, tried, and convicted Israel before the bench of divine judgment for its legal transgressions. The Prophets, as one Bible scholar has observed, spoke "like lawyers quoting the law."

But surely, modern liberals insist, the Prophets stood for the rejection of cultic ritual in favor of individual morality, the repudiation of religious law for social justice, and the replacement of parochial nationalism with universal brotherhood (if not sisterhood). Outside Christian sources, however, there is little evidence to justify that claim. Although it was long an axiom of Bible scholarship that the Prophets superseded the priestly cult, ushering in the triumph of right over rite, this tidy evolutionary progression toward liberal Protestantism cannot be sustained. Both priest and prophet were entrusted with the task of teaching Torah. The Prophets complained, loudly, that the priests had elevated ritual above ethics, but they did not question the centrality of the cult or the Temple.

Given their attachment to the sacred law, it should come as no surprise that several of the classical Prophets maintained a close relationship to the priestly caste, to cultic ritual, and to the Temple. Isaiah was inspired to prophesy when an angel touched his lips with a burning coal, a familiar cultic purification ritual. Jeremiah explicitly identified himself with the priestly tradition and prophesied within the Temple grounds. The Prophets in exile, Ezekiel (a priest) and Deutero-Isaiah, held out the vision of national redemption *and* a rebuilt Temple to the "deaf" and "blind" Jews in *galut*. Haggai and Zechariah, after the return from Babylon, were vigorous advocates of cultic regeneration centered upon the holy sanctuary. It is hardly coincidental that the prophetic era closed with the rebuilding of the Temple.

The prophetic demand for justice is incomprehensible outside the context of the sacred law. Biblical *mishpat*, so frequently and inadequately translated as "justice," never was a standard external to law. At its broadest (as when Abraham, confronting God's intention to demolish Sodom, asked: "Shall not the Judge of all the earth do *mishpat*?" [Genesis 18:26]), it imposed upon God the obligation to make right judgments. More often it had a precise legal focus, as in the Covenant Code of Exodus, where *mishpatim* referred to the legal commands that God imposed upon Israel. Elsewhere, it meant a law that is just, or the right judgments of judges. *Mishpat* conveys the obligation to conform to God's just ordinances. "The ways of the Lord are right," Hosea reminded Israel, "and the just do walk in them" (Hosea 14:10).

The meaning of justice, in biblical Israel, was conformity to divine law. There could be no conflict (of the kind that torments liberal legal thought) between law and justice, because law emanated from a just God. The stringent requirement that Israel do justice—a requirement of Mosaic law no less than of prophecy—was the stipulation that Israel abide faithfully by the legal norms of the covenant. The idea that morality or justice might be independent of the "knowledge of God" (Hosea 4:1) was inconceivable to the Prophets who, after all, rested their claim to authority entirely upon divine command.

Finally, there is the familiar assertion that the Prophets broke the shackles of the parochial national religion to proclaim a new universal moral order. But prophetic universalism, as the Bible scholar Yehezkel Kaufmann wrote, was "always connected with the glorification of Israel, Jerusalem, and the Temple... All of prophetic universalism is suffused with national symbols." Even Isaiah's majestic anticipation of the end of days, when all nations would come to the mountain of the Lord, and "out of Zion shall go forth Torah and the word of God from Jerusalem" (Isaiah 2:3), is strikingly particularistic, which explains why Jews still recite it during the Torah service.

The exilic experience vividly illuminates the impulse behind prophetic "universalism." The exiled community in Babylon confronted a tormenting problem: "How shall we sing the Lord's song in a foreign land?" (Psalms 137:4). Hidden within the Psalmist's lament was an anxious question: had God accompanied Israel into exile or, once vacating the territorial boundaries of the promised land, had Israel left God behind? Anticipating a massive crisis of faith, Deutero-Isaiah offered reassurance that the divine reach, truly universal in scope, embraced His children even in the remote outpost of Babylon. The Prophet brought God to the exiled community, proclaiming the divine message:

"Look to me, and be saved, all the ends of the earth" (Isaiah 45:22). He reminded the people of God's unbounded presence, and of their own undiminished obligation to obey the revealed law.

How ironic that prophecy has captured a far more receptive audience in the modern era than it ever did in ancient Israel, where (except for the rebuilding of the Temple) its impact was negligible. But the attentiveness of Jewish liberals to the prophetic message may only suggest that they hear in prophecy what they want to hear, irrespective of what the Prophets said. In fact, the prophetic "tradition" of social justice and universalism (divorced from divine command) is barely a century old. That "tradition" can best be understood as part of the Jewish response to the terms of the emancipation bargain set in the Christian West: individual rights and civil equality in return for abandonment of the national religion of Judaism. Just as Jews conformed to Christian standards of dress, dietary preference, decorum, calendar observance, and religious ritual, so they reshaped their sacred-law tradition to conform to Enlightenment values. Hebrew prophecy provided a bridge, built in large measure by Christian exegetes, that Jews crossed in their exodus from the national religion to enlightened liberalism.

For Jews eager to acculturate, but unwilling to jettison their Jewish identity, prophecy eased their entry into Christian society. Severed from the particularism of the national religion, grafted to Christian theological precepts or to secular liberal politics, prophecy symbolized Jewish enlightenment. To Reform rabbis, the Prophets represented reason, progress, and American patriotism. To radical socialists the Prophets were nascent Marxists, denouncing class exploitation and proclaiming universal brotherhood. To political liberals they remain social-justice advocates, favoring the right (Left) side of any issue on the current political agenda. Prophecy, in its time a desperate cry to return to the ancient faith—"Ask for the old paths, where the good way is" (Jeremiah 6:16)—has become, in our time, an exit from the faith.

Prophecy has served as a passport to modernity—and not only for American Jews. Secular Zionists in Israel associated their state-building efforts with prophecy; not, of course, as a measure of their fidelity to the word of God but to justify their break with religious Judaism. David Ben-Gurion, presenting his first government to the Knesset, echoed Israel's Declaration of Independence, declaring: "Our activities and policy are guided...by a political and social vision that we have inherited from our Prophets." He hardly meant to imply that Israel was dedicated to the word of God, to the covenant, or to the sacred law. But secular Zionists (like their liberal American counterparts) still reflexively cite the Prophets as political allies, ironically in their struggle against the very conception of the sacred law that the Prophets so passionately defended.

It is a measure of their powerful eloquence that the Prophets became so available to all faiths in every political season. But irrespective of the varied uses to which prophecy has been put, history also has its claims. This is no mere fundamentalist exercise, akin to the effort of constitutionalists to discover in the "original intent" of the American Founding Fathers those simple truths which might restore the golden age of republican virtue. Secular liberals may make of prophecy what they will; and their imaginative transmutations provide fascinating insights into the changing sources of legitimation, both political and religious, for modern Jews. But the temptation to trim prophecy to current liberal fashion may only reflect modern anxieties, which require the reformulation of the Jewish tradition in contemporary terms. To recover the full impact of the prophetic message requires intellectual and spiritual resources that modern liberalism may not possess. Without them, however, it cannot recapture that delicate balance between faith and hope, order and change, divine command and human choice, which the classical unity of law and prophecy preserves.

7 · Rabbis and Lawyers

An influx of German Jews, arriving in the United States by the mid-nineteenth century, became the privileged beneficiaries of the unprecedented economic and civic opportunity that Jews enjoyed in American society. As they climbed the ladder of social mobility to affluence and influence, they began to construct a reformed Jewish identity that was compatible with American values. In a supreme irony of American Jewish history, Jews turned to the Puritans and Pilgrims as the authoritative interpreters of their own biblical heritage. Eager to identify themselves as Americans, they were led back to their own sacred texts as a guide to the American experience. From fragments of seventeenth-century Protestant thought, they constructed a unitary Judeo-American tradition that enabled them, as Jews, to become Americans.

The timing of their discovery was hardly coincidental. The arrival of the first wave of Jewish immigrants from Russia, after the czarist pogroms of 1881, aroused tremors of apprehension among the German Jews, who by then were settled, successful, and culturally integrated. So many impoverished, Yiddish-speaking, religiously observant newcomers, evidently foreign and distinctively Jewish, might call into question the place of all Jews in American society and even their loyalty to the United States.

The Constitutional centennial in 1887 provided an appropriate ceremonial opportunity for the first elaborate affirmation by a Jew of the Hebrew antecedents of American political values and institutions. Oscar S. Straus, one of the German Jewish luminaries of his generation (twice minister, and then ambassador, to Turkey, and the first Jew to serve in a presidential cabinet), was fascinated by the relationship between the Hebrew commonwealth and the American republic. Straus had emigrated from Bavaria as a youngster. Raised in a liberal Jewish family in a small town in Georgia (where he attended Baptist Sunday school), he delayed his entry into L. Straus & Sons, the lucrative family merchandising business, to attend college. But at Columbia, he recalled, "I was under many disadvantages...with no social standing and a Jew" He had, however, absorbed a sense of wondrous fulfillment of ancient Jewish ideals in modern American society—probably from the rabbis of his Reform temple. In 1885, after briefly practicing law, he published a long essay, *The Origin of Republican Form of Government in the United States of America*, which can best

---

Rabbis and Lawyers: The Journey from Torah to Constitution (1990, 2010), 12-21.

be understood as an effort to eradicate some of his "disadvantages" as a Jew.

It was "remarkable," Straus thought, that historians had overlooked the bonds between ancient Israel and the United States. The repeated references that Straus discovered in the revolutionary era to the biblical narrative, especially to the Book of Exodus, demonstrated that the history of Israel had served as "a glorious example and inspiring incentive to the American people" in their own "mighty struggle for the blessings of civil and religious liberty." Straus recognized the Puritan link between Israel and America: "Through the windows of the Puritan churches of New England," he wrote, "the new West looked back to the old East." The Hebrew and American peoples, although separated by two millennia, were united in their commitments to constitutionalism, democracy, and republicanism. Among the numerous parallels that Straus cited were the separation (with Aaron as high priest and Joshua as military commander) of church and state; the principle of federalism (government under the Judges, when each tribe had its own government yet sent "duly elected representatives to the national congress"); and resistance to monarchy (recounted in the Book of Samuel). Above all, there was "the divine supremacy of the law," the primary source of American liberty. To Straus, ancient Israel embodied "the spirit and essence" of American constitutionalism; and, reciprocally, "in the spirit and essence of our Constitution the influence of the Hebrew commonwealth was paramount." Israel had set "a divine precedent for a pure democracy." Truly, "the bright sun of Canaan" had risen again in America, where the spirit of Moses, Joshua, and Samuel, transmitted to Franklin, Washington, and Adams, was expressed in liberty, law, and constitutionalism.

The unity of Americanism and Judaism, proclaimed in Straus's book, molded his own identity as an American Jew. Yet as effortlessly as Straus drew the comparison, his persistent attempts to demonstrate the compatibility of Judaism and Americanism suggest some interior doubts that needed to be overcome—the legacy, perhaps, of the "disadvantages" Straus had experienced as a Jew in a predominantly Christian society. Whether in his writing, or in his commitment to the work of the American Jewish Historical Society and the American Jewish Committee, Straus made certain that "American" and "Jewish" always converged. He succeeded admirably—even to the point where, as a member of the New York delegation to the Progressive party convention in 1912, he could unselfconsciously lead the delegates in an impassioned rendition of "Onward Christian Soldiers" as they stood at their political Armageddon and waited for Theodore Roosevelt to lead them into their promised Progressive homeland. When Straus reflected upon American history he frequently returned to the Pilgrims and Puritans, who symbolized the best of the American tradition because they had absorbed the most from biblical Israel. Returning to his central theme in a subsequent book, *The American Spirit*, Straus noted "the Hebrew mortar that cemented the foundations of our American democracy." The United States, he reiterated, is "peculiarly a promised land wherein the spirit of the teachings of the ancient prophets inspired the work of the fathers of our country." So he could confidently conclude that "the American spirit and the spirit of American Judaism were nurtured in the same cradle of liberty, and were united in origins, in ideals, and in historical development." History clearly demonstrated to Straus that Jews were good Americans.

Straus was one of the first Jews to define the terms of convergence between the Jewish and American traditions. What remains of value in his effort is not its historical veracity but the claim itself, which has reverberated through a century of American history since Straus enunciated it. Resting upon a biblical idiom, it unquestioningly absorbed the Puritan self-identification with Israel without any recognition of the Christian triumphalist assumptions that framed it. The Puritan link enabled Straus to connect Israel and America to a common democratic tradition whose origins could be found in the Hebrew Bible. In a fascinating two-step process of identity formation, the Puritans affirmed their divine chosenness through Israel; then Jews affirmed themselves as Americans by reiterating the Puritan identification with the Hebrew biblical tradition. In that way, American Jews could not only demonstrate the inherent unity of the Jewish and America traditions but also claim the Puritans as "their" spiritual forbears. So American Jews became the last Puritans; the last Americans, that is, to take seriously the claim that the United States truly was the fulfillment of divine promise to Israel.

The myth of American biblical origins, woven by devout Protestants to substantiate their claims of providential blessing as the new Israel, ultimately found its most enthusiastic champions among Jews yearning to be recognized as Americans. During the year that Straus's book was published, Rabbi Kaufmann Kohler, the intellectual leader of Reform Judaism, concluded a series of lectures, on July 4th, by describing the United States as "the land where milk and honey flow for all." Rather than lament the destruction of the ancient Temple (as observant Jews would do on the approaching fast day of Tisha B'Av), Jews could fulfill their messianic yearnings in "the Holy Land of Freedom and Human Rights." Kohler heard "in the jubilant tocsin peals of American liberty the mighty resonance of Sinai's thunder." Divine revelation had become the precursor of American patriotism.

American ceremonial occasions provided recurrent opportunities for Jews to demonstrate the compatibility—indeed, unity—of the Jewish and American traditions. David Philipson, a member of the first graduating class of the Hebrew Union College and a nationally prominent Reform rabbi, delivered a Thanksgiving sermon in 1888 in which he proclaimed: "Israel's religion has gained a new foothold in a greater Zion, where the words of its prophets are finding their exemplification." Philipson long retained memories of his own visit to Plymouth where, discovering Hebrew words inscribed on the gravestone of Governor William Bradford, he identified with the very source of American civilization. Several decades later, at a celebration of the three hundredth anniversary of the Pilgrim landing, Philipson described the Pilgrims as "devout and earnest students of Israel's inspired chronicles," who had established "a home of religious freedom...for the latter-day children of Israel, outcasts and pariahs in every European land." In that striking demonstration of "poetic historical justice," the Pilgrims thereby repaid their debt to biblical Israel—and, it might be added, Jews repaid their debt to the United States.

Ever since the late nineteenth century, the identification of Judaism with Americanism has depended upon the Hebrew Bible as the source of their compatibility. This has aptly been described as a manifestation of "American Jewish apologetics," designed to justify Jewish legitimacy in American terms (which, earlier, had derived their legitimacy from Hebrew texts). Reform Jews were the first, but hardly the last, American Jews who "appropriated for themselves the American national myth of the Republic as the new Zion or Israel." But the biblical heritage, with special emphasis upon the writings of the Hebrew prophets, quickly overspread the Reform movement, inspiring successive generations of American Jews to rephrase Jewish tradition in modern American terms. In the process, the Hebrew Bible came to serve Jews who were least responsive to the claims of biblical authority.

For Jewish radicals, who strayed the farthest from religious tradition, "socialism was Judaism secularized." The fondness of Jewish socialists for biblical allusions might be taken as an indication of their commitment to Jewish tradition. As early as 1883, the poet Emma Lazarus (in her essay on "the Jewish Problem") insisted that socialism was rooted in provisions of Mosaic law that protected the rights of workers, assured a harvest portion to the needy, and restrained the property rights of landlords. Examples abound of Jewish socialists who cited the Bible, especially the prophetic writings, to support their denunciation of class exploitation. "For almost everything I write," a Jewish radical declared, "I have to thank that poet-preacher (Isaiah) who entered my heart and mind with love for...oppressed people." "Each era has its own Torah," wrote a socialist poet at the end of the nineteenth century; "Ours is one of freedom and justice." Biblical references aside, the vastly disproportionate number of Jewish socialists in the American (as in the European) movement around the turn of the century seems to suggest a special affinity between Jewish tradition and socialist consciousness.

Did the politics of Jewish socialists truly express deeply rooted traditional Jewish values? Was socialist messianism an adult expression of a youthful immersion in Torah and Talmud, demonstrating attachment to the values of righteousness and justice that may be found there? If so, American Jewish socialists can best be understood, one historian suggests, as "a prophetic minority, responding to biblical norms of social justice, interpreted in a modern context." To be sure, the rhetoric of Jewish socialists often incorporated prophetic and messianic themes. References to the "holy duty" and "sacred struggle" against "sinful" capitalism surely resonated with religious content. Jewish socialists who used such traditional allusions wished, however, to make an altogether different point. David Edelstadt, the Yiddish poet whose Torah was freedom and justice, referred to the "new prophets" who will "deliver us from exile." But he had in mind Karl Marx and Ferdinand Lassalle, not Amos and Isaiah. And Morris Winchevsky, who declared his debt to Isaiah, recalled that his "greatest pleasure" was "proving that Moses did not write the Torah."

Benjamin Feigenbaum, a leader among Lower East Side socialists, insisted that "the narrow 'Jewish spirit' has not produced any value that could not have been created—and created better—by the universal human spirit." To Feigenbaum, the greatest blessing, especially for Jews, was assimilation.

Despite the abundant references to Hebrew prophets by Jewish socialists, socialism was a political expression of Jewish renunciation. The prophets of socialism, Marx and Lassalle, had shown the way. Marx, notwithstanding the venerable tradition of rabbinical learning that distinguished his family history (preceding his father's conversion and his own baptism), was explicitly and maliciously hostile to Judaism. Whether Marx was a self-hating Jew or an anti-Semite is an inconsequential distinction. His notorious accusation—"Money is the jealous God of Israel"—and his yearning for "the emancipation of humanity from Judaism" speak for themselves. Lassalle, as a young man, took pride in Jewish religious culture, was attached to Reform, and identified with the struggle of the Maccabees for national independence. But once he rejected Judaism, Judeophobia burst forth as it did for Marx. Judaism, Lassalle wrote, represented "perfect ugliness" as an obsolescent, detestable faith which must be transcended. Lassalle saw in the Jewish people "nothing but the degenerate sons of a great, but long past epoch." For these radical prophets, socialism was less an expression of Judaism than an expression of its denial, pointing toward the ultimate disappearance of Judaism in socialist universalism. That prospect generated vastly more pleasure than sorrow among Jews who heeded their socialist prophets.

For all of its passion for justice, prophetic rhetoric, and messianism, socialism—except for its Labor Zionist variety—offered an alternative to a Jewish identity, an exit from Judaism rather than any modern restatement of ancient Jewish values. Perhaps the biblical idiom expressed a lingering, if tenuous, attachment to Judaism. But socialists, like Reform Jews with whom they otherwise shared nothing in common, used traditional Hebrew sources to break with Jewish tradition. They extracted from the legacy of biblical Israel what they needed to forge a modern identity.

Socialism had widespread appeal among new Jewish immigrants from Eastern Europe, but it was too foreign and shrill to appeal to acculturated German Jews. Their Reform, however, was too thoroughly Protestantized to appeal to the immigrants. Neither an upper-class religion, nor lower-class radicalism, could bridge the vast gulf between old and new immigrants. The reconciliation of Judaism with Americanism depended upon a different kind of synthesis, one that was insufficiently religious to offend the secular majority, but sufficiently American to attract the immigrant newcomers, whose growing numbers were rapidly transforming the demography of American Jewry.

Between 1906 and 1916 that new synthesis emerged as the formative statement of modern American Judaism. Articulated most persuasively by two lawyers, Louis Marshall and Louis Brandeis, it drew upon the centrality of law and justice in the Jewish and American traditions. During that prewar decade, lawyers challenged rabbis as the undisputed public leaders of the American

Jewish community. Their professional success, largely as counselors to wealthy and powerful corporate institutions, enabled them to ascend to influence in Jewish communal affairs. The identification of Judaism with Americanism, within a common tradition that emphasized the rule of law and the quest for social justice, was their singular contribution to the self-definition of American Jewry in the twentieth century.

Marshall's forum was the American Jewish Committee, organized in 1906 "to prevent infringement of the civil and religious rights of Jews." Galvanized by czarist pogroms, which cost tens of thousands of Jews their lives and property, the committee was a self-appointed elite of German Jews—predominantly lawyers and businessmen, with some Reform rabbis. Although they wrangled incessantly about how democratic an organization they wished to create, their decision to emphasize civil and religious rights demonstrated their unequivocal commitment to the language of American constitutionalism. That was Marshall's preferred emphasis. A distinguished New York corporate and constitutional lawyer, his Judaism was a religion only, without political or national content. He demanded of Jews unequivocal submission to the legal authority of the state, for respect for law demonstrated one of the abiding virtues of the Jewish people. The American Jewish Committee propelled Marshall to a pivotal position of communal leadership: no one was better able to define and defend Jewish interests within the framework of American patriotic and constitutional values. During more than two decades of his leadership, "Marshall law" governed American Jewish life.

It was Brandeis, however, who forged the most popular synthesis of Judaism to Americanism, through the seventeenth-century New England experience. Brandeis, like so many other German Jews (including Marshall), was deeply concerned about the patriotic allegiance of the new Jewish immigrants. It was virtually the only substantive Jewish issue, before 1914, that elicited public comment from him. By then, Brandeis had earned a glowing national reputation as a progressive reformer (and a considerable private fortune as counsel to corporations). A prominent lawyer and an outspoken liberal, a successful American Jew without any evident familiarity with Jewish tradition, ritual, or texts, he was ideally situated to synthesize Judaism and Americanism.

By 1914, Brandeis, the new leader of American Zionism, had become convinced that the "twentieth century ideals of America had been the age-old ideals of the Jews." No longer questioning the loyalty of immigrant Jews, he embraced the proposition that "there is no inconsistency between loyalty to America and loyalty to Jewry. The Jewish spirit...is essentially modern and essentially American." Jews had given to the world "reverence for law and highest conceptions of morality." The prophetic teachings of "brotherhood and righteousness," filtered through seventeenth-century New England (the Puritans, Brandeis believed, were finely honed to their task "by constant study of the prophets"), had become the modern liberal ideals of democracy and social justice. In a circuitous historical and conceptual journey, from prophecy through Puritanism, ancient Jewish ideals had become thoroughly Americanized. Brandeis's appointment to the

Supreme Court personified this synthesis. It was not merely that he was the first Jew to serve on the high court. For the first time in American history, a Jew was empowered to determine the final meaning of the American Constitution. The synthesis between Americanism and Judaism, between the biblical heritage of Torah and the American rule of law, had been forged.

Ever since Marshall and Brandeis formulated the compatibility of Judaism and American constitutionalism, rabbis, lawyers, and scholars have offered many variations on the theme. By now, it is virtually impossible for American Jews to understand themselves without locating the origins of American constitutionalism in the Hebrew Bible. This ingenious example of "social memory," with legitimacy defined by an imagined historical model, has taken on a life of its own—the ultimate testimony to its persuasive authority. The Constitution, as the reformulation of biblical ideas in an American idiom, became (even for Jews) the new testament of American democracy. The compatibility theme has become especially audible during wartime crises, when affirmations of patriotism were required, and on national celebratory occasions, to reaffirm Jewish identification with American values.

During World War I, for example, Rabbi Kaufmann Kohler proclaimed the continuity between Hebraic and American democratic ideals. Democracy, he declared, "found its classical expression in Israel's holy writings," where law was proclaimed as "the eternal source of liberty." The synthesis of liberty and law had come to fruition in America, where the Founding Fathers (as spiritual descendants of the Puritans) "took the heroes of ancient Israel as their models for the championship of liberty and democracy, framing their constitution on the principles underlying the Law of Sinai." In a single sentence, Kohler braided liberty, democracy, and law into a strand that connected the divine revelation at Sinai to the principles of American constitutionalism.

Twenty years later, the conjunction of the celebration of the one hundred and fiftieth anniversary of constitutional ratification with the impending crisis of another war, encouraged reaffirmation of the biblical origins of American democracy. "Hebrew learning," it was asserted, had come to America "on the Mayflower." Puritanism and Judaism "spoke the same spiritual language." So the Puritans' "intense, liberal, wholehearted acceptance of the Biblical laws" was transformed into the "sound political maxims" of the new nation, while "Hebraic law and legislation" was the foundation of American constitutionalism. In this way, "the Hebraic and biblical tradition," nourished in Massachusetts Bay in the seventeenth century and in the thirteen colonies during the revolutionary era, was the continuing inspiration for "American ideals and institutions" that must be protected against fascist challenge.

After the Second World War, Jews across the denominational spectrum affirmed the compatibility of the American and Jewish traditions. A Reform rabbi described American revolutionaries as the "heirs of the Prophets"; the Declaration of Independence "had the ring of Prophetic conviction" in its emphasis upon liberty and morality; while the Founding Fathers (concededly the children of the Enlightenment) were inspired by the God of Israel. The president of the Orthodox Yeshiva University denied any "serious conflict between our spiritual heritage and the American way of life, which is itself rooted in Hebraic spiritual values." American Jewish scholarship echoed their pronouncements. One excursion into political theory demonstrated the compatibility of Judaism with the American "democratic ideal." The constitution of ancient Israel was the Torah, under which rulers and citizens alike were "equally bound by the law." The fundamental principles of American political theory—especially "republican government within a democratic context"—were "directly related to the great moral values of Jewish tradition and, indeed, are taken predominantly from that tradition as it is expressed in the Bible."

Scholarly affirmation climaxed in a crescendo of enthusiasm during the bicentennials of the sacred texts of American liberty and law, the Declaration of Independence and the Constitution. Scholars repeatedly cited the affinities of two "Bible-rooted" cultures, noting the pervasive biblical imagery that had molded American democratic consciousness since the earliest Puritan settlements. The ancient Israelite experience of slavery and freedom, culminating in efforts "to build the good commonwealth," was taken as a paradigm for the development of "free American institutions." Americans and Jews shared "strikingly interesting historical affinities." Each people had experienced, at its national birth, "an unsurpassed moment of spiritual exaltation, which found embodiment in treasured and revered written documents." The Ten Commandments and the Declaration of Independence recorded "divinely inspired communications," when "ethical principles, and codes of law which presumably embodied them, were formally adopted." American democracy, "rooted in Judaism," implemented "the laws of justice and the principles of righteousness enunciated in the Torah."

Scattered through the literature of celebration was an occasional hint of uneasiness, a suggestion that, beneath surface affirmations of unity, American Jews might still experience some dissonance as Americans and Jews. One author expressed his discomfort with the idea that American Jews might be culturally schizophrenic, torn between "different and competing" worlds. Nothing in the Declaration of Independence or the Constitution, he insisted, "makes it impossible" to be an observant Jew in America—a revealing denial at a time when the contrary proposition was rarely affirmed. A legal scholar, returning to a subject he had begun to develop more than twenty-five years earlier, reiterated "the intertwining relationship of Judaism and the American Idea"—inalienable rights, equality, democracy, and "the law of justice." As a self-described "Hellenistic Jew," searching for a unified American Jewish tradition, he found it in his discovery that "The spirit, the inner values, the energies of democracy are right at the very heart of Judaism."

The Constitutional bicentennial, a decade later, provided an unprecedented opportunity for Jews to affirm the fulfillment of Jewish values in American constitutionalism. Legal scholar Milton Konvitz reiterated "the confluence of Torah and Constitution," a theme that had preoccupied him throughout his career. Together, he had written earlier, they expressed "the ideal of life under law"; the movement "from biblical covenant...to constitution," he now wrote, was the American expression of biblical themes. Political scientist Daniel Elazar (who, appropriately, held academic appointments in the United States and Israel) found a "strong commitment to constitutionalism and the rule of law" at the core of Jewish political consciousness. The Jewish political tradition, he wrote, combined federal and republican values "with strong democratic overtones." Constitutionalism was "central to the study of Jewish political history." Jewish history, for Elazar, was "constitutional history," with the Torah as the "foremost constitutional document" of Judaism. With that reading of Jewish history, the biblical origins of American institutions had all but been inverted into the American sources of biblical norms. No one articulated such patriotic piety, masked in Jewish symbols, more insistently than journalist Anthony Lewis (the son of a family of Jewish immigrants named Oshinsky). Lewis, long a devout worshipper at the shrines of American constitutionalism (especially the Supreme Court and Harvard Law School), climaxed his reverence with a celebration of American law and constitutionalism as "our rock and our redeemer"—terms that can refer, in Jewish liturgy, only to God.

Undergirding the discoveries of a unitary tradition were unabashed expressions of Jewish gratitude for American constitutional blessings. American Jews could find comfort in "the fact that the civilizations share several basic tenets, and that they have borrowed freely from each others." Jews were "overwhelmingly proud and grateful" for the opportunity to participate in "such a majestic and unique experiment in freedom and governance." Jewish gratitude was understandable, for under the Constitution "we have achieved more freedom and more justice than any other country in our history"—including, presumably, the Jewish State of Israel. (American Jews have taken great pains to demonstrate that *their* country, not Israel, is the true legatee of the biblical heritage, precisely as seventeenth-century Puritans had insisted.) With the Constitution duly proclaimed as "another Sinaitic covenant," American Jews could embrace it as the appropriate statement of their undiminished covenantal faith....

8 · Zionism as Americanism

The legend remains compelling: Louis D. Brandeis, the esteemed "people's attorney" and renowned Progressive reformer, who would become the first Jew to sit on the Supreme Court, shed his identity as an assimilated Jew and proclaimed himself a Zionist. His personal conversion, when he was past the age of fifty, triggered the momentous transformation of the American Zionist movement that followed his ascension to leadership. A moribund organization without members, leaders, resources, or ideas became the powerful, respected voice of American, even world, Zionism. The movement was the extended shadow of the man, still revered half a century after his death as the American Isaiah.

Like most legends, this one mixes fact and fiction. It implies that Brandeis experienced a deep personal conversion, leading to his strong self-affirmation as a Jew, and that his persuasive synthesis of Zionism and Americanism uncovered some deep truth about the movement for Jewish national restoration. His reconciliation of Zionism with American tradition continues to satisfy the strong need of American Jews to merge two national movements, each of which might legitimately claim their loyalty. But the mythical Brandeis is much less interesting than the real man, whose Zionist identification was not only belated but also spasmodic, hesitant, and constricted. The popular Brandeisian synthesis of Zionism and Americanism expressed the yearnings of American Jews, not Zionist ideology. Indeed, it suggests why Brandeis still retains his secure position in the pantheon of American Jewish heroes, the eminent American jurist whose Jewish leadership was largely symbolic. He made it possible for American Jews to be better Americans by becoming Zionists. Zion was still the promised land, but Brandeis located Zion in the United States, securely within the contours of American history.

Brandeis grew up in a Jewish family whose primary ethnic identification was German, as it long remained for Brandeis himself. Until shortly before his fiftieth birthday in 1906, the limit of his participation in Jewish affairs was defined by an occasional charitable donation. He evaded entreaties for deeper involvement, whether to attend a meeting with Israel Zangwill, the Jewish territorialist leader, or to speak on behalf of the victims of the terrible Kishinev pogroms. Not until 1905, when he accepted an invitation to commemorate the

Rabbis and Lawyers, 123-28, 148.

two hundred and fiftieth anniversary of Jewish settlement in the United States, did he deliver his first address to a Jewish audience. In a remarkable preview of his consuming concerns as a Zionist leader, he demanded loyalty "to American institutions and ideals." The eradication of class and ethnic distinctions was imperative; there was no place in the United States, he warned, for "hyphenated Americans." To be a good Jew required precisely the traits that distinguished loyal Americans: energy, perseverance, self-restraint, intelligence, and austerity. The description, more revealing of Brandeis than of Judaism, enabled him to celebrate the loyalty of Jews to the United States. With these words of warning and reassurance, Brandeis lapsed into public silence on Jewish issues. The limits of his Jewish identification were apparent: considered for nomination to the executive committee of the new American Jewish Committee, he was shunned because (in the judgment of its secretary) "he has not identified himself with Jewish Affairs and is rather inclined to side with the Ethical Culturists."

Five years later, in 1910, Brandeis was called to New York to mediate a garment workers' strike in an industry that was almost entirely Jewish. He was evidently intrigued by the struggle between socialist workers and capitalist employers, who not only argued vehemently about wages and unions but also denounced each other in Yiddish, citing biblical authorities to justify their demands. Like other German Jews of his time—including Judah Magnes, Stephen Wise, and even Herzl—Brandeis was attracted to the rambunctious *yiddishkeit* of the new immigrants, whose roots in Eastern Europe tapped centuries of vibrant Jewish tradition. Once again, however, he rearranged the ingredients of Jewish identity to fit his American mold. Brandeis discovered within the garment workers "the qualities which, to my mind, make for the best American citizenship,…a true democratic feeling and a deep appreciation of the elements of social justice," a compatibility attributable "to the fact that twentieth century ideals of America had been the age-old ideals of the Jews."

Shortly after the strike Brandeis, who devised the protocol that established new terms of industrial self-government, was the subject of an interview in which he significantly expanded his identification as a Jew. He commended the enduring mission of the Jewish people "to struggle for truth and righteousness to-day just as the ancient prophets did." He reiterated his concern that Jews should demonstrate "above all things loyalty to American institutions," warning once again that "habits of living, of thought which tend to keep alive difference of origin or to classify men according to their religious beliefs are inconsistent with the American idea of brotherhood and are disloyal." Brandeis commended the Zionists, who "are entitled to the respect and appreciation of the entire Jewish people." But, he asserted firmly, "I believe that the opportunities for members of my race are greater here than in any other country."

Brandeis's ambivalent pattern of identification and retreat persisted. It was heightened by political circumstance in 1913, when he was considered for an appointment in Woodrow Wilson's cabinet. Business and banking interests resented his advocacy of corporate regulation; their hostility, especially in Boston financial circles, was tinged with anti-Semitism. Prominent Jewish leaders, most of whom were conservative Republicans, were diffident to his appointment. Jacob Schiff, declaring that Brandeis was, "without doubt, a representative American," could only provide "a qualified reply" to the question whether Brandeis was a representative Jew. So Brandeis, too Jewish for the Brahmin bankers and insufficiently Jewish for Schiff, lost the support of both—and the cabinet position. Stung by anti-Semitism and rebuffed by Jews, he remained at the periphery of American Jewish life.

Two chance encounters with committed Zionists, during the spring of that year, seem to have affected Brandeis deeply. At a dinner to honor Nahum Sokolow, the European Zionist leader, Brandeis was stirred by his appeal to American Jews to participate in the effort to "recreate Zion." Brandeis confided to Sokolow, "You have brought me back to my people." Some weeks later, Brandeis met Aaron Aaronsohn, the Palestinian Zionist who was on one of his frequent fundraising tours for his agricultural field station near Haifa. Brandeis, who knew of Aaronsohn's work (which had excited Brandeis's interest in "the possibilities of scientific agriculture"), was fascinated by the man. During a discussion about the recent "unpleasant" implication of New York Jews in prostitution and assorted gangster activities, Aaronsohn contrasted "the little communities" of law-abiding, industrious Jews that flourished in Palestine. Brandeis was inspired by the example. In a public address, some weeks later, he cited it as "a lesson which must apply to Jews all over the world." American Jews, he urged, must identify with the "noble traditions" that inspired the Palestinian pioneers.

Once again, however, Brandeisian rhetoric was unsupported by activity. Preoccupied with his Boston law practice and his advisory role to President Wilson, Brandeis continued to demonstrate slight interest in Jewish affairs. But for the outbreak of the war in Europe during the summer of 1914, there is every reason to believe that his inattention would have persisted, punctuated by an occasional public address that demonstrated the intellectual and emotional distance that separated Brandeis from Jewish history, tradition, and faith. The war, however, crippled the Zionist organization in Europe, endangered Jewish communities in Palestine, shifted the center of Zionist activity to the United States, and propelled Brandeis to the forefront of the American Zionist movement.

The initiative did not come from Brandeis, nor was there a personal conversion to account for his deepened involvement in Zionism. With the European Zionist organization, whose headquarters were in Berlin, all but incapacitated by the war, the movement desperately needed a safe geographical haven, which only the United States could provide. But why Brandeis? A far more intriguing question than why Brandeis became a Zionist is why Zionists should have wanted Brandeis as their leader. It was not a random selection; there are some hints of a "very careful analysis of his career which was made before we presumed to ask him to lead us." But surely that search would not have disclosed a significantly stronger identification with Judaism than the American Jewish Committee had discovered a decade earlier. Only Brandeis's national prominence in American public affairs could have accounted for his appeal. American Zionists, among them the philosopher Horace Kallen who played an important role in recruiting Brandeis to the movement, had their own American agenda to promote. They were surely attracted to a Jew who was respected, above all, for his American credentials, who could dilute the Jewish national zeal of Zionism. World War I provided the opportunity; Brandeis was the perfect choice.

When Brandeis assumed the mantle of Zionist leadership he confessed, candidly and accurately, "I have been to a great extent separated from Jews. I am very ignorant in things Jewish." He had given but passing attention to Zionism, "far as it was from me." Yet precisely these deficiencies, in conjunction with Brandeis's towering stature as a liberal reformer, qualified him to lead the American Zionist movement from obscurity to respectability, from its preoccupation with urgent issues of Jewish identity to a far more secure identification with American history and liberal policies.

Biographers have long been fascinated by Brandeis's Zionist conversion. Why should this very prototype of an assimilated German Jew, who emulated the Boston Brahmins in all but his political preferences, suddenly identify with the most nationalistic expression of Judaism? Sharing Brandeis's secular liberal political orientation, they posit the natural affinity of Zionism with progressivism. Once Brandeis understood that Zionism was the Jewish expression of democracy and social justice, and that fundamental Jewish and American values were indistinguishable, he turned to Zionism as the Jewish expression of his progressive commitments. It has even been suggested that Brandeis, who deeply admired the Athenian polis as the institutionalized ideal of political virtue, found in Zionism the appropriate link to ancient Greek democracy, the very source of Western humanism. Inspired by Alfred Zimmern's *The Greek Commonwealth* (Zimmern, a half-Jew, scattered references to the Bible, the Hebrew Prophets, and ancient Palestine in his 1912 book), Brandeis embraced Zionism, not only as a progressive reform, but as the modern recreation of the values of Periclean Athens.

It has occasionally been recognized (usually by less reverential Israeli scholars) that even Brandeis did not function exclusively at such abstract levels of intellect and principle. His austere exterior, reinforced by a thick veil of privacy, was (and remains) a barrier to access. But there is no reason to believe that Brandeis, more than anyone else, was impervious to ambition, immune to criticism, or indifferent to the implications of mass Jewish immigration for his own place in American society. His identification with Zionism (after years of apathy, moderated only by vacillation) and his willingness to lead the American movement (after resisting repeated efforts to enlist his participation) had to do with more than an ideal, a book, or a reform, as compelling as these surely were to Brandeis. By 1914, Brandeis had been twice spurned: by the Brahmins for his liberalism (to say nothing of the fact that he was a Jew); and by the German Jews for his tepid identification as a Jew (to say nothing of his liberalism). Zionism may have offered Brandeis an escape from his impasse. Rebuffed for a cabinet appointment in 1913, he almost immediately thereafter made known his commitment to Zionism. Within two years, by the time Wilson nominated him to the Supreme Court, Brandeis had displayed his own credentials as an American Jew—so impeccably that even Schiff could acknowledge him as "one of our most eminent co-religionists."

But political opportunism is no more satisfactory an explanation of Brandeis's Zionist conversion than the assumption of a natural affinity between Zionism and progressivism. In 1914, an identification with Zionism was hardly the passport to expanded career opportunities, which Brandeis, as a political figure of national prominence, surely did not need. Furthermore, if Zionism, progressivism, and Americanism were as compatible as many Brandeis biographers (echoing Brandeis) suggest, then one is left wondering why Brandeis did not become a Zionist a decade earlier, when he first became the champion of progressive causes. In the end, neither "explanation" truly explains, because both focus on the wrong issue. The fundamental issue is not why Brandeis became a Zionist, but what kind of a Zionist Brandeis became. He was neither the clever opportunist that cynics decry, nor the pure idealist that hero-worshippers cherish. He made a calculated choice, based upon assumptions about the compatibility of Zionism and Americanism. It proved to be persuasive, indeed decisive, because Brandeis, sharing the abiding anxieties of his generation about Jewish identity and American loyalty, personified the terms of reconciliation between them.

The years between 1912 and 1914 were especially crucial to this formulation. There was a decisive relationship between Brandeis's public career and his Jewish concerns. It seems paradoxical that the more conspicuous a national figure that Brandeis became, the more clearly he articulated the content of his Zionist identification. Given the times and context, one would anticipate that the higher Brandeis rose in American government circles the more he would wish to distance himself from Jewish nationalism. Yet as he reached his apogee as a nationally active progressive—the proponent of Wilson's New Freedom, a prospective cabinet member, and a presidential adviser—he strongly identified with Zionism. But—and this is the critical point—he defined it in a way that left no doubt that American Jews, even Zionists, were patriotic Americans. As he explained, in the single sentence that became the motto of Brandeisian Zionism: "To be good Americans, we must be better Jews, and to be better Jews, we must become Zionists." With that astonishing *non sequitur* Brandeis became the leader of the American Zionist movement. Indeed, it qualified him for leadership because no other prominent American Jew so unerringly identified, and immediately resolved, the implicit conflict between Jewish and American loyalties that defined the nagging dilemma of American Jewish life. Zionism as Americanism was the Brandeisian resolution of that dilemma....

Brandeis closely resembled another assimilated, successful Jew who, from the periphery of Jewish life, inspired the Jewish masses to identify Zionism with the values of enlightened liberalism. In the United States, as in Europe, "the urbane assimilationist...became the savior of the suffering chosen people." Just as Brandeisian Zionism was largely devoid of Jewish content, so Theodor Herzl's model state was "not a Jewish Utopia," as Carl Schorske has noted, "but a liberal one. The dreams of assimilation which could not be realized in Europe would be realized in Zion." The state that Herzl envisioned was a state inhabited by Jews ("just another modern secular state," Ahad Ha-'Am complained), not a Jewish state. Yet Herzl, like Brandeis, won a passionate following among the Jewish masses who found in that definition of Zionism the satisfactory reconciliation of Jewish distinctiveness *and* normalization. Herzl, the Jew as Viennese aristocrat, favored a state for the Jews, a Jewish Switzerland with cricket and tennis, where "we shall keep our priests within the confines of their temples." Brandeis, the Jew as Boston Brahmin, envisioned a Jewish Denmark, populated by modern Pilgrims and Puritans. Herzl was the charismatic leader, propelled by the sheer force of his vision into the company of sultans and kings who might assist him in realizing his dream. Brandeis was the American Isaiah, who prophesied the reconciliation of Zionism and Americanism through liberal reform.

9 · Exodus and Return

The remarkable voyage of the *Exodus* remains a heartbreaking and inspiring symbol of Jewish yearning, Zionist tenacity, and British perfidy. The rickety ship was an unlikely choice for a heroic, or even historic, journey. As the S.S. *President Warfield*, built in 1928, it was designed solely for inland water traffic. After years as a Chesapeake Bay honeymoon cruise ship, it had been requisitioned for transport service during World War II. Refitted early in 1947 for the Haganah, it had barely left port in Baltimore when a hurricane battered it back to dry dock. After extensive repairs, it finally resumed its ill-fated mission to transport nearly five thousand Jewish refugees from the charnelhouse of Europe to their destination of hope in Eretz Israel.

The *Exodus* crew was an incongruous mix of experienced seamen and adventurous novices. Among them was first mate Bill Bernstein, a 23-year-old former Merchant Marine sailor from San Francisco. Bernstein, only recently discharged from the Navy, was restless. As he patiently explained to his mother, "if I tried to settle down I would only get into trouble and bring misery to you and God knows what to myself." He conceded the blessings of "a nice wife and children and a good job," but he knew that he was not ready for "a normal married, clean living life right now."

Bernstein, who had been raised by his older brother Morris, had no Jewish education or affiliation. Palestine was a geographic, not a spiritual, destination. His commitment was to adventure, not to Zionism. During a brief port stop in Italy, accompanied by a Protestant minister who was his crew mate, he found time to buy a rosary for his Catholic girlfriend. Shipboard photographs depict a ruddy, curly-haired, playful young man.

"There was no fanaticism in our makeup," recalled Eli Kalm, another crew member; "we were too typically American to worship the Martyr clause in the Haganah Contract." But, Kahn marveled, en route to Palestine Bernstein was transformed: "He got it; this crazy bug Eretz."

Bill's letters, reprinted here without corrections or editing, to Moe his older brother back in San Francisco, tell his story.

[no date, 1947]
Dear Moe,

I'm writing this letter from ship board. A ship like none I've seen before.

" 'Exodus' and Return," *Jewish Spectator* (Winter 1992-93), 45-47.

There's so much to describe that I just don't know where to begin. Well, I'll forget the actual physical characteristics of the ship itself, and devote some time to describing the crew. I'll write to you from Europe and in one of those letters I'll give you the word on what the tub looks like.

But the crew. God! We have everything aboard except sailors. Everyone has a different reason for making the voyage, altho a good number of the boys intend to remain in Palestine.

Every one aboard is a Jew with the exception of the Captain, Chief Engineer, Steward, and one ordinary seaman. We'll drop the Captain, Chief Engineer, and Steward in Europe before we make the run into Palestine. However, the gentile sailor whose's shipping as ordinary seaman will make the run with us. I referred to him as a sailor, but actually in civilian life he's a priest. You ain't heard nothing yet. I've eaten in the crew's mess hall on many a ship but in all the time I've spent at sea I have never yet heard the kind of talk I've heard here. The ordinary run of conversation on the average ship stems from the subject of women and the various means of enjoying them. Not here.

If you don't know integral calculus, at least one-third of the conversation at the dinner table is lost to you. If you don't know what Aristotle told his mother on his sixth birthday, another slice of the conversation is lost. And if, God forbid, you shouldn't know what opera played in Pittsberg two years ago, or worse yet, how many caluses Yosha Heifitz has on the index finger of his left hand, you are completely ignored. You might just as well not exist. Should one commit the cardinal sin and interrupt this light trend of conversation to mutter that it isn't completely unpleasant to sleep with girls, he's politely told to quit acting like a Gentile.

Incidentally the word "Gentile" is never mentioned here. Instead the Jewish word for Gentile is used i.e. "Goy." As a matter of fact to really understand every thing that's going on about you one should have a good working knowledge of Yiddish plus a smattering of Hebrew. It's the god-damndest thing!!!!!! The chief mate's name is Yitzhuk; he's a Palestinian. I still jump when I hear some one shout his name.

To hear the bosun give an order in Yiddish, and have everyone comply as tho there's nothing strange or funny about it.

God damn it! I just can't describe what it feels like.

Regards...

Bill

❖ ❖ ❖

March 9, 1947
Dear Moe,

Arrived safely Porta Del Gada-Azores (Island of San Miguel).

Our only purpose in stopping here is to refuel. As soon as we bunker, we'll be off. So far, we've been here two days trying to cut through the red-tape. So far no luck.

Incidentally, the motley mess of philosophers, mathamaticians, socialist and assorted intellects have begun to shape up into some sort of half-assed crew. More team work. The ship is beginning to run like a ship and the sailors are beginning to act like seamen. (I even caught one thinking of girls.)

Seriously tho, the crew is really catching on.

Regards

Bill

❖ ❖ ❖

April 15, 1947
Dear Moe,

Just arrived in Marseilles. Everything running smoothly. No hitch. Weather coming over was good. Trip was uneventful. The crew has finally moulded into a good working bunch of seamen.

As far as I know, I'll be here about six to eight weeks and then I'll make the run to Haifa. As my plans stand today I should be back in the States by September. I expect to spend a few months looking around Palestine and I suppose on my way back I'll drop back into Europe again for a quick look around. After I hit Palestine all I'm entitled to is a fast trip back to the States, but I understand there's plenty of work in Palestine so that will keep me going a while....

Will write again soon.

Bill

❖ ❖ ❖

April 21, 1947
Dear Moe,

Today is our last day in Marseille; we sail tomorrow for Italy.

From what I understand, we'll pull into some small port in Southern Italy and remain there for about five weeks while berthing facilities are put up. We've already loaded the lumber and other materials here in Marseilles. Incidentally, the Italian government doesn't permit these "goings on" ever since the British counsel was blown up in Rome about 6 months ago. Consequently we have to go into port as a "black" ship i.e. unregistered, undeclared, and unentered. We do it by [paying] off the local small time petty custom officials and politicians. The money for all this graft comes from the black market sales of the strippings of the ship. In other words we strip the ship of everything that isn't absolutely essential for the functioning of the ship, and then sell it.

We do the stripping and the shoo shoo [Haganah] does the selling.... I think they're justified! None of them do it for they're own personal gain. Our people have only one burning desire here,—ALIYAH BETH! The *second deliverence to Eretz Israel. The first migration was supposedly the handiwork of God, the second one we fight for. If we can fuck some goyem up in the process, all the better.*

Three days ago the Jews here in Marseille and aboard my ship celebrated the fourth anniversary of the resistance of the Warsaw Ghetto. Every one of 60,000 Jews were massacred there defending a street with small arms against the German army. We held it for five days. Only five days of resistance in 4,000 years of persecution. Something we should be ashamed of. However the time isn't far off when we'll redeem our honor. Perhaps you and I won't be around when it happens but I can see it building all around me. The base of the pyramid is slow being built, but the pinnacle comes quickly.

I was at the refugee camp on the outskirts of Marseille yesterday. I saw practically all young men and women, boys and girls. They all speak Jewish, some speak Hebrew and all will eventually be in Eretz raising Sabras on good communal farms stolen from the desert. A good many of those kids have numbers tattood on there arms as proof of the life they have lead for four years.

I don't know if be able to mail any letters in my next port so don't worry if you don't hear from me for a few weeks. I'm about positive that no one will be allowed ashore. I'm feeling fine. Say hello to everyone for me.

Bill

❖ ❖ ❖

July 9, 1947
Dear Moe,

This is it! After working, hiding and chasing all over Europe for months, we've finally cleared the way for a seven day voyage.

I'm not sure, but I think that by the time you receive this letter, my ship will be in. Chances are very slim as far as getting through the English are concerned. Of course we'll do our best. But the important thing is that these people are out of Europe and will definately end up amongst their own people in their own country sooner or later. This is the biggest ship to do this kind of work and consequently we're carrying the greatest number of people ever transported in one ship.

Regards to everyone.

Bill

As his letters reveal, Bill Bernstein experienced a remarkable metamorphosis. He began his odyssey as an innocent abroad, a naïve American Jew who did not comprehend the Jewish passion and Zionist fervor that swirled around him. In Marseilles, however, his encounter with Holocaust survivors, young Jews like himself, and their commemoration of the Warsaw Ghetto uprising, converted him to the Zionist cause. Bernstein, until then a bemused observer, suddenly became a committed participant.

Early in the morning of July 18 the *Exodus*, accompanied by British destroyers that had tracked it through the Mediterranean, approached Rafah. The ship, still in international waters, was twenty miles off the coast of Palestine. Bernstein, who had begun his watch at midnight, had just made his log entries. Ike Aronowitz, the young Haganah ship captain, joined him in the wheelhouse. The clock struck five bells (2:30 a.m.). Suddenly the sky lit up as British searchlights illuminated the *Exodus* from bow to stern. Bernstein seized the ship whistle; its "great wail sounded like the shriek of an animal caught by beasts of prey."

British destroyers repeatedly rammed the fragile ship, before sending armed sailors and marines aboard to capture it. As they raced for the bridge and wheelhouse a frenzied battle began, with refugees and crew members hurling tin cans and potatoes, their only weapons, at the British invaders. Hours later, after dozens of serious injuries, the Haganah conceded that further resistance was futile and the captain surrendered.

The "war-battered" *Exodus* was escorted into Haifa just before 4:00 p. m. on the Jewish Sabbath, "its deck black with people," according to the Palestine *Post*. There were "huge gashes" in its deck walls, as though it had been "blitzed." It took twelve hours, in sweltering heat, to remove all the passengers. Stretcher bearers, the *Post* reported, "were kept busy." That evening three British prison ships, loaded with nearly five thousand Jewish refugees, sailed back to Europe.

Not everyone on board the *Exodus* made the return trip. Scores of wounded were hospitalized in Haifa. Two passengers, Hirsch Yakubovich, 15, from Poland, and Mordecai Baumstein, 23, from a displaced persons camp in Germany, had been killed by British pistol shots during the struggle. Bill Bernstein, forcibly ejected from the wheel-house, had grabbed a fire extinguisher to squirt as a weapon as he fought his way back inside. A British marine, wielding a steel-tipped truncheon, clubbed him on the side of his head. Bernstein suffered a serious concussion, lying unconscious in the captain's cabin until the *Exodus* docked more than thirteen hours later.

The last letter to Bernstein's brother Moe came from the Haganah:

> *We regret to inform you that Naval Officer William Bernstein was killed on the high seas in a brutal manner by sailors of the British Navy who were carrying out the ruthless policy of the British White Paper Government. The Haganah stands at attention at his fresh grave and pays a last tribute of respect to this young American Jew who made the supreme sacrifice while helping to bring the remnants of our people to our homeland.... American Jewry has lost one of its heroic soldiers.*

Bill Bernstein, the fun-loving adventurer, was wrapped in an American flag and buried in the Martyr's Row of Haifa cemetery, near other Zionists whose cause he belatedly shared but passionately defended.

10 · *Altalena*: The Pariah Ship

Barely a month after the birth of the State of Israel on May 14, 1948, the fledgling nation approached the brink of civil war. Amid its desperate struggle for survival against invading armies from five Arab countries, the arrival of a ship named *Altalena* provoked a violent and traumatic confrontation. For some embattled participants it even evoked memories of Jerusalem in the 1st century, when a Jewish civil war shredded national sovereignty for nearly two thousand years. The dark shadow of the *Altalena* still hovers over Israel more than six decades later, raising vital issues of political legitimacy that have yet to be resolved in the Jewish state.

The *Altalena* story braids themes that are woven into ancient Jewish sources and modern Jewish experiences. The book of Genesis recounts that in the beginning, after Creation went awry, Noah's ark—the first ship to be mentioned in a Jewish text—transported a righteous man and his family from impending disaster to safety. Jews sailed to safe haven in America as early as 1654, when twenty-three refugees from Brazil landed in New Amsterdam. In the mid-19th century, as many as 200,000 German Jewish immigrants arrived in the United States. Then, during the decades surrounding the turn of the twentieth century, nearly two million Jews fled from poverty and persecution in Eastern Europe. Packed on board teeming immigrant ships, those uprooted Jews were among the "huddled masses yearning to breathe free"—in the memorable words of Emma Lazarus that were engraved beneath the Statue of Liberty. Their flight from danger, combined with their yearning for freedom in a safe homeland, is deeply embedded in American Jewish history.

With Adolf Hitler's ascent to power in Germany in 1933, and the inexorable spread of Nazi terror throughout Europe, frantic Jews tried to flee from imminent danger and looming annihilation. They rarely succeeded. Restrictive American immigration laws, government indifference to the plight of European Jewry, and the fearful timidity of American Jews kept them away. For all but a fortunate few, the possibility of reaching the *goldene medina*, their American Zion, vanished. By the end of the Thirties, British restrictions on Jewish immigration had also placed Palestine, where Zionists were building a new society in the biblical homeland of the Jewish people, beyond reach.

After the Holocaust barely a surviving Jewish remnant remained alive to

---

Brothers at War: Israel and the Tragedy of the Altalena (2011), 1-9.

seek refuge in Palestine. Once again, ships attempted to transport Jews to safety and freedom. But unrelenting Arab hostility to Jewish immigration was reinforced by British capitulation (fed by lurking anti-Semitism) to Arab demands. The yearning of Jews for Zion, where they could build a state of their own, was repeatedly and cruelly thwarted.

The inspirational journey of one ship, the *Exodus*, has testified ever since to the fierce determination of Holocaust survivors to reach "*Altneuland*," the old-new land of Theodor Herzl's dream. The story of the *Exodus* has been endlessly told, retold, celebrated—and popularized in the romantic novel by Leon Uris that was transformed into an iconic Hollywood movie. The poignant journey of its passengers in 1947—from France to Palestine, then back to France and, finally, to displaced persons camps in Germany—came to symbolize the desperate yearning of the Jewish people. It remains embedded in the heroic narrative of the creation of the State of Israel—and the history of British perfidy.

One year later, barely a month after proclaiming its independence, the new Jewish state was besieged by invading Arab armies determined to destroy it. Amid its desperate struggle for survival the *Altalena*, a ship dispatched by the Irgun Zvai Leumi (National Military Organization), led by Menachem Begin, arrived in Israel with more than nine hundred fighters and desperately needed weapons and munitions. But Prime Minister David Ben-Gurion, perceiving a menacing challenge to the state and to his authority, seized the opportunity to quash his detested right wing political rivals. Claiming that the *Altalena* was the spearhead of a *putsch*, an attempt to overthrow the government, he ordered the Israel Defense Forces to destroy it.

If the *Exodus* was revered as the valiant ship, the *Altalena* became the reviled pariah ship. It arrived with the permission of the Israeli government at Kfar Vitkin, north of Netanya, on June 21. As weapons were unloaded passenger Dov Shilansky encountered an Israeli soldier in a command car. "I spoke to him in Hebrew," he recalled. "It was my first speech in Israel." Shilansky told him: "We've just arrived. We survived the Holocaust. We've come here to fight by your side. The homeland is in danger. We will join the army." The soldier instructed him to go no further. Shilansky responded: "We have no other way. I won't go back to Dachau. If we can't come to Israel, we'll go back to the sea." The soldier replied: "I don't care. Go back to the sea."

Under orders from Ben-Gurion Israeli soldiers had surrounded the beachhead, preparing to seize the weapons. Later that afternoon, as Begin spoke to his assembled fighters, Israeli soldiers raked the beach with machine-gun bullets and mortar shells. Yaacov Meridor, Begin's second in command, ordered: "Don't shoot back." An Irgun fighter realized: "I couldn't shoot. My brother was on the other side." Another newcomer was uncomprehending: "instead of welcoming us they were killing and wounding many of our men whose only purpose was to help." Six Irgun men died in the fighting.

The next day, after the *Altalena* ran aground off the Tel Aviv shore, Ben-Gurion ordered the Israel Defense Forces to destroy it. Some IDF soldiers refused to obey. An officer protested: "I'm here to fight the enemy. I won't fight another Jew." He instructed the soldiers in his squad: "Do what your conscience tells you." (He became one of eight soldiers to be court-martialed for their disobedience that day.) An hour-long battle raged. An Irgun fighter remembered: "If Begin had told us to fight we would have, but he did not want war between brothers and we accepted his leadership." Irgun fighters heeded his command not to return fire.

Yet Ben-Gurion was convinced—without a shred of supporting evidence (then or since)—that the Irgun was planning to overthrow his government. Late that afternoon, he ordered cannons to fire on the ship. Hilary Dilesky, a volunteer from South Africa who had arrived in Israel only two months earlier, commanded the cannon battery that was chosen to fire the first shot. Receiving his orders, he recalled, "I suddenly was struck with a heavy, deep feeling that I didn't want to shoot." Dilesky approached his corps commander, telling him—in English, for he could not yet speak Hebrew: "I hadn't come to Israel to fight Jews." The commander yelled back that his job was to obey orders. It was, Dilesky recalled, "a fateful moment" when he realized that "following orders was the right thing to do." But "my heart was broken when we began firing," he confessed. "This has been a burden all my life," he recalled nearly fifty years later, "and still is."

With the *Altalena* ablaze from a direct hit, and the explosion of its munitions imminent, Irgun leaders (including Begin) and members of the crew jumped overboard, filling lifeboats and swimming ashore. From the bridge of the *Altalena* an astonished American crew member observed that "continuous small arms fire from shore...was directed at everyone in the water." A 17-year-old Haganah soldier on the beach never forgot that "there were people on our side who waited until they saw heads above water, and then they fired at them."

A Palmach soldier recalled: "Firing on each other: it seemed illogical, unbelievable." He confessed: "I had many doubts, when I pointed the gun at the approaching boat filled with Jews." But he overcame them. "You tell yourself, you are guarding Israeli democracy. And with this belief, you shoot." Another Palmach soldier was stunned by what he saw: "Before my eyes was waged a war between brothers. Jews are shooting Jews—in order to kill!" That day, ten more Irgun men were killed. After the battle Ben-Gurion enthusiastically blessed the "holy cannon" that destroyed the *Altalena*. He denied as false rumors eyewitness reports from soldiers and journalists at the site of the Tel Aviv battle that Israeli soldiers on the beach had fired on desperate swimmers. Eighteen *Altalena* fighters subsequently died fighting for their country during the War of Independence.

The story of the *Altalena*, with its bloody climax, reveals another enduring theme in Jewish history, the recurrent tragedy of sibling rivalry and fratricide. That, too, is grounded in the biblical narrative. Cain murdered Abel. Isaac robbed Ishmael of his inheritance. Jacob's deception gained him Esau's birthright. Joseph's brothers, tormented by jealousy, abandoned him to die in a deep pit. In 1st century Jerusalem, Jewish Zealots ruthlessly slaughtered their fellow Jews in a civil war that destroyed the Temple, the revered religious and symbolic center of Jewish life and, with it, national sovereignty.

Ever since 1948, the *Altalena* tragedy has remained a sorrowful reminder that baseless hatred—known ever since the destruction of the Second Temple in 70 CE as *sinat hinam*—continued to torment the Jewish people, even at their wondrous moment of national rebirth. The bloody confrontation over the *Altalena*, and the killing of Jews by Jews that accompanied it, remains a lingering, self-inflicted wound from Israel's brave struggle for independence. It is a memory that still cuts to the very core of the enduring struggle over national identity and political legitimacy in the Jewish state.

11 · American Home or Jewish Homeland

American Jews have always asserted their independence from the historical and ideological implications of Zionism. Even American Zionists, guided by the claim of Louis D. Brandeis that Zionism was Americanism, responded to the imperatives of assimilation. They did not live in galut; aliyah was not their obligation; "they never believed that the laws of Jewish destiny formulated by Herzl and Pinsker applied to them." The establishment of a Jewish state, which sharpened their identity conflicts, elicited vigorous affirmations of American loyalty. "We American Zionists know that Zionism is good Americanism," declared the *New Palestine* within two weeks of Israeli independence. The new Jewish state, it predicted, would promote "the American ideals of freedom, peace, and prosperity."

The American Zionist movement, Ben-Gurion observed several months later, still had not adjusted to "the revolutionary fact" of the State of Israel. Relations between Israel and the Diaspora, he concluded, "cannot remain the same as before the establishment of the State." In the end, however, it was the Prime Minister who was forced to accommodate to American Jewish imperatives. As the young Jewish state struggled desperately to absorb hundreds of thousands of newcomers, especially refugees from Arab countries, Ben-Gurion looked desperately to the United States for an infusion of Jews whose youthful energy, scientific training, and managerial expertise would enable Israel to cope with its enormous tasks of resettlement and development. In September 1949 the Jewish Telegraphic Agency reported an appeal from the Prime Minister to American parents to send their children to settle in Israel. Even if the parents declined, Ben-Gurion allegedly told a *Histadrut* delegation, "we will bring the youth to Israel." A storm of protest erupted in the American Jewish community, aghast at the prospect that a pied piper in Tel Aviv would lure their children away to the strains of *Hatikvah*.

Leaders of the American Jewish Committee were incensed. The Committee, a venerable stronghold of wealthy, assimilated, anti-Zionist Jews of German ancestry, belatedly and reluctantly had made its peace with the idea of a Jewish state. Joseph M. Proskauer, a corporate lawyer who was Committee president between 1943 and 1949, had earlier denounced a Jewish state as "a Jewish catastrophe." He remained adamantly opposed to statehood until it was

---

"American Home or Jewish Homeland," *Forum on the Jewish People, Zionism and Israel* (Summer 1983), 59-63.

endorsed by the American government, a policy commitment that removed the sting of dual loyalty. But American Jews, Proskauer reminded Ben-Gurion after word of his *Histadrut* remarks reached New York, "suffer from no political schizophrenia.... We are bone of the bone and flesh of the flesh of America."

Ben-Gurion, informed (by Abba Eban) that Proskauer was "fuming," wrote a long, soothing letter in which he tried to reconcile Zionist principles, Israeli needs, and American Jewish sensibilities. A Zionist, Ben-Gurion insisted, was a Jew with "an inner need, and not on material grounds alone, to live a full Jewish life; a Jew who feels impelled to live in the land of the Jews, use the Jewish language (Hebrew), labour in a Jewish economy, under Jewish cultural conditions and in the Jewish Home." Not every Jew, he knew, possessed this "inner moral need." Lacking it, a Jew should be permitted "to remain a Jew and live on terms of equality with all others, wherever he may be." A Jew living outside Israel "owes no political or legal allegiance to Israel." As Ben-Gurion acknowledged: "There is, indeed there can be, no contradiction between an American Jew's duty to his country and his relation as a Jew to the State of Israel."

But Israel, Ben-Gurion told Proskauer, confronted "gigantic" problems of immigrant absorption that were "almost beyond the strength of this small and young state." It desperately needed something other than money from American Jews. Mass emigration was not the issue, for Ben-Gurion realized the futility of that prospect. But an infusion of American know-how was vital. "We feel that engineers, chemists, technicians, works-managers and other experts, especially among the young may wish to find among us an outlet for their talents...[and] help us to set up a democratic civilization."

The Committee was not mollified. (Even American Zionists were uncomfortable with reports of Ben-Gurion's appeal, but they eagerly accepted his distinction between technological experts and mass aliyah.) In the summer of 1950 Jacob Blaustein, the American Oil Company director who had succeeded Proskauer as AJC president, visited Israel as a guest of the government. After protracted negotiations, and careful orchestration, a luncheon was arranged in his honor at the King David hotel. Ben-Gurion, in a speech expressing understanding of the proper relationship between American Jews and Israel, said precisely what the American Jewish Committee wanted to hear.

"As a community and as individuals," Ben-Gurion reiterated, American Jews "have only one political attachment and that is to the United States of America. They owe no political allegiance to Israel." The Jewish state respected their right "to develop their own mode of life and their indigenous social, economic and cultural institutions in accordance with their own needs and aspirations." Ben-Gurion conceded that Israel depended upon "our cooperation with, and on the strength of, the great Jewish community of the United States, and, we, therefore, are anxious that nothing should be said or done which could in the slightest degree undermine the sense of security and stability of American Jewry." The decision to emigrate to Israel, Ben-Gurion concluded, "rests with the free discretion of each American Jew himself. It is entirely a matter of his own volition."

Blaustein sounded a firm note of caution to the Israelis, reminding them of their responsibility for "not affecting adversely the sensibilities of Jews who are citizens of other states by what it says or does." American Jews "vigorously repudiate any suggestion or implication that they are in exile.... To American Jews, America is home." Blaustein proclaimed the "influence and...strength" of American Jewry, upon which the future of Israel ("spiritual, social as well as economic") depended. He concluded with a pointed request for "unmistakable evidence that the responsible leaders of Israel," who had already harmed "the sense of security of the American Jewish community," would in the future respect "the feelings and needs" of American Jews.

It was a revealing exchange. Blaustein, representing a private organization with a long history of anti-Zionism, demanded that Israeli policy be constrained by the apprehensions of assimilated American Jews. In turn, Ben-Gurion, the Zionist Prime Minister of a sovereign Jewish state, accepted the limitations set by the Americans. He relinquished basic Zionist tenets of Diaspora nationalism (the national unity of the Jewish People) and *aliyah* (the ingathering of exiles) to conform to the security needs of Americans Jews—as Americans. The Prime Minister's statement, as Blaustein subsequently acknowledged, was crucial to free American Jews "in the minds of other Americans from the serious charge of dual-nationality."

Ben-Gurion's concessions set the standard against which subsequent Israeli statements were measured for their conformity to American Jewish interests. A year later, Blaustein was "distressed and amazed" by press reports that Ben-Gurion, at a World Zionist Organization conference, had insisted that Zionist groups were obligated to aid Israel even at the risk of opposing the policies of their own national governments. Blaustein reminded Ben-Gurion that American Jews "unalterably oppose" the idea that "Jews everywhere constitute one nation." Although Ben-Gurion claimed that his statement was consistent with their prior understanding, Blaustein demanded additional reassurances: "nothing be said or done by Israel that would create, or give the impression of creating, any dual loyalty on the part of American Jews"; references to the ingathering of exiles must specifically exempt "Jews in the democracies such as the United States (who certainly are not in exile)"; Israel would refrain from efforts to promote mass immigration "from the United States and other democracies."

Blaustein was not only worried about the loyalty issue; he was evidently concerned lest Ben-Gurion's reassertion of Zionist obligations (especially at a World Zionist Organization conference) weaken the AJC relative to American Zionist groups. He cautioned Ben-Gurion that "the really effective tangible aid" to Israel came from the non-Zionists (specifically the Committee and the United Jewish Appeal). He reminded the Prime Minister that Committee leaders enjoyed access to American government officials, a privilege that translated into generous government aid to Israel. "Virtually all we ask—and this is fundamental with us—is that Israel observe the proper relationship toward Jews in other countries, and that Israel continue to develop within a democratic framework."

The Prime Minister tried to reassure Blaustein that his "apprehensions about dual loyalty are...unfounded. The State of Israel has authority over its citizens only. It does not represent Jews living outside its boundaries and is not authorized to impose upon them any obligations whatsoever." For the first time, however, a note of irritation intruded. "As a Zionist," Ben-Gurion wrote, "I believe that there is one Jewish People in the world, and as a Zionist I reserve the right to express my Zionist convictions."

Precisely these convictions made the Committee uneasy. In a resolution drafted by Proskauer and endorsed by the executive committee, the AJC restated its American creed: "America is our home.... We oppose as completely false and unrealistic any view that American Jews can be convinced that Israel is the only place where Jews can live in security and dignity. We reject the notion...that American Jews are in any sense 'exiles.'" Blaustein added his personal objection to any Israeli policy that would "affect adversely the position of American Jews."

Ben-Gurion was less conciliatory than he had been a year earlier. He described the AJC resolution as "excessively apologetic" (although, he admitted, "Possibly...I lack a full comprehension of the feelings of an American Jew"). He suggested to Blaustein that dual loyalty was not exclusively an American problem, nor need it be quite so terrifying as American Jews claimed. Israelis, the Prime Minister suggested, also experienced dual loyalties: to the Jewish People and to the State of Israel. Indeed, Ben-Gurion confessed, "the bonds of my loyalty with the Jewish People lie deeper even than those with the State of Israel." Ben-Gurion expressed his wish for the continued prosperity of American Jews, but he remained skeptical of their unflagging optimism with regard to their future in the United States. Their expressions of security reminded him (although he minimized the comparison) of German Jews; he feared that still another Jewish community would follow its own self-delusions to destruction.

The controversy finally dimmed after 1951, although Blaustein demanded periodic reassurances whenever Israeli leaders touched his sensitive loyalty nerve. When Israel protested a rash of swastika-paintings in the West, Blaustein complained about its infringements upon the autonomy of the victimized Jewish communities. Unsettled by the remarks of Golda Meir and Moshe Dayan about relations between Israel and Diaspora Jewry, he warned against Israeli provocations that would arouse its enemies or displease its financial benefactors. In 1960, when Ben-Gurion declared that Western Judaism "faces the kiss of death, a slow and, imperceptible decline into the abyss of assimilation," AJC leaders protested with sufficient impact to compel him to reaffirm his 1950 agreement—thereby provoking an Israeli cabinet motion of censure for the deference of the Prime Minister to non-Zionist sensibilities.

Ben-Gurion always understood that the source of their disagreement was their divergent conceptions of Jewish peoplehood. To Blaustein, American Jews were Americans first, a conception of Jewishness that Ben-Gurion found unacceptable. For Ben-Gurion, Jews comprised a single entity, unified across time and space; every Jew, at the irreducible core of identity, was a Jew. Although Ben-Gurion yielded on occasion to American pressure, he could not accept Blaustein's terms and remain a committed Zionist. (Nor, however, could Blaustein accept the implications of Zionism and preserve his security as an American Jew.) But once Ben-Gurion was stuck in the quagmire of American squeamishness about divided loyalty, he could placate American Jews, or Zionists in Israel, but not both simultaneously. So, like any successful politician, he told each group what it wanted to hear. In Israel, or among Zionists, he remained committed to the unity of the Jewish People and to the imperative of *aliyah*. When American Jews complained, he conceded the freedom of individual choice that they demanded, as an entitlement of their American birthright (although, in one of his more candid moments, he described Diaspora Jews as "human debris")....

There may be an imperative of history, virtually as old as the Jewish people, that preserves the tension between Israel and the Diaspora. But in this complex but compelling relationship, new definitions are always welcome. Surely it is no longer legitimate for Israelis to dismiss two thousand years of Jewish history in the Diaspora as though it was the dark ages (or, given the extent of *yeridah*, to retain *aliyah* as the sole test of Zionist commitment). But neither is it appropriate for American Jews to retreat into the isolationism that their privileged Diaspora affluence invites (breaking their silence only to demand renewed demonstration of Israeli moral rectitude).

As long as there is a Jewish state and a Jewish Diaspora, loyalty issues (and echoes of the Ben-Gurion-Blaustein dialogue) will resonate among Jews. It is futile to wish them away. Dual loyalty defines the essence of Diaspora life; the problem does not disappear (as Blaustein discovered) because American Jews insist that the Diaspora does not exist or that they do not inhabit it. But, as Ben-Gurion suggested (and as persistent conflict between traditional Judaism and Israeli modernism demonstrates), divided loyalties can also torment Jews in Israel. Quite possibly, American Jews and Israelis will find mutual exploration to be mutually beneficial. It may even demonstrate that they cannot sever the reciprocal bonds of identity that unite them, collectively, as one people—or, if that is too American a word, one nation.

12 · Americans in Israel

During the "golden decade" of rising opportunity and prosperity following the end of World War II, American Jews seemed comfortably reconciled to the new state of Israel. "We American Zionists know that Zionism is good Americanism," declared *New Palestine* editors after independence. The new Jewish state, they predicted, would promote "the American ideals of freedom, peace and prosperity"—a curious purpose, indeed, for a Jewish state. But as long as it did so, American Jews were content...

In 1949, the Zionist Organization of America published what may have been the first American travel guide to the new State of Israel. In this "concise and handy guide for the American tourist," the ZOA effusively encouraged American Jews to realize their "dream of a lifetime" by visiting the new Jewish state. But it prudently warned visitors not to impose an American framework upon this "valiant little country"—even as its description of Israel reinforced their inclination to do precisely that.

Prospective American visitors were instructed that Zionists had transformed a "neglected wilderness" into "a healthy, prosperous land," whose political institutions rested "on the ideals of social justice." But "woe" to any visitor who "compares everything with America, to the constant advantage of the latter." Israelis could be "helpful and friendly" to American visitors. But if their stunning achievements were measured by American standards, they were inclined to turn "cold, argumentative, and narrow." If American travelers did not find "a bed of roses" in the land of milk and honey, that was not attributable to Zionist deficiencies but to British indifference to the "progress or prosperity" of the pre-state *yishuv*.

The ZOA found its own prescription for cultural tolerance difficult to follow. Israeli delicatessens, the guidebook noted, were likely to be "a great disappointment" to American tourists, while Israeli ice cream "does not approach American standards." Americans were forewarned that religious observance might also be problematic. Tourists were unlikely to find any familiar Conservative synagogues in Israel. Indeed, American Jewish sensibilities were "apt to be disturbed by the rather free and easy attitude of the [Orthodox] congregants," which contrasted sharply with American conceptions of synagogue decorum. And, the guide noted with discernible regret, in Israeli synagogues there are "no

Are We One? Jewish Identity in the United States and Israel (2001), 82-87.

sermons."

Israeli cities received mixed reviews. Tel Aviv, the burgeoning Zionist metropolis, was built by "indomitable will," but it must not be measured by sophisticated American urban standards. Jaffa was a "panorama of dress, language, and modes of life," but it had little to offer of Jewish interest. Jerusalem was "most interesting," with its "memorable landmarks," "beautiful residential sections," and "some touches of medieval Europe." But it sounded more like a provincial French town than the holy city of the Jews.

No trip to Israel in the early years was complete without a visit to a kibbutz, the shining symbol of Zionist pioneering achievement. Kibbutz "settlers" (in those days, an honorable designation among Israelis) were lauded as genuine pioneers who deserved the highest respect of Americans. But tourists were warned, yet again, not to measure the struggling kibbutz "settlements"—some of which "have not yet eliminated flies"—by the hygienic standards of American farms.

The ZOA tourist guide was soon followed into print by two popular guides to the young state, written by journalist Ruth Gruber. She urged American Jews to "Go now" to Israel, where they could witness the rebirth of "a once broken people and a once broken land." In Israel, she wrote excitedly, the Diaspora Jew is "transformed...into a new type of man: a tiller of the soil in peace, a fighter in war." Here was a people "released from fear," a country "built out of death for life."

Gruber's Israel closely resembled a mythologized America of bygone frontier days. In the Jewish state, American tourists were invited to glimpse "the growing pains of young Americans freeing themselves from British law." Not only did Israel resemble colonial America on the eve of independence; it would also remind Americans of their own "Wild West of the 1880s." (The Negev outpost of Beer Sheva resembled "Lost Gulch or Deadman's Creek.") Israel is "like America," Gruber wrote reassuringly, where "you can find almost everything you look for"—even "the comforts and pleasures" of Florida.

After barely a decade of national life, Gruber proudly reported, Israel conspicuously displayed "its Yankee ways." American cars abounded. Frosted milk shakes and self-service laundries (with American washing machines) were available to satisfy tourist needs. In a Habonim kibbutz, Gruber was delighted to discover American-style toilets. Israeli children, she noted, learned the facts of life from Hollywood movies. Jerusalem, she wrote reassuringly, was "the Washington, D.C. of the Jewish State." Israel might be "a small frontier land making brave new experiments," but Gruber reminded Jewish women to bring their hats "for tea parties and afternoon receptions."

Early travel guides invariably depicted Israel as a newer, smaller, only vaguely Jewish version of the United States. The Zionist revolution might be creating bold, brave Jews, "suntanned, and determined, strong and beautiful," as one enraptured American wrote; and American visitors were encouraged to observe them in their native kibbutz habitat (variously described by visiting journalist Judd Teller as a "boy scout utopia," "a summer camp," and "a coal mine"). But there were constant reassurances that the new Jewish state fit snugly into American preconceptions and expectations.

The tour-guide profile of Israel in its early years of statehood conspicuously omitted anything of Jewish content or consequence. The dominant frame of reference was the American historical experience, not biblical sources or Jewish history. A young American-born instructor at the Hebrew University complained that American Jews who declined to make aliya lacked "the true, pioneering American spirit"—not Zionist will. There were "few better places in the world to study essential 'American history,'" he wrote, than Israel during its nation-building years.

The Americanized rendition of Israel was a reflex of self-affirmation by American Jews. A Zionist, it seemed, was a hardy American pioneer reborn in the Middle East. "Of all the countries that one may visit in Europe or Asia," wrote an American visitor, "Israel is the only one which gives a similar feeling of tempo and spirit to that felt in the United States." Israel, after all, must affirm the compatibility of Zionism with Americanism, the staple of American Jewish life ever since Jews in the Brandeis era first confronted the Zionist challenge.

The initial spasm of American Zionist enthusiasm for Israel should not be exaggerated. To the overwhelming majority of American Jews, Israel was geographically and spiritually remote. They paid little attention to it. In his classic survey of American Judaism, Nathan Glazer observed in 1957: "The two greatest events in modern Jewish history, the murder of six million Jews by Hitler and the creation of the Jewish State in Palestine, have had remarkably slight effects on the inner life of American Jewry." ...

13 · The Long Shadow of 1977

By 1948, for American Jews, liberalism and Judaism were ideologically indistinguishable. That may explain why Israel won more favor from Jews as an embattled democratic nation than as a distinctively Jewish state. Jews might idolize Ben-Gurion as the founding father of Jewish statehood, embrace Golda Meir as their Jewish grandmother, and admire Moshe Dayan as a modern Maccabee. But only as long as Israel remained faithful to liberal norms could American Jews safely identify with it.

All that changed in 1977. For the first time, Israel had a Revisionist prime minister who symbolized nationalism and religious orthodoxy, an ancient Jewish synthesis that contradicted fundamental modern liberal tenets. Even before Menachem Begin took office, American media images depicted him as a symbol of reckless terrorism, unyielding fanaticism, and dangerous demagoguery. The *New York Times* described him as "a former guerrilla" with "a fiery past." That august newspaper, whose venerable anti-Zionism had guided editorial policy for decades, drew solace only from the prospect that the new government "may not last long." *Time*, even less restrained, labeled Begin in successive issues as a "terrorist," "superhawk," and "strong-willed little Polish immigrant," whose name, it crassly noted, "rhymes with Fagin."

Although American Jewish leaders quickly pledged their "support and commitment," affirming "the indissoluble ties" that bound American Jews to Israel, their uneasiness with Begin was evident. The most they could bring themselves to say about the Israeli political transformation was that it had occurred "freely and peacefully," demonstrating "the democratic process at work."

Begin, to be sure, sharply contradicted romantic American images of Israel as the land of muscular kibbutzniks, descended from Amos and Isaiah, who wore *kova tembels* by day, danced the horah all night, and piloted their planes and tanks to astonishing military victories early the next morning. Instead, Begin resembled a missing Old World uncle who had suddenly reemerged from the shadows of Diaspora history. His ill-fitting suits, Yiddish-accented English, and frequent Holocaust analogies touched deep, often discomforting, feelings among American Jews. His lost world of Eastern European Jewry was, after all, the Old Country that American Jewry had abandoned.

As Begin grafted explicitly Jewish symbols onto Israeli public life, the state

---

"Are We One? Menachem Begin and the Long Shadow of 1977," *Envisioning Israel* (1996), 340-51.

of the Jews—at least iconographically—actually began to resemble a Jewish state. He was the first prime minister of Israel, one of his biographers observed, to identify himself "as a Jew rather than as an Israeli." His post-election visit to the *Kotel* graphically symbolized his claim to be not only prime minister of Israel but leader of the Jewish people. One of his first acts as prime minister was to visit a new Jewish settlement outside Shechem (Nablus). There he pledged "many Elon Morehs," claiming Judea and Samaria as part of Israel and insisting that the land be known by its biblical names. Like a vision from Ezekiel, Begin pointedly reminded Jews of their historical attachment to their ancient biblical homeland.

In the process, Begin antagonized the president of the United States. Jimmy Carter found statements by the new prime minister "frightening." Even before the Israeli election, Carter's political sympathies were evident. Urging Israeli withdrawal from nearly all the territory acquired in 1967, he had called for a Palestinian homeland and asked for reparations for displaced Arab refugees—which even Arab leaders had not yet demanded. Begin, aware of the disquiet that his image generated in Washington, publicly discounted the president's hostility. "Carter knows the Bible," the prime minister declared, "and that will make it easier for him to know whose land this is."

As Begin prepared for his first Washington visit, American Jewish leaders were palpably uneasy. Their effectiveness, after all, depended on an absence of friction between Israel and the United States. They were accustomed to Israeli prime ministers who did not make excessive demands on them as Jews; Ben-Gurion, Golda Meir, and Yitzhak Rabin usually permitted American Jews to identify with the Jewish state, or ignore it, without undue discomfort. With Begin, however, that flexibility diminished. He was, wrote an Israeli journalist, "a different kind of Prime Minister": "a more 'Jewish' leader." The more directly that Begin, speaking as a Jew, implicated American Jewry in the Jewish state, the more fragile became those "indissoluble links" between American Jews and Israel.

The first Begin-Carter visit, in the summer of 1977, was not quite the disaster that many had anticipated. Within weeks, however, the surface geniality between the two leaders dissolved. An Israeli announcement that three West Bank military bases would be converted into settlements provoked sharp criticism from the State Department. The Israeli government, in turn, challenged any assertion that Jewish settlement "in the Land of Israel" could be regarded as illegal. Published reports that the Carter administration was "increasingly alarmed" over Begin's "intransigent views" were followed by predictable White House denials that the United States and Israel were following a "collision course." But even the diplomatic success they shared with President Sadat of Egypt, two years later at Camp David, could not ease their mutual suspicion.

American pressure on the Begin government eased during Ronald Reagan's first term. Reagan lacked Carter's determination to resolve the Palestinian problem contrary to Israel's interests; and he welcomed Israel's role as a counterweight to Soviet influence the Middle East. Consequently, Begin enjoyed greater diplomatic freedom to implement his most controversial policy decisions—to expand settlements, bomb the Iraqi nuclear reactor, annex the Golan, and wage war in Lebanon.

Even Reagan's forbearance, however, had its limits. After the nuclear reactor bombing at Osiraq, the American government suspended its delivery of F-16 fighters. Administration criticism of the Golan annexation provoked Begin's most intemperate outburst. He complained indignantly to American ambassador Samuel Lewis: "Are we a vassal state? A banana republic?" Nobody, Begin predicted, "will frighten the great and free [Jewish] community in the United States. They will stand by us, this is the land of their forefathers. They have the right and duty to support [Israel]."

Begin's assertion of transcendent Jewish unity, irrespective of national identity and citizenship, upset the fragile consensus that enabled American Jews to identify with the Jewish state. As long as Israel was a staunch American ally, a democratic obstacle to Soviet influence in the Middle East, American Jews could comfortably assert a mutuality of interest between the two countries. But once Begin invited them to respond to Israel as Jews, not as Americans or liberals, they backed off. "Anxious American Jews," like children whose parents had begun to quarrel incessantly, were stretched between their attachments to liberal universalism and Jewish particularism.

Until Begin's election, criticism of Israel had largely been confined to the political margins, where New Left anti-Zionism intersected with Black Power anti-Semitism. With Begin in power, the liberal Jewish critique sharpened. Journalist I. F. Stone, who had traveled to Palestine in 1946 with illegal Jewish immigrants, complained in 1978 that the "moral gravity" of Zionism had shifted toward Begin's "cold-blooded nationalistic calculation." How, Stone asked, "can we talk of human rights and ignore them for the Palestinian Arabs?" To retain both his liberal and Zionist credentials, Stone pledged allegiance to "the other Zionism," a Zionism of "the deepest ethical motives," which he located in "that spirit of fraternity and justice and conciliation that the Prophets preached."

Rabbi Arthur Hertzberg, responding to Begin's tongue-lashing of Ambassador Lewis, wondered how American Jews could support "a different country from the one its founders had intended," one no longer based on "a moral passion for a better Jewish people." Did Begin, Hertzberg wondered, "define the true meaning of Zionism and will American Jews follow him?" The basic commitment of American Jewry, the American rabbi insisted, was to "the liberal dreams" of Israel's founders, to "a benign society that could be 'a light unto the nations.'" Israel must remain "a moral cause, consonant with America's highest ideals." Liberalism, for Hertzberg, must remain the true priority of American Jews.

With Yitzhak Shamir's accession to power, the dilemma of Israel intensified for American Jews. Especially after the eruption of the Intifada, when Israel was routinely pilloried in the American media, liberal Jews joined (and often led) the chorus of denunciation. In a remarkable confession in the *New York Times*, Reform spokesman Albert Vorspan offered an explanation. American

Jews, he wrote, were "traumatized" by events in Israel. Suffering "shame and stress," they wanted "to crawl into a hole," where they might escape guilt by association with "the political and moral bankruptcy" of Israeli policy. American Jews, Vorspan insisted, were "implicated" by the actions of the Jewish state. "It's about us."

Implicated by Israel, liberal Jews turned bitterly against it to preserve their liberal credentials. A refrain of liberal disaffection, shading into a myth of Israeli betrayal, emerged. On the Op-Ed page of the *New York Times*, Anthony Lewis relentlessly hectored Israel for its infidelity to the liberal precepts of Brandeis and Isaiah. The magazine *Tikkun* was founded to save the world from neoconservative defenders of Israel like Norman Podhoretz. A stream of books offered variations on the theme of fallen Israel, compromised by its abandonment of liberal values. The moral decline and fall of Jewish state became the irresistible allegation of disaffected Jewish liberals.

The theme of this moral melodrama was labeled, by one author, "the tragedy of Zionism." In his story of Zionist decline from liberal democratic promise to Revisionist holy land, Bernard Avishai described the ascendance of an "utterly nationalist, self-absorbed" Zionism, menacingly identified with "power, Bible, defiance, [and] settlement." Journalist Milton Viorst recounted how Israel, after 1967, had wandered into "a moral desert." Ruled by a coalition of Sephardi Jews accustomed to "mob politics," and Orthodox Jews who gave theological legitimacy to Begin's "'muscular Zionism,'" a once "humane" Israel had descended into the moral abyss of militarism and imperialism.

The popularity of this polemical genre reached its apogee with Thomas Friedman's *From Beirut to Jerusalem*.... Propelling his book up the best-seller list, Friedman offered variations on the theme of Israeli betrayal and his own Jewish disillusionment. Friedman described himself as "a Jew who was raised on...all the myths about Israel," only to witness "an Israel he had deeply believed in...recede from gilded, heroic mythology to the shadows of bleak reality." Projecting the self-image of a morally anguished innocent, who suffered a "personal crisis" as the once "heroic" Israel stripped his "illusion" away, Friedman could only conclude that "something had gone terribly wrong" in the Jewish state.

What had "gone wrong," of course, was the Begin political revolution. As an unholy alliance of Revisionists and Sephardim, joined by rabbis and settlers, swept into power, Israel as a light unto the nations became a Jewish state shadowed by political darkness and religious fanaticism. One might have thought that the democratization of Israeli politics, to say nothing of Israel's first peace treaty with a neighboring Arab state, would have elicited a measure of liberal approval for the government whose conspicuous achievements these were. But even as the Sephardi underclass finally entered the Israeli political mainstream, gaining a measure of the recognition that successive Labor governments had denied it, and as land was traded for peace with Egypt, liberal criticism intensified. Israel became a conditional Jewish commitment, endlessly castigated for its violations of liberal norms.

Liberalism, for American Jews, had become a double-edged ideology.

Before 1977, it had cut the knot of dual loyalty, persuading them that they were better Jews—and better Americans—the more liberal they became. At the time, liberalism had facilitated their identification with Israel. But once the Israeli political balance shifted to the right, American Jews experienced "the pains of dual loyalty"—not, as in the classical model, between Israel and America, but between Israel and liberalism. Their commitment to liberalism, for so long a source of identification with Israel, swiftly provoked their sharpened criticism of the Jewish state.

Harmony between liberalism and Judaism, and between American Jews and Israel, was not restored until the Israeli election of 1992. The Rabin victory resolved the nagging dilemma of American Jewish liberals. Once again they could support Israel as good Jews, committed liberals, and loyal Americans. Allegations of disloyalty subsided. No longer were there complaints about Israel's "Amen" corner in Congress. Instead, there were audible sighs of relief from American Jewish liberals. "Now we can be friends of the government," declared Peter Edelman of Americans for Peace Now. He meant the Israeli government. But his eagerness to suppress the dual-loyalty nightmare, a conflict between American Jews and their own government, was evident.

While liberalism is not nearly as salient in Israeli conceptions of Judaism as it is for American Jews, the identical tension between Judaism and liberalism tormented the Israeli left during the Begin era. That tension, historically rooted in Jewish emancipation and in the process of Western assimilation that it encouraged, erupted after Likud came to power. A decade ago, Amos Oz, with characteristic eloquence, denounced the challenge of "fanatical tribalism" to "the union between Jewish tradition and Western humanism." That rendezvous, he insisted, was "formative" and "irrevocable." Nobody, Oz warned, "will force us to choose...between our Judaism and humanism," for they are "one and the same." More recently, the young writer David Grossman despaired that an "enlightened" Israel had trained itself "to live as a conqueror." He registered a plea for the liberal virtues of "humanity and morality," which encouraged his startling literary transformation of Palestinians into Jews. Oz and Grossman, needless to say, have reached an appreciative audience of American Jewish liberals.

The Israeli literary critique was accompanied by a New Left historiography of Israel. It narrated how the very founding of the Jewish state was sullied by "original sin": the denial to Palestinian Arabs of their country and national identity. Consistent with this moral homily of Israeli political declension, "the decline of Israeli democracy" during the 1980s has been attributed to the growth of a radical right. From its founding to the present, according to the new Israeli scholarship, Israel has betrayed its democratic promise.

In their chastisement of Israel, Israeli and American writers and scholars spoke the common language of liberalism. American magazines and newspapers opened their pages to criticism of Israel during the Begin years—and in the *New Yorker*, the *New York Review of Books*, and the *New York Times*, Oz, Grossman, Meron Benvenisti, Avishai Margalit, and Amos Elon, among others, were delighted to prove it. So, too, were their American counterparts: liberal rabbis, professors, and journalists, far too numerous to mention, who incessantly wondered whether Israel had lost its soul. With liberalism as their shared ideological heritage, it became all but impossible to distinguish their substantive ideological positions by their national identities.

It is difficult to exaggerate Menachem Begin's role as symbolic catalyst for liberal Jewish disaffection with the Jewish state. He was, after all, a disciple of Jabotinsky with a vision of Israel within the biblical boundaries of Eretz Israel, a Jew who wore a *kipa* and prayed at the *Kotel*. American Jews always preferred Israeli statesmen who spoke with a British accent, or who capitulated graciously to American definitions of Israel's best interests. Certainly they were uncomfortable when Begin identified himself to President Carter as a proud Jew who would bend his knee only to God. Begin activated some of their deepest concerns about their loyalty as Americans, their identity as Jews, and their credentials as liberals.

Begin era politics, between 1977-1992, offered American Jews disturbing glimpses of an Israeli Judaism that contradicted their understanding of their Jewish identity. Instead of the Hebrew prophets, whose jeremiads for justice made them the patron saints of Jewish liberals in the modern era, they heard disconcerting calls for the Land of Israel for the people of Israel according to the Torah of Israel. The fundamental premises of Diaspora liberalism were challenged. Liberal ideology, which had once encouraged American Jews to identify with Israel, now undermined their attachment to the Jewish state. Once Israel turned right, Jewish liberals turned away.

For American Jews, the momentous Israeli political transformation of 1977 sharply challenged their conventional understanding of Israel, Zionism, Judaism, and ultimately themselves. Once Orthodox nationalism competed actively with secular liberalism as a legitimate expression of Zionism, the American Diaspora was forced to redefine its relation to the Jewish state. The Begin era remains a prism for viewing the inherently unstable relations between Israel and the Diaspora. It invites us to replace the confident assertion, "We Are One!", with the far more troubling question with which any analysis of Israel-Diaspora relations should begin: "Are We One?"

14 · Zionism Without Judaism

Six months after the stunning handshake on the White House lawn, any lingering vestiges of September euphoria were obliterated.... A "peace process" has triggered the bloodiest internecine fighting between Arabs and Jews since the birth of Israel.

September 13 [1993] certainly seemed like a good day to invest in plowshares. To most, it was an astonishing moment of prophetic fulfillment, when "nation shall not lift up sword against nation." Only the most churlish Jews, in Israel and the Diaspora, dared to wonder whether peace now foreshadowed yet another catastrophic "peace in our time."

Back in September, I watched faces, not hands. Yasir Arafat exulted. And why not: his PLO, wracked by internal conflict, verging on financial ruin, spurned by Arab states, and diminished in the media by newer claimants to superior victim status, had been rescued from terminal collapse by the government of Israel. Arafat, teetering at the edge of political oblivion, suddenly had reemerged as an international hero, a statesman entitled to all the fawning media coverage, diplomatic favors, and financial largesse that his newly-inflated stature commanded.

Rabin, by contrast, was funereal. And why not: after a year of fruitless negotiation, while repeated Israeli concessions proved insufficient, he was prepared to relinquish the geographical and historical cradle of Jewish civilization. Indeed, the Rabin government seemed to exist for no reason other than to divest the Jewish state of its Biblical homeland. The day after the signing, as if to affirm the body language in Washington, Palestinian flags fluttered over the Old City of Jerusalem.

This was hardly "a peace of the brave," as President Clinton and assorted pundits proclaimed, but a peace of the weak, who needed to lean upon each other to avoid imminent political collapse. The Palestinian national movement, always drawing upon Zionism for its own identity, seemed incapable of sustaining itself. And Zionism, quite evidently, had lost its will to continue the struggle against its rival claimant for the land of Israel. Amid the aftershocks from the Yom Kippur war and the *intifada*, secular Israelis embraced Western liberalism and American materialism in an effort to compensate for their loss of Zionist passion and purpose. It is understandable that decades of ceaseless conflict

---

"Rest in Peace: Zionism, 1967-1993," *Jewish Spectator* (Spring 1994), 32-34.

should have ground Israelis into political and spiritual exhaustion. They had endured unremitting Arab enmity and vicious Palestinian terror for so long that even a glimmer—or the mirage—of peaceful normality was irresistible. Most Israelis, after all, yearn for nothing more daring than a comfortable and secure life for themselves and their children—a Zionism no riskier than a short Shabbat drive to the nearest beach or newest shopping-mall. Wary of peace, they were nonetheless weary of war.

Rabin defended his peace accord as a momentous Zionist victory, the crowning achievement of the generation that had come of age forty-five years earlier in a desperate battle for Jewish statehood. But in the Samarian settlement of Ofra, on the September day when Zionism, according to one resident, "died of its own will," Jews tore their clothes in mourning. Zionism, an Ofra settler declared, "has given up on itself." Now, six months later, how is the Israeli-PLO accord to be understood? Even before the events in Hebron, and their violent reverberations, imploded upon the peace accord, was that September moment a Zionist triumph or a Zionist tragedy?

The answer is embedded in the lingering paradox of Jewish emancipation, and the persistent flight from Judaism that accompanied it. Early in the nineteenth century, as newly emancipated Jews began to infiltrate Western Christian society, Judaism was drastically reformed. Once a way of life, it became the diminished identity of Jews who were increasingly remote from their own religious and national antecedents as a people. Yet no matter how avidly Jews assimilated, they remained potentially disloyal aliens; like French captain Alfred Dreyfus, forever suspect. Therefore, Zionism: the reassertion of Jewish nationality as the necessary precursor of Jewish normality. Zionism offered an alternative to traditional Judaism, rooted in rabbinical Orthodoxy, and a sanctuary from the spreading ravages of anti-Semitism, endemic even in the most enlightened sectors of Christian culture. A "fundamental revolution in Jewish life," as Shlomo Avineri aptly described Zionism (*The Zionist Revolution* [1981]), it represented the Jewish "quest for self-determination and liberation under the modern conditions of secularization and liberalism."

Yet Zionism absorbed, and still exudes, the Western secular liberalism that generated it. With scattered and conspicuous exceptions, the boldest Zionist theoreticians—from Hess and Pinsker through Herzl to Ben-Gurion and Jabotinsky—all plundered Western political ideology for their assorted nationalist and socialist justifications for the Zionist struggle.

Zionists like Ahad Ha'Am and Rabbi Kook, among the few who tapped Jewish cultural or religious sources, long remained misguided prophets without honor in the nascent Jewish state. For all the power of his assertion that the Jews were one people, constituting a single nation, Herzl (who would have settled for Uganda) yearned for a Jewish Switzerland. There Western bourgeois norms would confine Jewish "priests" to their irrelevant temples. A Jewish state, that is, without Judaism—a fitting vision for an assimilated Viennese gentleman.

Herzl's dream of Jewish normalization was realized in modern Israel. Ben-Gurion would consort with Orthodox politicians to secure his ruling coalition. And, on ceremonial occasions, there might even be obligatory references to Amos, Isaiah, or Jeremiah. (Zionists, like nineteenth century Reform Jews, glibly converted ancient Hebrew prophecy into the Jewish source of modern liberalism.) But founders and sons, by and large, were unrelenting secularists.

Labor Zionists translated the Jewish national struggle into a quest for secular normality. Most Israelis grew up as abysmally ignorant as most Diaspora Jews of two millennia of Jewish history after the destruction of the Second Temple in 70 C.E. While the ultra-Orthodox berated Zionists for forcing God's hand, with the Godless State of Israel as the inevitable consequence, secular Zionists, with equivalent intolerance, denounced the galut mentality of Orthodoxy. And, since God is said to favor the side with the largest battalions, Labor Zionists easily carried the day. The Israeli pursuit of Jewish normality was abruptly and profoundly interrupted in June 1967. Jews throughout the world shared Rabbi Abraham J. Heschel's startling discovery, in words that now sound almost quaint with naive passion: "I had not known how deeply Jewish I was." Battle-weary Israeli soldiers, educated to think of themselves as normal people in a normal country, realized quite unexpectedly that they were Jews. For the first time, they understood the Jewishness of Israel. Even Yitzhak Rabin, speaking in Jerusalem after the war, expressed "the sense of salvation and of direct confrontation with Jewish history" that Israel had just experienced.

Nineteen sixty-seven has been described as a covenantal moment, an instant of "abiding astonishment" in Jewish history like the crossing of the Red Sea. The ancient covenant of the Jewish people, Harold Fisch wrote soon afterward (*The Zionist Revolution* [1978]), had always rested on "a triad of relationships: God, land and people." With the heartland of Biblical Israel, and Jerusalem, finally restored to the Jewish people, Jews "were suddenly living in the fullness of our own covenant history." After June 1967, Zionism and Judaism were fused.

Even covenantal moments, however, are fleeting. What is remarkable, in retrospect, is that after 1967 there actually were Jews who acted upon the realization that Zionism without Judaism was hollow nationalism, certain to hasten the inevitable drift, even in Israel, from emancipation to assimilation. Throughout Judea and Samaria (formerly Jordan's West Bank and, long before, the ancient homeland of the Jewish people), clusters of Jews fused Zionism and Judaism. The return of these newest *halutzim* to homeland and covenant was rooted in the most ancient themes of Jewish history. It was (as Fisch noted) "what Zionism is all about." For without "the theological dimension," Fisch warned, Zionism "turns to ashes."

Most Israelis, resolutely secular, would vigorously disagree. None has been more eloquently critical than Amos Oz, the novelist whose political commentary (*In the Land of Israel* [1983]) illuminated the fierce struggle within Zionism, since 1967, to define the identity of the Jewish people in the Jewish state. Oz graphically evoked "the elusive cunning of the Biblical charm" of Judea and Samaria, only to reject this land as "Arab, through and through."

Israelis, like Moses, were fated to see their Promised Land only from afar. For once they entered it, Oz warned, "the Biblical charm will fade like a dream. The penetration will not be one of harmony, but of occupation and capitulation and destruction."

If the Biblical landscape of Judea and Samaria no longer enticed Oz, Jews who resettled there viscerally repelled him. Nineteen sixty-seven, he lamented, signified the triumph of "yeshiva students" over "kibbutzniks": "values, ideals, conscience, world view," which Oz associated with secular Zionism, suddenly were challenged by "victory and miracles, Redemption and the coming of the Messiah." Religious Zionists arrogantly portrayed themselves "the heirs of the pioneering spark that had dimmed"; and Oz, for good reason, was concerned that they were correct. Adding insult to injury, they dismissed their secular opponents as Bohemian lightweights, wearied of Zionist exertion and eager, like their American exemplars, to make love, not war.

The struggle after 1967, as Oz insisted, was "over the nature of Zionism and even the meaning of Jewish destiny." He offered a passionate defense of the fateful modern rendezvous of Judaism with enlightened Western humanism. It was, he insisted, "formative" and "irrevocable"—and altogether distinguishable from the process of Hellenization that once had diluted Jewish civilization in the land of Israel. Why? Because Western humanism, especially its liberal and socialist varieties, contains "Jewish genes." By now, at least for Oz, Judaism and Western humanism were "one and the same." The only alternative was "fanatical tribalism, brutal and closed," a Jewish "museum" civilization rigidly fixated upon its ancient heritage.

Oz's Zionism is the secular Israeli variant of the pro-choice Judaism that is now rampant among contemporary Americans. Accordingly, any Western fashion becomes "Jewish" once Jews absorb and display it. So, without any discernible embarrassment, Oz has demanded for Zionism that most enticing freedom of modern emancipated Jews: intermarriage (the "marriage" metaphor is his) between the Jewish heritage and Western humanism. By now, he rejoiced, modern Jews have "assimilated" Judaism and humanism. For Oz, there can be no turning back.

The consequences of Israeli assimilation are readily apparent. Secular Israelis, like those newly emancipated Jews who once avidly copied the manners and mores of their Christian exemplars, have delighted in mimicking Western cultural and intellectual fashion. From the boutiques and cafes of Tel Aviv, where beautiful sabras faithfully worship at their shrines of Western hedonism, to the lofty heights of Mt. Scopus in Jerusalem, where alienated Jewish intellectuals gather on the Middle Eastern edge of the upper West Side, Israelis yearn for their own version of the American dream, with little discernible Jewish content.

Did 1967, then, mark a momentous step toward the fulfillment of Zionist destiny, finally unfolding within the ancient homeland of the Jewish people? Or did it signify regressive tribalism and immoral domination? This is not an idle question, for upon its answer turns the meaning of the fateful events of 1993. If the covenantal moment of 1967 was merely a mirage, yet another self-destructive example of Jewish messianism ("the Bar Kokhba syndrome," as Yehoshua Harkabi labeled it), then the Rabin government has indeed acted with consummate wisdom, even as it prepares to transform the Biblical Jewish homeland into a Palestinian state. If not, however, it has abjectly surrendered the historical patrimony of the Jewish people.

Since September, the peace process has degenerated into brutal violence. With each Israeli concession, Palestinian terror attacks escalated. Before Hebron, Hamas had declared open season on Israelis, littering the peace process with their corpses. As the Rabin government contemplates the return of the Golan Heights to Syria, the transfer of Jews from Judea and Samaria (or their abandonment to the new state of Palestine), and shared sovereignty in Jerusalem with the PLO—still committed to the destruction of Israel "in stages"—the exorbitant price of its peace fantasies is apparent. For the Rabin government is promising to divest Israel of much that is most distinctively Jewish about it—including its Biblical heritage, its ancient homeland, and its covenantal identity.

That is why the Israeli-PLO accord of 1993 signifies the peril, not the promise, of Jewish emancipation; the repudiation, not the embrace, of Jewish covenantal history and memory; the collapse, not the fulfillment, of Zionism. Yitzhak Rabin, the first native-born Prime Minister of Israel, exemplifies the constricted boundaries of contemporary Zionist normality, a Zionism without Judaism. Where, one wonders, are those who understand that Israel cannot remain the land of Jewish destiny if Judaism atrophies in Zion?

15 · Israel's Shadow Line

September 11, 2001 marks the terrible shadow line that defines before and after in the American war against terrorism. Now, a year after the heinous Palestinian suicide bombing in Netanya at the Park Hotel Seder, we can better understand that atrocity as a defining moment for Israel.

The Passover massacre, killing twenty-nine Israelis and wounding more than one hundred, was the climactic act in a month of horrific suicide bombings that illustrated the very essence of terrorism: the intentional targeting of innocent civilians for political purposes.

But it was not merely the cruelty of the deed, nor even the human carnage, that sent ripples of metaphysical horror through world Jewry. Like the premeditated Arab attack against Israel in October 1973, the Netanya bombing was activated by the Jewish calendar. It was, precisely as Harold Fisch described the outbreak of war on Yom Kippur in *The Zionist Revolution* (1978), a stark "covenantal moment" when Jews could fully grasp the true nature of the war that is being waged against us.

The Arab-Israeli, or Israeli-Palestinian, conflict has never, of course, been "merely" a war between peoples, or even a normal struggle between nations. At its very core, as Fisch grasped twenty-five years ago, it is "a holy war," a religious war for "the liquidation of the Jewish entity in Palestine in the name of the integrity of Islam." The enemy is not merely Israel, but Judaism, and Jews. Just as the Yom Kippur war was launched "at the most sacred hour of the Jewish year," so the Passover massacre reminded even the most secular Jew that there are Palestinians, at least, who take the Jewish calendar seriously. Sufficiently seriously, in fact, to plunge the joyous annual celebration of Jewish freedom into a paroxysm of grief and lamentation....

In the days that followed, reverberations from the Passover massacre rippled from Israel throughout the world like the aftershocks of an earthquake. They spread through the festering terrorist enclaves under Palestinian Authority rule, and on the Arab "street," where suicide bombings were celebrated; in chic European intellectual circles, where suicide bombers were exonerated; within a divided and ambivalent Bush administration, where on Mondays, Wednesdays, and Fridays government officials condemned terrorism but on Tuesdays, Thursdays, and Saturdays they condemned Israel for responding to

"Israel's Shadow Line," *Midstream* (April 2003), 12-15.

terrorism; in American universities, where anti-Zionism, anti-Semitism, and anti-Americanism were converging to become the new litany of the Left. Jews everywhere were understandably apprehensive about the gathering storm of international anti-Semitism, by far the worst since the Nazi era.

I absorbed the gruesome details of the Seder slaughter with a grim, unwanted sense of confirmation. For nearly a decade, I had been a resolute opponent of the Oslo process. My belief had never wavered that Yasir Arafat, the most notorious killer of Jews since Hitler, was unrepentant, and that the Palestinian goal was not merely the rollback of Jewish settlements from "occupied" lands in the Biblical homeland of the Jewish people in Judea and Samaria, but the ultimate obliteration of the largest Jewish "settlement" in the Middle East, the State of Israel.

The Oslo process both symbolized and accelerated the malady of post-Zionism, the corrosive attempt by Israelis on the secular Left to expunge both Judaism and Zionism from Israeli history and culture. The waning of Zionist energy through the Nineties was sadly evident. With Israelis so palpably eager to Americanize, the very meaning of Jewish distinctiveness and destiny seemed in danger of obliteration. Only the futile negotiations presided over by President Clinton at Camp David, when Prime Minister Barak seemed eager to give away so much of the Land of Israel to an unreceptive Arafat, finally, if belatedly, brought a halt to Zionist surrender. The outbreak of the renewed *intifada* did the rest. Yet even Ariel Sharon, as it happened, seemed initially inclined to heed cautionary warnings from the American administration that, in effect, preserved the fiction—so eagerly swallowed by the Israeli Left and the American State Department—that peace now was just around the corner, if only Ararat were granted one more chance.

It was one thing, before September 11, for Israel to capitulate to American pressure in pursuit of this flight of fancy. Thereafter, however, anyone who was not willfully blind to reality could understand that if the war against terrorism properly targeted Osama bin Laden and Al Qaeda, it must also target Yasir Arafat and his Palestinian terror brigades, along with Hamas, Islamic Jihad, and Hezbollah. Any attempt to distinguish between these varieties of Islamic terrorism, whether directed against the Great Satan of the West (the United States) or its ally the Little Satan of the Middle East (Israel), was delusional and, worse yet, perhaps willfully malevolent.

But Sharon, long beset by a fractured Cabinet (of his choosing), dithered, even when the State Department skirted the alluring swamp of moral equivalence in which terrorism and retaliation were so often condemned in the same breath. The prime minister might speak loudly, as in his biting denunciation (October, 2001) of Bush administration "appeasement"; nevertheless, he carried an olive branch.

But the Passover massacre climaxed yet another wave of deadly terror, which had already claimed the lives of nearly three dozen Israelis in March 2002 alone. Israelis were finally roused to the realization that they were engaged in a war for their very survival as a people against a vicious, unrelenting enemy, the

Palestinian face of militant Islam. The incessant terrorist attacks within Israel's pre-1967 boundaries belied Palestinian proclamations of "occupation" as the *casus belli*. It was not merely West Bank "settlers," but Israelis and Israel, Jews and Judaism, who defined the targets of Islamic fury.

When Israel finally retaliated, Jews suddenly confronted waves of anti-Zionist and anti-Semitic demonization, not only in the Arab Middle East but throughout Western Europe. It was bad enough, according to frenzied accounts in the French, German, British, Italian, and Norwegian media, that the Israeli army confined Yasir Arafat to house arrest in Ramallah, and surrounded Palestinian terrorists who had taken refuge in the Church of the Nativity in Bethlehem. (One can only imagine the outrage had Israel, not the Palestinians, seized one of Christianity's holiest places.) But once the Israel Defense Forces finally assaulted the Palestinian terrorist network entrenched in the Jenin refugee camp, the outpouring of anti-Zionism and anti-Semitism expressed depths of Jew-hatred that had not been heard in more than half a century.

The Jenin "massacre," the massacre that happened only in the inflamed Arab imagination and in hostile Western media, simultaneously expressed and fueled the newest war against the Jews. Partisan journalists were only too eager to convict the Israeli army of "human-rights" violations, while ignoring the Israeli soldiers who paid with their lives for fastidiously maximizing danger to themselves to reduce risks to Palestinian civilians. They overlooked the cruelty of Palestinians toward their own people (under the averted eyes of UNRWA): neighborhoods honeycombed with bomb factories and booby-traps; the use of civilians as human shields; and desperately needed ambulances routinely converted into taxis for terrorists. To say nothing of the Palestinian insistence, ever since 1948, upon holding its own people hostage in these camps for political purposes.

Framing the onslaught in Europe, where synagogues were destroyed, Torah scrolls desecrated, and Jews assaulted, were the most ancient and ugly canards of anti-Semitic vituperation. Among the more grotesque examples, surely, was the Italian newspaper cartoon depicting the baby Jesus sighting an Israeli tank and imploring, "Don't tell me they want to kill me again." Not to be outdone, *Al-Riyadh*, the Saudi government-controlled newspaper, referred to "Jewish vampires" who used gentile blood for their Purim baking. Everywhere, as Gabriel Schoenfeld wrote in *Commentary*, it was the same story: "Israel, a country victimized by terrorism, stands accused of perpetuating terrorism; the Jews, having suffered the most determined and thoroughgoing genocide in history, stand accused of perpetrating genocide."

Some American academic precincts were similarly hate-infested. At San Francisco State University last spring, a mob of pro-Palestinian demonstrators threatened to kill Jewish students if they did not "return to Russia." The San Francisco Police Department had to be called in to lead the students to safety. In Berkeley, the womb of the Free Speech Movement of the 1960s, the English Department offered a course on the "brutal Israeli military occupation of Palestinians" from which "conservative thinkers" were advised to absent themselves.

Even in the normally decorous academic precincts of Wellesley College, which I inhabit, a Muslim student offered a heartfelt poem describing Jews as "Judas," while another circulated a photograph of Israeli soldiers with the caption "Three Jewish Animals." In academic circles, as Harvard professor Ruth Wisse noted, Jews are "the only minority it is trendy to denigrate."

While Israel was relentlessly pilloried for "war crimes," there was evidence among its soldiers of a powerful reconnection to Jewish history. One of them, identified only as Alon, described Yom Hashoah in the Nablus casbah, where his unit was surrounded by Palestinian snipers: "It was the most moving experience of my life. It began when we stood around in a circle and began reading texts we wrote for the day about the Holocaust.... At the end of the reading ceremony we all stood and sang the *Hatikvah*, and all I could think of during this 30 or so minutes was how much this means for all the 6 million people to have a voice, an army of trained soldiers, people to protect the exact concept that so many have tried to finish—Judaism.... You should feel special as a Jew, you should feel that you are carrying the torch for all those that have been murdered for just being a—Jew. I am not a religious person, yet there is something unique in what we are."

Something unique, indeed. And perhaps it is not absurd to suggest that precisely this uniqueness—which includes, but is hardly limited to, reverence for the life of an enemy even when one's own life is threatened—drove so much of the world wild with fury against Jews. Of the recrudescence of Christian anti-Semitism, no one said it better, or more passionately, than Oriana Fallaci, the Italian journalist. In April 2002, at the height of European anti-Semitic frenzy, she wrote: "I find it shameful that [*l'Osservatore Romano*] the newspaper of the Pope...accuses of extermination a people who were exterminated in the millions by Christians.... I find it shameful that in the name of Jesus Christ...the priests of our parishes...flirt with the assassins of those in Jerusalem who cannot go to eat a pizza or buy some eggs without being blown up.... I find it shameful that in part through the fault of the left...Jews in Italian cities are once again afraid. And in French cities and Dutch cities and Danish cities and German cities, it is the same."

With the alarming convergence of "Christ-killer" and *jihad* with Leftist politics, Jews understandably felt vulnerable. "Hitler is dead," Leon Wieseltier pointedly reminded his *New Republic* readers, cautioning against overreaction. But that was hardly reassuring when enemies of the Jews remained alive, active, numerous, empowered, and, in Israel at least, eager to transform themselves into *shahids* (martyrs). Oslo enthusiasts, such as Wieseltier, who had pilloried the Israeli Right for doubting Palestinian intentions, came rather belatedly, if at all, to an appreciation of the very real dangers to Jews from the Palestinian terror war. Hitler might indeed be dead, but so, too, were many hundreds of Jews brutally murdered by Arafat's terrorists.

Among the prominent pundits whose misplaced Oslo euphoria was, at least momentarily, punctured by the new terrorist realities, Thomas Friedman of *The New York Times* was conspicuous. Back in February, Friedman had famously reported his dinner with Crown Prince Abdullah of Saudi Arabia in which, miraculously, a "Friedman Plan" was embraced by the Saudi leader as the recipe for peace in the Middle East. It required nothing more from Israel than full withdrawal from *all* territory acquired in the Six-Day War. In return for Palestinian statehood, Israel would receive diplomatic relations, normalized trade, and security guarantees that were presumably stronger than those that had been cavalierly violated by the Palestinian Authority ever since the Oslo accords were signed.

Friedman seemed genuinely euphoric to have been kidnapped by the Saudis for their own post-September 11 public-relations purposes. He suddenly found himself a media and diplomatic star for proposing a "peace plan" that was so dangerous to Israel that even the United Nations, back in 1967, had rejected the return of all territories for the less inclusive "return of territories." It was quite easy for Friedman to relinquish Judea and Samaria and the settlements on Israel's behalf. For Israel, however, such surrender would be nothing less than an act of national mutilation—historically, strategically, and politically. If one million Arabs can live inside Israel, as citizens of the Jewish state, there is no reason—aside from Jew-hatred—why several hundred thousand Jews cannot live in Judea and Samaria, the Biblical homeland of the Jewish people.

The primary obstacles to peace in the Middle East, contrary to the conventional wisdom, remain Palestinian refugee camps, not Jewish settlements. As long as Palestinians are confined to these wretched slums, impoverished, politically voiceless, and deprived of hope and opportunity, terrorism against Israel festers. Then the familiar scenario plays itself out: terrorists get a free ride from world public opinion, while Israel is pilloried for responding....

Israeli strength and American firmness are the prerequisites for waging war effectively against Islamic terrorism. Operation Determined Path could not provide absolute safety for Israelis, but after the devastating terror-bombing at Hebrew University on July 31, in which five Americans were killed, the Israeli military response, this time with Bush administration support, brought Israel a six-week respite from terror attacks. As the new Chief of Staff explained, a continued military presence in the populated areas of Judea and Samaria "is like a blanket over a fire. If we take away the blanket, the fire will burst forth."

As always, however, Israel remained vulnerable to American diplomatic pressure. President Bush's commitment to Israel's role in the war against terrorism, in which Israel has for so long been the front line, has wavered. His evident fury after the Hebrew University bombing, which killed more Americans than Israelis, was reassuring. But his intermittent determination to restrain Israel, the better to placate Arabs opposed to an American war against Iraq, may yet bode ill for the Jewish State.

Indeed, with deadly predictability, whenever Israel lifted the blanket of its military presence, the fire of Palestinian terrorism raged. Through the late summer and early fall, Israeli military and diplomatic firmness showed evident signs of success. In Nablus, previously a hotbed of terrorism, no successful Palestinian attack originated in more than two months. As the Israeli colonel in charge explained, "We're in the middle of a hundred-years war." The Palestinians, he predicted, "will suffer until they understand.... When they will say 'enough,' they can live in peace and quiet."

Under these circumstances, it would be foolhardy for Israel even to consider any further divestment of land west of the Jordan River. The Oslo process, rightly identified by Minister Dani Naveh as "the biggest strategic mistake ever made by Israel," is now a sobering reminder of the price that Israel pays by whetting Palestinian appetites for surrenders and concessions. Only when the cost of terrorism becomes unbearable to Palestinians—not only to those who plan and fund it but to family members of those who practice it—will the lives of Israelis be secure. That, after all, is the meaning of a war against terrorism.

It just may be that the Passover massacre last March, simultaneously an attack against Israelis and an assault on the Jewish calendar, unmasked the true intentions of the Palestinian national movement. Perhaps, in all its horror, it finally stripped away the persistent Israeli willingness, evident since 1993, to accommodate its terrorist enemy. If so, that tragic event will have served as a desperately needed wake-up call whose message must not be forgotten....

Ultimately, defeating terrorism depends upon the determination of Israelis to endure, to resist, and to fight when necessary, even while preserving their moral compass. To be sure, international opprobrium is all but assured whenever Israel retaliates, or acts pre-emptively. The United Nations and the European Union will continue to blur the vital distinction between the unintentional killing of innocents by Israelis and the intentional murder of civilians by Palestinian suicide bombers. With such moral equivalency, however, the war against terrorism loses its moral credibility.

In its own war against terrorism, the United States finally resorted to the targeted assassination of Al Qaeda leaders in Yemen, a tactic it vigorously condemned when used by Israel against Palestinian terrorists. State Department spokesman Richard Boucher fumbled to explain how "the situation with regard to Israeli-Palestinian issues and the prospects of peace and the prospects of negotiation, the need to create an atmosphere for progress, a lot of different things come into play there." But this was standard State Department doublespeak. As an F.B.I. official declared: "this is a kind of war which requires us to fight on multiple fronts with all the weapons at our disposal." That remains no less true for Israel than for the United States.

The costs to Israel of placating the United States by pursuing a "peace" agenda were readily apparent. In mid-November, just two weeks after the Israel Defense Forces in Hebron were thinned out (in part, to serve Defense Minister Ben Eliezer's political ambitions), a horrific Shabbat massacre killed a dozen soldiers, border police, and security guards. As Israel's ambassador to the United States explained, "Whenever we leave an area, the terror bounces back." The following week, as if to illustrate his point, a suicide bomber from Bethlehem (another city from which the IDF had withdrawn) killed eleven Israelis, including four children, by exploding himself on a Jerusalem bus. When Israeli soldiers immediately returned in force to Hebron and Bethlehem, terrorism quickly subsided.

    I saw this pattern with my own eyes in Hebron, where I visited in early November to celebrate Shabbat *Chaye Sarah*, recounting the purchase by Abraham of the first Jewish foothold in the land of Israel. For that day, at least, the Israeli army had returned to Hebron to protect some 20,000 Jews who joined the Jewish communities of Kiryat Arba and Hebron in observance and celebration. To watch thousands of fellow Jews flow down the hill from Kiryat Arba to Me'arat ha-Machpelah for Shabbat prayer, securely protected by Israeli soldiers, was a memorable experience, even before I joined the overflowing crowds of worshipers inside for *Kabbalat Shabbat* and Shabbat services. To hear the joyous sounds of Jewish prayer echoing throughout the massive Herodian structure was to be reminded of the dynamic fusion of Judaism and Zionism, if only all Jews and Zionists could allow themselves to be energized by it. But after Shabbat, predictably, the IDF pulled back; precisely two weeks later, at the exact spot and time where we had walked, the massacre occurred.

16 · Zionism vs. Judaism

Historically, Zionism meant the national liberation of the Jewish people in their own homeland—free from foreign domination. But there is a fundamental, perhaps irreconcilable, tension between Zionism, a revolutionary political movement in pursuit of normalization, and Judaism, the distinctive faith tradition of the Jewish people—a people, according to the biblical text (which, after all, is the ultimate source of Zionism), destined to dwell alone, set apart from the other nations of the world...

Zionists, after all, were Jews who refused to wait for the messiah. They believed in action, now. With extraordinary determination and courage, driven by the confluence of historical events both too horrific and too wondrous to anticipate, they achieved what was historically unprecedented—some might even say miraculous. They actually reconstructed the national identity of a dispersed, powerless, and landless people. Who cannot be awed by the singular majesty of their accomplishment?

But the stunning Zionist achievement was not without its serious blemishes, which are already debilitating and may yet become fatal. This has nothing to do with the politically fashionable indictment of Zionism for its "theft" of "Palestinian" land, or its "oppression" of the Palestinian people. Rarely, if ever, in history has any "conquest" or "occupation" secured so much freedom for its beleaguered victims. (The prolonged encounter between pioneers and American Indians was far more exploitative, brutal, mendacious, and destructive than anything done by Zionists to Palestinians.) It is little wonder that the Palestinian national movement, from its claim of biblical antecedents to its language of ingathering exiles and its obsession with Jerusalem, has faithfully mimicked the very Zionism that it so fervently despises.

The real problem is the abiding and deepening hostility within the Jewish state toward Jews and Judaism. The normalization impulse among secular Israelis, so deeply embedded in their Zionist inheritance, is relentlessly driving Israel from its origins in Jewish nationalism and its pursuit of Jewish freedom. The future is already clearly discernible: Israel as an American cultural outpost in the Middle East, clamoring for admission to the global American village.

To be sure, the Americanization impulse—which has included everything from Big Macs and Levis to the Michaels Jordan and Jackson—has all but be-

Are We One? (2001), 113-15, 171-73, 189-91, 200-02.

come a worldwide stampede. But Israel alone, among the nations, has assumed responsibility for preserving the Jewish people in its own national home. Yet its mission is undermined by the inherent ambiguity of Zionist "normalization." Was Zionism intended to make Jews like everyone else, or to enable them, as Jews, to live normal lives?...

The split Zionist vision—a Jewish state depleted of Jewish content—is nowhere more vividly on display than in the Israeli rendition of a tale of two cities. Long before Zionism, of course, there was "Zion." Jerusalem, as decayed and barren as it might be in reality, remained the spiritual centerpiece of return. Even today, for all the garish excesses of its modern architecture—the obtrusive glass towers and ponderous public buildings—Jerusalem still turns Jews inward upon their own history as a people. The twisted alleys of its shtetl neighborhoods, transplanted from the decimated Eastern European centers of Orthodoxy, lure visitors from modernity into a maze of Jewish memory that winds all the way back to the Second Temple and beyond, to King David's ancient city.

Isaiah's prophecy proclaimed that the word of God would go forth from Jerusalem. This unique city of myth and metaphor demands fidelity to Jewish history, religion, tradition, and memory. Yet the literature of modern Zionism, virtually from its beginning, displayed what has aptly been called a resentful "demystification" of the holy city. Among Zionist writers for nearly a century now, the "irrelevance" of Jerusalem has been a persistent theme.

From Leo Pinsker and Ahad Ha'Am (who, despite his yearning for a cultural center for Judaism, preferred to live in Tel Aviv), through Chaim Nahman Bialik and Yosef Chaim Brenner, into the era of statehood and down to our own time, the Zionist literary imagination has remained hostile to Jerusalem as the repository of Jewish memory. Even among contemporary Israeli writers—once again, Amos Oz comes conspicuously to mind—Jerusalem is little more than a dismal symbol of Jewish "national deformity and impotence," a wandering ground for demented religious mystics and zealots.

Zionist political leaders displayed similar indifference to Jerusalem. The Knesset, the seat of government power, was located there but Ben-Gurion commuted from Tel Aviv. During Golda Meir's years in office, the prime minister's residence in Jerusalem rarely was occupied. Only in 1967 did Jerusalem begin to assume the spiritual and emotional centrality in Zionism that it had always enjoyed in Judaism. The city that Ben-Gurion would not fight for in 1948 became, twenty years later, the city that Israel would never abandon.

Even today, despite its high-rise apartment and office buildings, luxury hotels, and state-of-the-art shopping mall, Jerusalem still stands slightly apart from modern Israel. Astride the hills of Zion and Moriah, at the end of the road from Tel Aviv, it remains too Jewish to fit altogether comfortably into a Zionist state. Secular Israeli visitors often seem uncomfortable in Jerusalem, where they are surrounded by too many Jews whose very presence is an "encroachment." Even Jerusalem residents are prone to complain bitterly about the "takeover" of the city by "black hats," as though ultra-Orthodox Jews constitute an invading foreign army.

Tel Aviv, by contrast, is the consummate Zionist city, brashly asserting Israeli normality. Its very existence repudiates Jewish memory. Built early in this century on the shifting sand dunes (both real and metaphorical) that covered all traces of the Jewish past, it literally turned its back on the geographical cradle of Jewish history. Facing away from the Samarian hills, it focuses Israeli longing toward the Mediterranean and beyond, to the glittering West. Its most distinctive historic architecture is the cluster of Bauhaus buildings in the old city center. A Western import, they were as definitively modern as they were unambiguously foreign.

Tel Aviv is the secular, liberal, hedonistic fulfillment of Herzl's dream, a magnet for Israelis who crave relief from spiritual yearning, historical claims, and divine command. Here Yom Kippur can be just another (holy) day at the beach, a fast day that is as likely as not to prompt a lavish meal behind discreetly closed shutters. So insulated are Tel Avivians from Judaism by their cosmopolitanism that they have occasionally been stunned, whether by scud missiles or terror bombings, into the astonishing realization that to enemies of the Jews they, too, are the Jewish enemy...

The most important Zionist story by the mid-nineties, according to *The Jerusalem Report*, was the "Americanization of Israel." When a McDonald's opened in Rishon l'Tzion, the very first Zionist settlement, an Israeli exulted: "This is America, but better... Now we have it all." In Herzliya (named to honor the Zionist prophet), Chinese takeout and pizza were available in a sparkling new shopping mall, where a country-and-western band was booked for Texas Jack's on the sabbath.

The "fast-food invasion" of Israel—not only the requisite McDonald's but Burger King, Pizza Hut, and Kenny Rogers' Roasters—stimulated the appetite of Israelis for rampant American-style consumerism. Tel Avivians could hardly contain their delight with Tower Records, the Gap, and Toys "R" Us. Prosperous Israeli suburbanites took time away from their villas and swimming pools to shop at Ace Hardware and Office Depot. By 1995, the newest status symbol no longer was a VCR, or even a computer, but the ubiquitous cell phone. With cable TV, Israelis could move beyond *Dallas* to a wider range of American sitcoms. That December, to heighten holiday cheer, shops in Tel Aviv displayed Christmas decorations.

The younger generation of Israelis was all but indistinguishable from its American counterpart. Children tested their roller blades on Yom Kippur, when the streets were empty of heavy traffic. Teenagers in designer jeans flocked to the Hard Rock Café. At the Hebrew University, where courses in business and Asian studies were oversubscribed, the Institute of Jewish Studies, for decades the intellectual core of the university, confronted an enrollment crisis. As the head of the Hebrew literature department explained sorrowfully, "There is an alienation from everything connected to Judaism."

The author of the *Jerusalem Report* survey, Stuart Schoffman, himself a transplanted American Jew, admitted to conflicted feelings of pride and dismay.

The "homogenized consumer culture" of shopping malls, tennis clubs, and computerized fitness machines seemed somehow inspiring. Consumerism, after all, "implies choice, opportunity, a sense of openness and freedom." Indeed, "with any luck Israel will become much more Americanized." Yet Schoffman could not help but wonder, "What becomes of tradition, Judaism, self-sacrifice—of Zionism itself?" Might the "ugly Israeli," he mused, fulfill both definitions of *goy*, the Hebrew word that not only means "nation" but "Gentile"?

If secular Israelis exulted over *normaliut*, defined as Americanization, Israelis with Zionist memory despaired. The "rising tide of self-doubt" among Zionist intellectuals, Aharon Meged concluded, had finally encouraged Israelis to doubt "our right to be here." Post-Zionist normalization, added Yoram Hazony, a young political analyst in Jerusalem, meant "the end of Zionism." The Rabin government could divest Israel of its biblical homeland because the "near-total collapse" of Zionist ideology had prepared the way. Western cultural imports were merely symptomatic of the Zionist malaise; the debilitating malady that sapped Zionist vitality was the loss of Jewish memory and the evisceration of Jewish identity...

The pursuit of Jewish normality may once have been the glory of Zionism, anchoring it to the ennobling tasks of ingathering Jewish exiles and state-building. For most contemporary Israelis, however (as for most Diaspora Jews), the prospect of belonging to a distinctive people who dwell alone in a covenantal relationship with God is slightly embarrassing, if not altogether unappealing. Encouraged by their politicians, public intellectuals, entertainers, journalists, and writers, they yearn for Israel to become the chic Mediterranean vacation spa, consumer paradise, and hi-tech center of a "new" Middle East.

In the Diaspora, it took nearly two centuries for emancipation to eviscerate Jewish life. In Israel, however, fifty years of statehood has sufficed. As Israel becomes a nation like other nations, the Zionist dream is fulfilled—yet Zionism becomes increasingly indistinguishable from Jewish assimilation. Israelis may (or may not) be spared the Diaspora plague of intermarriage, but Israel's cultural intermarriage with the West already seems all but irreversible.

By the end of the nineties, the signs of Zionist disintegration were everywhere apparent. Slouching toward its fiftieth birthday in the spring of 1998, Israel could hardly bring itself to celebrate its own Jubilee. Never had the country been more despairing over its history, identity, or destiny. Rejecting the heroic "founding myths" of Zionist achievement against seemingly insurmountable historical odds that had once inspired so much struggle and sacrifice from so many, secular Israelis yearned for little more than a culture of self-gratification modeled on American hedonistic norms.

Two highly touted books by Israeli academics offered post-Zionist variations on this familiar theme. Ze'ev Sternhell, analyzing "the founding myths of Israel," brusquely dismissed "the sanctity of the Jewish heritage" (so much for Judaism) and "the mystique of the land" (so much for Zionism). In *Rubber Bullets*, Yaron Ezrahi celebrated the emergence of Israeli individualism, finally liberated from the encumbrances of Jewish memory, religion, and nationalism.

Seeking nothing less than "a retreat from Jewish history," Ezrahi avidly embraced "the private values of the self."

Such signs of Zionist exhaustion were reaffirmed by some astonishing statements from Israeli public officials. Not long before the Jubilee, Labor party leader Ehud Barak told a television interviewer that had he been born a Palestinian, he probably would have "joined a terrorist organization." Killing Jews, in other words, is a legitimate Palestinian activity. (Just days later, a Hamas terrorist, on trial for killing eleven Israelis, took the cue and justified his murderous actions by quoting Barak.) Shlomo Gazit, the former head of army intelligence, compared the knitted *kipot* worn by religious soldiers to the Nazi swastika. Judaism, in other words, is fascism.

What does it say, after fifty years of statehood, that respected Israeli leaders cannot distinguish Zionism from terrorism or Judaism from Nazism? Or that academic luminaries at the university in Jerusalem that once was a symbol of the revival of Jewish culture are mesmerized by life in *galut*? It says, sadly, that secular Zionism, the Zionism of Jewish normalization, has reached a dead end. For once Zionism is depleted of Jewish content, it bears an uncanny resemblance to Diaspora materialism, consumerism, and individualism. Well might another Josiah mournfully proclaim: "Great is the wrath of the Lord that is poured out upon us, because our fathers have not kept the word of the Lord, to do according to all that is written in this book." This time, however, "the book" is *The Jewish State*, not the Torah; and Zionists have faithfully obeyed Herzl's urgent command that Jews become a normal people.

17 · Welcome to Palisdan

It had been a long time since Jacob had visited Israel. With its fateful decision to squander the covenantal legacy of the Jewish people, Israel had relinquished its claim upon his allegiance. He stopped following news from the Middle East. For thirty years, he did not return. But in 2023, when he was past eighty, he reconsidered. Despite his undiminished disillusionment with Zionism, Jacob felt an irrepressible urge to visit the homeland of the Jews one more time. In preparation, he reread *Altneuland*, Herzl's fantasy of the Jewish state in the distant future of 1923.

Herzl's utopia, predictably, was a Jewish Vienna. "We only had to take the inventions of the Western world and use them," explained David Litwak, Herzl's prototypical Israeli, to a foreign visitor. In *Altneuland*, Litwak continued, the "inherited dead-weight" of the Jewish past had finally been lifted from the Jewish people. Here, in the "New Society," Jews were governed by the laws of "all civilized European countries." Arabs and Jews lived together harmoniously, indeed indistinguishably. No embarrassing questions of identity intruded "about anyone's race or religion." Symbolized by "All Nations Square" in Haifa, there was "a new feeling of brotherhood" in the land.

Lingering traces of a vestigial Judaism managed to survive in *Altneuland*. But they were well concealed, and Herzl bad little to say about them. A great new Temple (singularly bereft of Jewish content) had been built in cosmopolitan Jerusalem, which—like Herzl's Vienna—was a modern city of boulevards, institutes, and "splendid public buildings and places of amusement."

The Temple, Herzl's modest gesture to Jewish parochialism, was more than balanced in splendor by a nearby "Peace Palace." The squalid Old City, once inhabited by religious Jews, had become "an international centre which all nations might regard as their home." Litwak's visitor was impressed with *Altneuland*. Here Judaism no longer was "ashamed of itself," and Jews were "proud and free"—if indistinguishable from everyone else. *Altneuland* was "a free commonwealth in which [Jews] could work for the good of mankind."

Herzl had once imagined that the Jewish Question, the place of Jews in modern society, could be solved by the mass conversion of Jews to Christianity. *Altneuland* suggested that Zionism had become his preferred instrument of transformation. But the result was the same. Zionism would complete the

---

Are We One? (2001), 214-20.

process of assimilation that emancipation had begun a century earlier.

Jacob feared that Israel had fulfilled the assimilationist dream of its prophetic founder. With considerable trepidation, he decided to see for himself.

"Welcome to the New Middle East," read the flashing strobe-lit sign at the Palisdan International Airport. Inside the terminal, which resembled a Giza pyramid, Jacob was bewildered by the array of unfamiliar local destinations: Palisdan-by-the-Sea. Canaan. Palestine Province. Bedu-Negev. Galilee Autonomous Zone. Judah. He spotted, an enormous map, labeled "Palisdan," which looked suspiciously like Israel, Judea, Samaria, and Jordan—even parts of Lebanon and Syria—all merged together. Could it be, Jacob wondered in astonishment, that Israel had finally found a way to reverse its slide into Jewish oblivion and regain its biblical patrimony?

Interrupting his reverie, a young woman in uniform identified herself as an international guide to Palisdan. She led him to her desk, clicked on her computer for a detailed map of the region, and asked Jacob where he wished to travel. When he replied "Israel," she seemed bemused. In the New Middle East, she explained gently (for she had considerable experience with elderly American Jews who still used archaic place names from their youth), the former Israel had merged into the confederation of Palisdan—uniting Palestine, Israel, and Jordan—which was about to celebrate its twentieth birthday.

Perhaps, she continued solicitously, Jacob would permit her to suggest an itinerary. Fatigued by his journey, already dispirited, and confronting the labyrinth of unfamiliar place names, he readily consented. He might go north, she told him, but not beyond Safed, which marked the international border with Lebanon. How, Jacob wondered aloud, could the border have moved so far south? It had been a small price for Israel to pay, she replied, for peace now in the north.

Nor, she reminded him, could he visit the Golan Heights without a Syraqi visa. While she would not presume to inquire into his race or religion, he should know that Jews were not welcome there. Furthermore, all traces of Jewish history and habitation had been obliterated after Israel had relinquished the Golan and transferred its Jewish residents.

Indeed, she continued, he might even find it a bit uncomfortable in the Galilee Autonomous Zone, stretching from Afula to Safed. Jacob was confused; could it be that the fertile Galilee, once home to so many flourishing Zionist kibbutzim, no longer was part of Israel? That, his guide explained, exemplified Israel's commitment to democratic principles. For once Israel had granted the right of return to Palestinian refugees, which post-Zionist logic required, there no longer was a Jewish majority in the Galilee. According to democratic precedent, by which Judea and Samaria had been relinquished back in 2003, the Galilee Arab majority also enjoyed the right of self-government. There remained, however, one mixed Israeli-Arab city, Kfar Kalkilya, where modest traces of pre-Palisdanian Israeli culture could still be found.

For anything more than that, the guide suggested helpfully, Jacob should visit Canaan, surrounding old Tel Aviv on the Mediterranean coast. Its fine restaurants, luxurious resort hotels, fashionable boutiques, enticing gambling casinos, and computerized work-and-play centers gave the Palisdan-by-the-Sea district of Canaan international renown. Its people, too, were most unusual: the grandchildren of Israelis, they were proud of their identity as Hebrew-speaking Gentiles, insisting upon the right to dwell apart and be called Canaanites.

There was also Bedu-Negev, stretching from Beer Sheva south to Eilat. The Bedu-Negevians had gained autonomy under the Indigenous Peoples Resolution, sponsored by Israel in return for some gestures of international approval from the United Nations. They were a most engaging people, who welcomed visitors to their hospitality villas. There, volunteers fondly reminisced about the enlightened Zionist government that had severed the Negev from Israel to enable Arabs to build a land bridge that stretched all the way from Gaza to Baghdad. It was, the government had insisted at the time, a small price to pay for peace.

Jacob's guide strongly recommended a brief stopover in Jerusalem, on his way to the desert reserve of Husseinia beyond the Jordan River. He would marvel at its transformation from the provincial capital of Israel, inhabited mostly by Jews, into the multi-ethnic, transdenominational United Nations City. There he should be sure to visit the magnificent Raperfat Peace Center—named, of course, in recognition of the exemplary cooperation, back in the nineties, between Rabin, Peres, and Arafat, the foundation for the New Middle East with Palisdan as its keystone.

A forlorn Jacob asked whether, anywhere in Palisdan, he might still find any Jews. His guide hesitated, before recalling from her training program that an occasional Jewish tourist might still ask that embarrassing question. Certainly, she responded; at the Peace Center, he could obtain a one-day visa to Judah, located by the terebinths of Mamre in biblical Hebron. There, some ten thousand Jews still lived according to Jewish law in the Jewish homeland, as though Zionism had never happened.

Jacob was tempted. Before the collapse of Zionism he had frequently visited their communities, where he had always been inspired by the strength of their Jewish commitment. They were, he believed, the last true Zionists, whose undiminished attachment to the Land of Israel might somehow inspire other Jews to defend their historic homeland. Abandoned by the government of Israel, they resolutely declared autonomy, renaming their ghetto Judah to commemorate the last stronghold of Jewish national independence in the First Temple era.

But Jacob could not, in the end, bear to witness the humiliation of this proud and ancient community of Jews. He remembered the story of the elderly European rabbi who had finally met the obligation incumbent upon Jews to return to Zion. Landing at Jaffa, he had stepped ashore and paced the four els required to fulfill his *halakhic* obligation. Then, to the astonishment of his students, who could hardly contain their eagerness to guide him to Jerusalem, he returned to his ship to await its departure to the Diaspora.

Thanking his guide for sparing him a wrenching encounter with Palisdan in the New Middle East, Jacob boarded the next flight home. As his plane crossed the Mediterranean, he sorrowfully pondered the remarkable rise—and astonishing collapse—of Zionism in his own lifetime. Once a revolutionary ideology of Jewish renewal, Zionism had reduced itself to a whimper of Jewish normalization. Within seventy-five years of the birth of Israel, assimilation was as rampant in Tel Aviv, the first Zionist city, as anywhere in the American Diaspora. Everywhere, Jews lived in *galut*.

Had Zionism, Jacob wondered, been fatally flawed from the outset? The Zionists, after all, rejected the religious faith that alone could explain why Jews must rebuild their national home in Zion, and only there. So avidly did secular Zionists repudiate Jewish history, memory, and ritual that even their claim to Jewish land finally proved too onerous to defend. Palisdan gave the lie to the incessant claim of secular Israelis, at the beginning of the twenty-first century, that they could have it all: give land to the Arabs, make peace, join the New Middle East, and still retain their own distinctive national identity. Instead, they had won the argument—and lost the Jewish state. What newly emancipated Jews had wanted as individuals—freedom from Judaism and integration into Gentile society—the State of Israel had finally assured to all its Jewish citizens....

Jacob realized, with a sigh of sorrow, that the journey of modern Jews, from emancipation through Zionism to assimilation, was over.

18 · Are Settlements Illegal?

With the recent election of a liberal American president and a conservative Israeli prime minister, pressure on Israel to reach a final agreement with the Palestinian Authority is likely to intensify. According to the conventional political wisdom, peace will require substantial Israeli concessions to the Palestinian Authority regarding the status of Jerusalem, the return of refugees, and the future of Jewish settlements. But the problem that has eluded resolution for sixty years remains: demarcating the permanent, recognized borders of the Jewish state.

Settlements have been a deeply polarizing issue, in Israel and elsewhere, ever since the Israel Defense Forces swept triumphantly through the West Bank of the Kingdom of Jordan in June 1967. Before long, clusters of religious Zionists returned to the once inhabited, then tragically decimated, sites of Gush Etzion and Hebron, south of Jerusalem. They were the vanguard of a growing movement to restore a Jewish presence throughout Judea and Samaria, the Biblical homeland of the Jewish people.

Settlement of the Land of Israel, after all, had defined Zionism ever since the founding of Rishon l'Tzion, the first settlement, in 1882. The "tower and stockade" settlements built overnight by *kibbutzniks* under British Mandatory rule remained legendary achievements in Zionist annals. With its stunning victory in the Six-Day War, Israel unexpectedly confronted new possibilities to fulfill ancient dreams and, it is seldom recognized, long-deferred international commitments.

Now, four decades after the first settlers blazed the trail of return, nearly 300,000 Israelis live in more than one hundred settlement communities amid 1.5 million Palestinian Arabs. No Jews anywhere in the world have been as persistently maligned—indeed, as maliciously vilified—as these Jewish settlers. Everyone from Yasir Arafat to Jimmy Carter (who has made a new career of hectoring Israel) has condemned them for occupying Palestinian land and violating fundamental principles of international law, to say nothing of impeding peace efforts.

This allegation has been incessantly propagated by Israeli critics of settlement and by enraged Palestinians who claim that Jewish settlers have stolen "their" land. In *Lords of the Land* (2007), the first comprehensive survey of

---

"Are Settlements Illegal?" *Midstream* (Spring 2009), 4-7.

the Jewish settlement movement, Israeli historian Idith Zertal and *Ha'aretz* journalist Akiva Eldar lacerated settlers for their illegal occupation, plunder, destruction, and lawlessness. The "malignancy of occupation," they wrote, "in contravention of international law," has "brought Israel's democracy...to the brink of an abyss." By now, *The New York Times* has reported, "Much of the world" regards "all Israeli settlements in land occupied in the 1967 war to be illegal under international law."

At the core of the settlement critique is the incessant allegation, rarely scrutinized or challenged, that Israeli settlements established in "occupied" territory since 1967 are illegal. It surfaced within Israeli government circles three months after the Six-Day War when Theodor Meron, legal counsel for the Foreign Ministry, sent a memo to Foreign Minister Abba Eban, a copy of which he forwarded to Prime Minister Levi Eshkol. "My conclusion," Meron wrote, "is that civilian settlement in the administered territories contravenes the explicit provisions of the Fourth Geneva Convention."

The Geneva Convention, adopted in 1949 in the shadow of World War II atrocities, declared that an "occupying Power shall not deport or transfer parts of its own civilian population into the territory it occupies." According to Meron, this provision (Article 49) was intended to forever prevent repetition of the notorious Nazi forced transfers of civilian populations—for "political and racial reasons"—from conquered territory to slave labor and extermination camps. As a youthful prisoner in a Nazi labor camp, Meron had painful personal memories of such population transfers, when hundreds of thousands of Jews were deported from their homes and replaced by foreign nationals. He insisted that the Geneva prohibition was "categorical and is not conditioned on the motives or purposes of the transfer."

Meron's legal opinion, recently rediscovered by journalist Gershom Gorenberg during his research for a critical study of the early years of Jewish settlement, was filed and forgotten—for good reason. It was neither persuasive to his superiors nor an accurate appraisal of the applicability of the Geneva Convention to new Israeli settlements in the former West Bank of the Kingdom of Jordan. Military Advocate General Meir Shamgar, who subsequently became attorney general and then chief judge of the Supreme Court, asserted, "The legal applicability of the Fourth Geneva Convention to these territories is in doubt." For legitimate legal reasons, no government of Israel has ever accepted the validity of Meron's argument.

To the contrary: Israeli settlement throughout the West Bank is explicitly protected by international agreements dating from the World War I era, subsequently reaffirmed after World War II, and never revoked since. The Balfour Declaration of 1917, calling for "the establishment in Palestine of a national home for the Jewish people," was endorsed by the League of Nations Mandate for Palestine, drafted at the San Remo Conference in 1920, and adopted unanimously two years later. The mandate recognized "the historical connection of the Jewish people with Palestine" and "the grounds for reconstituting their national home in that country." Jews were guaranteed the right of "close settlement" throughout "Palestine," geographically defined by the mandate as comprising land both east and west of the Jordan River (which ultimately became Jordan, the West Bank, and Israel). This was not framed as a gift to the Jewish people; rather, based on recognition of historical rights reaching back into antiquity, it was their entitlement.

Jewish settlement throughout Palestine was limited by the mandate in only one respect: Great Britain, the Mandatory Trustee, acting in conjunction with the League of Nations Council, retained the discretion to "postpone" or "withhold" the right of Jews to settle east—but not west—of the Jordan River. Consistent with that solitary exception, and to placate the ambitions of the Hashemite Sheikh Abdullah for his own territory to rule, Colonial Secretary Winston Churchill removed the land east of the river from the borders of Palestine.

Churchill anticipated that the newly demarcated territory, comprising three-quarters of Mandatory Palestine, would become a future Arab state. With the establishment of Transjordan in 1922, the British prohibited Jewish settlement there. But the status of Jewish settlement west of the Jordan River remained unchanged. Under the terms of the mandate, the internationally guaranteed legal right of Jews to settle anywhere in this truncated quarter of Palestine and build their national home there remained in force.

Never further modified, abridged, or terminated, the Mandate for Palestine outlived the League of Nations. In the Charter of the United Nations, drafted in 1945, Article 80 explicitly protected the rights of "any peoples" and "the terms of existing international instruments to which members of the United Nations may respectively be parties." Drafted at the founding conference of the United Nations by Jewish legal representatives—including liberal American Rabbi Stephen S. Wise, Peter Bergson from the right-wing Irgun, and Ben-Zion Netanyahu (father of the future prime minister)—Article 80 became known as "the Palestine clause."

It preserved the rights of the Jewish people to "close settlement" throughout the remaining portion of their Palestinian homeland west of the Jordan River, precisely as the mandate had affirmed. But those settlement rights were flagrantly violated when Jordan invaded Israel in 1948. The military aggression of the Hashemite kingdom effectively obliterated U.N. Resolution 181, adopted the preceding year, which had called for the partition of (western) Palestine into Arab and Jewish states. Jordan's claim to the West Bank, recognized only by Great Britain and Pakistan, had no international legal standing.

Contrary to Theodor Meron's citation of Article 49, the Geneva Convention did not restrict Jewish settlement in the West Bank, acquired by Israel during the Six-Day War. As Eugene V. Rostow, formerly dean of Yale Law School and undersecretary of state for political affairs between 1966 and 1969, noted, the government of Israel neither "deported" Palestinians nor "transferred" Israelis during or after 1967. (Indeed, beginning with the return of Jews to Hebron the following year, settlers invariably acted on their own volition without government authorization.) Furthermore, Rostow noted, the Geneva Convention applied only to acts by one signatory "carried out on the territory of another." The West Bank, however, did not belong to any signatory power, for Jordan had no sovereign rights or legal claims there. Its legal status was defined as "an unallocated part of the British Mandate."

With Jordan's defeat in 1967, a "vacuum in sovereignty" existed on the West Bank. Under international law, the Israeli military administration became the custodian of territories until their return to the original sovereign—according to the League of Nations mandate, reinforced by Article 80 of the U.N. Charter—the Jewish people for their "national home in Palestine." Israeli settlement was not prohibited; indeed, under the terms of the mandate, it was explicitly protected. Jews retained the same legal right to settle in the West Bank that they enjoyed in Tel Aviv, Haifa, or the Galilee.

After the Six-Day War, a new UN resolution—which Rostow was instrumental in drafting—specifically applied to the territory acquired by Israel. According to Security Council Resolution 242 (superseding Resolution 181 from 1947), Israel was permitted to administer the land until "a just and lasting peace in the Middle East" was achieved. Even then, Israel would be required to withdraw its armed forces only "from territories"—not from "the territories" or "all the territories"—that it administered.

The absence of "the," the famous missing definite article, was neither an accident nor an afterthought; it resulted from what Rostow described as more than five months of "vehement public diplomacy" to clarify the meaning of Resolution 242. Israel would not be required to withdraw from all the territory that it had acquired during the Six-Day War; indeed, precisely such proposals were defeated in both the Security Council and the General Assembly. No prohibition on Jewish settlement, wherever it had been guaranteed by the Mandate for Palestine forty-five years earlier, was adopted.

"The Jewish right of settlement in the area," Rostow concluded, "is equivalent in every way to the right of the existing [Palestinian] population to live there." Furthermore, as Stephen Schwebel, a judge on the International Court of Justice between 1981 and 2000, explicitly noted, territory acquired in a war of self-defense (waged by Israel in 1967) must be distinguished from territory acquired through "aggressive conquest" (waged by Germany during World War II). Consequently, the provisions of the Mandate for Palestine, allocating all the land west of the Jordan River to the Jewish people for their national home, remained in force until sovereignty was finally determined by a peace treaty between the contending parties—now Israel and the Palestinians. Until then, the disputed West Bank, claimed by two peoples, remained open to Jewish settlement.

In sum, the right of the Jewish people to "close settlement" throughout Mandatory Palestine, except for the land siphoned off as Transjordan in 1922, has never been abrogated. Nor has the legal right of Jews to settle in Judea and Samaria, indisputably part of western "Palestine," ever been relinquished. The persistent effort to undermine the legitimacy of Israeli settlements, according to international law expert Julius Stone, has been nothing less than a "subversion...of basic international law principles," in which the government of Israel, at best ambivalent about the settlements, has often been a willing accomplice. In the continuing absence of a "just and lasting peace," with an accompanying determination of the scope of Israeli withdrawal from "territories," Israel is under no legal obligation to limit settlement.

World opinion, of course, is another matter. (In his uncritical embrace of Meron's flawed conclusion, Gorenberg cited "the court of world diplomacy" as "the court that mattered.") Ever since the Six-Day war, settlements have provoked unrelenting international hostility toward Israel. A triumphant Jewish state could hardly be expected to win approval from intractable Arab neighbors who had not recognized Israel even before settlements. An international community that in 1975 perceived Zionism as "racism" continues to see Palestinians only as "victims" of Jewish "conquest" and "occupation." Secular Zionists on the political left—long the ruling elite in Israeli intellectual, academic and media circles—are hardly receptive to challenges to their own cultural hegemony from religious nationalist settlers.

So, ever since 1967, Jewish settlements have been widely and loudly—and erroneously—trumpeted as the major obstacle to Middle Eastern peace. They are convenient surrogates for the deep and enduring hostility to the very existence of a Jewish state. That hostility long antedated 1967 and, as Hamas, Islamic Jihad, Hezbollah, and President Ahmadinajad of Iran endlessly reiterate, it is likely to endure for as long as Israel exists within any boundaries. But neither in the court of world opinion, nor in the State of Israel, are settlement critics entitled to ignore the firm protection for Jewish settlements afforded by international legal guarantees extending back nearly a century, frequently affirmed ever since, and never rescinded.

19 · Hebron Letters

To Hebron Jews:

You must know that you are the crazy Jews. Zealots. Fundamentalists. Hamas in *tsitsit*. You are Baruch Goldstein and Yigal Amir: murderers with Uzis and pistols, poised to shed innocent blood, sabotage the peace process, assassinate the prime minister, even plunge Israel into civil war in demented pursuit of your Jewish *jihad*.

Among all the "settlers" tainted with illegitimacy for their return to the biblical homeland of the Jewish people, you are the Jews whom other Jews most delight in despising. Indeed, you are the only Jews, anywhere in the world, whom it is permissible to loathe, revile, and slander without being accused of anti-Semitism. No sooner had Prime Minister Rabin been tragically murdered than you were blamed for nurturing the virus of Jewish hate that infected the assassin. That Yigal Amir came from the Tel Aviv suburb of Herzliya, not Hebron, seemed inconsequential.

I think I know why you are so viscerally hated. To the prochoice Jews of modernity, who borrow every passing fashion and call it Judaism, you are an embarrassment. You cling too tenaciously to Jewish memory. You display far too much Zionist passion. You remind diaspora Jews in the fleshpots of galut, and Israelis along the shorefront of the ancient Philistines, where the land of their ancestors truly is. That makes them uncomfortable. No wonder they have vilified and abandoned you, the better to exorcise the claims of Jewish history that you assert.

Where, after all, does Jewish memory extend further in time or place than Hebron? When God summoned Abraham to leave his father's house in Ur, to make the journey to Canaan that began Jewish history, Abraham went to the terebinths of Mamre, in Hebron. There, after Sarah's death, he purchased the burial caves that became the first foothold of the Jewish people in the Land of Israel. Abraham, the Torah reminds us, did not steal the land from Palestinians. Or occupy it. Or settle it. He purchased it for 400 shekels of silver, the full asking price of Ephron the Hittite, who most assuredly was not Yasir Arafat's ancestor.

The book of *Joshua* recounts a poignant moment that locates the significance of Hebron in Jewish history and theology. Only Caleb, along with Joshua, had survived the 40 years of wilderness wandering. Among the spies sent by Moses into Canaan, Caleb alone had rejected the counsel of fear and flight that condemned an entire generation to die in the desert. Now an old man, Caleb

---

"Hebron Letters," *Midstream* (January 1996), 12-14.

remains steadfast, still willing to fight to secure the promised land for the Israelites. Joshua acknowledges his fidelity, blesses him, and gives him Hebron for an inheritance. Why Hebron? Because Caleb "wholly followed the Lord, the God of Israel." (*Joshua* 14:14)

Hebron, to be sure, became a Canaanite city. But after the death of Saul, when it was time for David to return to Judah, God commanded him to establish his kingdom in Hebron. There he was anointed king; there six sons were born. "And the length of time which David was king in Hebron over the house of Judah, was seven years and six months." (2 *Samuel* 2:11)

Once David left Hebron to conquer Jerusalem and unify the kingdom, we hear little more of it in biblical history. The geographical balance of Jewish holiness tilted decisively toward Jerusalem. But Hebron remained one of the four holy cities of Israel. Jews lived there and returned to worship at the tombs of their patriarchs and matriarchs. With the Muslim conquest, however, Jewish claims were relentlessly suppressed. Just as the Dome of the Rock in Jerusalem was built on the site of the Temple ruins, so the tombs in Hebron were enclosed within the walls of a mosque. In both places Jewish worship was forbidden; at Machpelah in Hebron, Jews were forbidden to climb above the seventh step to the entrance. But Hebron Jews did not abandon their holy sites, their homes, their historical claims, or Jewish memory.

Hebron returned to history in a spasm of modern brutality. During the Arab riots in 1929, the Jewish community of Hebron was decimated. Rampaging Arab mobs slaughtered nearly 70 residents and rabbis. Jews were expelled; Jewish property, with title dating as far back as the 16th century, was abandoned. Hebron became *Judenrein* until 1968. Then Rabbi Moshe Levinger—your leader and the rabbi (now that Meir Kahane is dead) whom everyone most loves to hate—brought a group of Jews to the Park Hotel for Passover. The seder ended, but you remained in Hebron to ignite the Zionist return to Judea and Samaria.

I have visited your community, and your Jewish neighbors in Kiryat Arba, several times. Even when I was still a liberal zealot, burning with indignation for every victim of prejudice or discrimination who happened not to be Jewish, you always welcomed me with generous hospitality, in the tradition of Abraham greeting the strangers. In Beit Hadassah, the old medical clinic, in the 500-year-old Avraham Avinu synagogue, and in the Tel Rumeida ridge above the city, you responded courteously and thoughtfully to my most ignorant, perhaps even insulting, questions about why any Jew would wish to live in a city filled with Muslims whose fury at the presence of a single Jew in their midst is palpable.

I remember our encounters. We argued for hours about the fusion of Zionism and Orthodoxy. We debated endlessly whether the arrival of the messiah could be hastened with violence. We explored, from our different perspectives, the fateful struggle within Zionism between Judaism and liberalism. I came to respect your devotion to Jewish history, your mastery of Jewish sources, and the analytical rigor—and Jewish passion—of your arguments. Indeed, you were far more tolerant of your Jewish opponents than the liberal zealots, castigating your politics from the cafés of Tel Aviv and the bookstores in Harvard Square, ever were.

Certainly I encountered fanatics among you. I confess to discomfort when one of my guides to Machpelah swaggered down the street, brandishing his Uzi to clear traffic from our path. But when I stood outside the entrance to the Avraham Avinu synagogue, and felt the searing Arab venom rising from the casbah behind us, I was grateful for his presence. I could understand why Israelis might prefer Haifa or Hadera to Hebron. But I never learned why Arab hostility should determine where Jews could live in the Land of Israel.

You are, I realize, a sharp bone in the Arab throat—and the throat of every Jew for Palestine on the Jewish left. As the peace process proceeds, and a Palestinian state seems ever likelier in Judea and Samaria, how can 450 Jews (especially Jews like you), living amid 100,000 Hebron Arabs, be permitted to thwart the government of Israel? To say nothing of enlightened world opinion according to the *New York Times*, which continues to treat the death of a single Palestinian as far worthier news to print than it ever did the death of six million Jews.

A tiny Jewish enclave like yours, surrounded by a sea of hostile Arabs, makes absolutely no sense. Such zeal may once have been a source of inspiration in the Zionist world we have lost, when "settler" was a badge of honor reserved for Jews who bulldozed their way overnight into watchtower-and-stockade kibbutzim in the Galilee (where Arabs also lived). Your besieged community may even resemble, in miniature, the Jewish state itself, surely the largest and least welcome Jewish "settlement" in the Muslim Middle East.

But Zionist history is now slightly embarrassing to secular Israelis, preoccupied with their cellular phones and Big Macs, their Volvos and VCRs. Besides, Palestinians were long ago anointed world-class victims. Their contrived national history, often with symbols appropriated from Zionism, must—for historical justice, no less—override Jewish claims. Even Zionists understand that.

You are so despised, I suspect, because you see the absurdity, even the obscenity, in such distorted history and bogus morality. What was Zionism, ever, but the return of Jews to the Land of Israel? Where is the Land of Israel if not Judea and Samaria? And what is the ultimate mandate for Zionism—as even the resolutely secular David Ben-Gurion once conceded—if not Torah? These truths have been all but forgotten, so pervasive is the loss of Jewish and Zionist memory in our time. Yet you still take seriously the covenantal history of the Jewish people. No wonder that forgetful Jews yearn to transfer you to a place where you will leave them alone.

That brings me to another point, almost too painful to mention. But I know that you have thought about it, agonized over it, perhaps even prepared for it. I am referring, of course, to the day when, God forbid, a government of Israel decides that an irrepressible yearning for peace in our time, or American dollars, or a new Middle East, requires your expulsion from Hebron. I recognize the portents in Peace Now declarations, *Ha'aretz* editorials, and Knesset speeches, to say nothing of the malicious venom directed against you since the

Rabin assassination.

Meretz is already campaigning for electoral support as the party that will rid Hebron of you. B'tselem, which proclaims itself a "human-rights" organization, calls for your removal because Hebron (a holy city to Jews since time immemorial) is a "Palestinian" city. But it is not difficult to imagine how B'tselem, Peace Now, *Ha'aretz*, or Meretz ministers would respond if you were to demand the transfer of Arabs from Israel because it is a Jewish state.

The world, even the Jewish world these days, turns on the axis of its own double standards. That is why your insistence upon the right of Jews to resettle and renew Hebron will continue to fall on deaf ears. Hebron Jews, as you rightly point out, are targeted for discrimination only because you are Jews who wish to live on Jewish land in the biblical Land of Israel. I do not wish to insult you, but it almost sounds quaintly liberal when you declare that the most basic individual and national right, after all, is the right of a people to live in its own homeland with no discrimination based on race or religion. How the liberals must hate you for that.

For now, I will not dwell on my most ominous foreboding: that some day soon the Israeli army will receive orders to remove you forcibly from your homes. I know that more than a thousand reserve officers have already declared their intention to disobey such orders. And I believe that many Jews will come to Hebron to support your cause. But images of other desperate last stands by besieged Jewish zealots come readily to mind: in Jerusalem and Masada against the Romans; in Warsaw against the Nazis. Hebron may yet join that list, this time with Jews fighting against Israelis.

If that happens, it will mean that the Jewish nation has once again destroyed itself with *sinat hinam*, causeless hatred. The Jewish people, you insist, "will never separate itself from its roots, the city of the Patriarchs and Matriarchs, the city of Abraham, Isaac, Jacob, Sarah, Rebecca and Leah." I fervently hope that you are right. But there are abundant indications, better known to you than to anyone else, that Israel may yet decide to trade its biblical birthright for a mess of post-Zionist pottage.

To Hebron Arabs:

We all know that something terrible has happened in our neighborhood. Jews live among us. Real Jews. Jews with beards. Jews who study Torah. Jews with children. Lots of children. Jews who pray at the tombs of their patriarchs and matriarchs. Jews who remember that Hebron was a holy city in Judaism long before Islam existed. Jews who know what terrible things our grandfathers did to them in 1929, when we slaughtered them like sheep. Why? Because they were Jews.

Those Jews were bad enough. But these Jews are far worse. They do not wait passively for God to save them. Nor are they enlightened Zionists with beautiful souls, who are so nice to us because they crave world approval. These Hebron Jews do not even care if they make diaspora Jews squirm with the discomfort of guilt by association. They are real Jews. They are very dangerous.

In our town, our quietly zealous and gently fanatical town, we only want a neighborhood that is *Judenrein*. Is that wrong? We are normal people. Read all the stories about us in American newspapers and see us on TV. Our men sit in cafés. They smoke pipes and play *sheshbesh*. They sell vegetables. Our women stay at home. Yes, some of our young hotheads occasionally throw stones at Jews. Sometimes Jews are even stabbed and shot. Who knows how such things happen? Perhaps Jews do it to themselves. Since we are never blamed, surely we have done nothing wrong. Violence must be expected when Jews move next door and walk through our streets. All would be well in Hebron if only there were no Jews.

Not even a single Jew should be permitted to live here. Especially Jews who always remind us that we are the real usurpers. Of course we built our mosque over a Jewish holy place here in Hebron. We did that in Jerusalem, too. Is that wrong? Nobody cares. Except these Jews. It seems only right that we should pray on their Temple Mount in Jerusalem, while their own government prevents them from praying there. The Dome of the Rock, after all, is our third holiest shrine in our third holiest city. (But we must forget whose holiest city Jerusalem is.) Our holy places surely take priority over their spurious claims.

We were all troubled here in Hebron on that awful Jewish Sabbath in mid-November when *Chaye Sarah* was read from their Torah. It is a subversive text. It tells how our father Abraham purchased burial caves from Ephron the Hittite, who (as we know) was the third Palestinian, may his name be cursed in memory. Ever since, Jews have had the temerity to claim that Machpelah was the first Jewish land purchase in the Land of Israel. On that very Sabbath, three thousand Jews from all over Israel actually came to Hebron in a gesture of solidarity to pray at Machpelah. Can you believe it!

Do not imagine, however, that these foolish Jewish zealots will get what they want, the opportunity to live in Hebron. If we repeat the Big Lie often enough—"Hebron is a Palestinian city" and "Hebron is a Muslim town"—most Jews, and nearly every journalist, will believe us. They will even come here to make films and write stories blaming the Jews for our unrelenting hostility to them. We can always depend on Jews to depict their own people as the real villains.

These days, the Zionists are especially good at this. Since Rabin's assassination, many more of them are willing, indeed eager, to transfer these Jews from Hebron. Rest assured: we will never remind them that Herzliya, where the murderer lived, is not Hebron. And remember: just months from now, in March, almost all of Hebron will be ours. The Jews will be isolated, alone—and at our mercy. That is our reward for our undisguised loathing of them.

I know how impatient you are. But rest assured that Jews will be our best collaborators. Zionists will condemn their own people, the Jews of Hebron, as "zealots," "fundamentalists," and "murderous inciters." Peace Now will defend our right to their holy city. And American Jews will cheer them on and give us money for an interfaith community center. They know, after all, that all we are saying is give peace a chance. Truly it seems incredible that a people would ever relinquish its own homeland and holy places. Among Arabs and Muslims that is unimaginable. You do not believe that the Jews will abandon their own people in Hebron? Just wait.

20 · Inventing "Palestine"

If the UN should decide to recognize a "State of Palestine" in the biblical homeland of the Jewish people it would endorse a bizarre irony. Why? Because Palestinian national identity borrows so extensively from Jewish and Zionist sources as to virtually constitute historical plagiarism.

"Palestine" emerged as an abbreviation of "Syria Palaestina." The name was imposed by Roman conquerors to obliterate the connection of Jews to their land after the Bar Kochba rebellion collapsed in 135 CE. During four hundred years of Ottoman rule, Arabs considered it to be part of Syria-Palestine, not a separate entity. A remote and neglected imperial province, it was loosely administered from Beirut or Damascus.

Modern conceptions of "Palestine" began to emerge in the mid-19th century once the Holy Land, as it became known to European visitors, entered Western consciousness. The veil began to lift after Edinburgh-born artist David Roberts followed the trail of the ancient Israelites from Egypt through the Sinai wilderness to the promised land in 1838-39. During his journey into the past Roberts sketched the lithographs that filled *The Holy Land* (1842), his magnificent three-volume collection that for modern critics defines the Orientalist vision of intrusive Westerners.

"If God spares me in life and health," Roberts wrote in his journal, "I expect to bring home with me the most interesting collection of sketches that has ever left the East." Riveted by ancient city gates, walls, tombs, churches, mosques, barren wilderness landscape, and the exotic local inhabitants, his lithographs remain unrivaled romantic depictions of sacred memory.

A year after *The Holy Land* appeared, another Scotsman, Rev. Alexander Keith, published his own book about the land of Israel. Keith had also traveled to the Holy Land in 1839; there he came to believe that Christians should bring to fulfillment the biblical prophecy that Jews would return to their ancient homeland. His book, *The Land of Israel According to the Covenant with Abraham, with Isaac, and with Jacob*, included a phrase that has reverberated ever since. The Jews, he wrote, are "a people without a country; even as their own land...is in a great measure, a country without a people." Slightly altered by the book reviewer for a Scottish Free Church magazine, it became the iconic phrase:

"Inventing 'Palestine,'" *The Jewish Press* (August 10, 2011), 1.

"A land without a people and a people without a land."

Rev. Keith's words were reiterated several years later in a letter from Lord Shaftesbury (Anthony Ashley-Cooper) to Lord Palmerston, the British Foreign Minister. Ashley-Cooper pondered the future of "Greater Syria" (as the land of the ancient Israelites was then commonly identified) after the Crimean War. He rephrased Keith's description as "a country without a nation" needing "a nation without a country." He wondered: "Is there such a thing?" before answering his own question affirmatively: "the ancient and rightful lords of the soil, the Jews!"

Rev. Keith's phrase continued to recur in the writings of Christian Zionists, especially once pogroms erupted in Russia during the 1880s. Evangelist William Blackstone, concerned over the plight of Russian Jews, referred to an "astonishing anomaly—a land without a people, and a people without a land." In 1897 John Lawson Stoddard published a travel guide exhorting Jews: "You are a people without a country; there is a country without a people...Go back, go back to the land of Abraham."

An American visitor to Palestine chose different words to describe the barrenness of the land for literary posterity. In *The Innocents Abroad* (1881), Samuel Clemens (better known as Mark Twain) described Palestine as "a desolate country.... We never saw a human being on the whole route.... There was hardly a tree or shrub anywhere. Even the olive and the cactus, those fast friends of the worthless soil, had almost deserted the country."

Curiously, Rev. Keith's persistent phrase rarely appeared in Zionist speeches or writings. A conspicuous exception was Israel Zangwill, who wrote in the *New Liberal Review* (1901) that "Palestine is a country without a people; the Jews are a people without a country." Ironically, Zangwill soon turned away from Zionism and came to the United States where, in flight from Judaism, he wrote *The Melting Pot*, the strikingly successful play that celebrated the alluring prospect of assimilation for Jewish immigrants in their new "*goldene medina*".

On the eve of World War I, Chaim Weizmann, destined to become the first president of the State of Israel, said: "there is a country which happens to be called Palestine, a country without a people, and, on the other hand, there exists the Jewish people, and it has no country. What else is necessary, then, than to fit the gem into the ring, to unite this people with this country?" But few other Zionists seem to have used the phrase, preferring to refer more succinctly to the "Jewish national home."

Official visitors documented the barrenness, stagnation and decay in the land. A British Royal Commission reported in 1913: "The area was underpopulated the 1880's." It was "Jewish development of the country," the commissioners noted, that had attracted "large numbers of other immigrants—both Jewish and Arab."

Even during the British Mandatory period following World War I local Arabs demonstrated little awareness of a distinctive Palestinian identity. As historian Diana Muir writes (in her careful scrutiny of "land without a people" mythology), they "neither perceived Palestine as a distinct country, nor Palestinians as a people." Testifying before the British Peel Commission in 1937, Syrian leader Auni Bey Abdul-Nadi asserted: "There is no such country as Palestine.... Our country was for centuries part of Syria. 'Palestine' is alien to us. It is the Zionists who introduced it."

Two years later Walter Clay Lowdermilk, assistant chief of the United States Soil Conservation Service, arrived in Palestine for three months of intensive field study. A dedicated land conservationist, he discovered the consequences of centuries of neglect, exploitation, and waste until the first wave of Zionists arrived to settle and rebuild the land. His careful analysis was entitled *Palestine Land of Promise*, a promise conspicuously unfulfilled by its Arab inhabitants.

"Like the Children of Israel" during their exodus, Lowdermilk wrote—and like Roberts nearly a century earlier—he journeyed from Egypt through the Sinai desert to Palestine. Traveling throughout the land, he covered nearly 2500 miles by car. Along the way he discovered "Jewish settlers who fled to Palestine from the hatreds and persecutions of Europe" confronting the despoliation and desolation caused by centuries of neglect from "backward native populations." British officials, he learned, had little success encouraging local Arabs to plant trees, even with donated seedlings. Progress was impeded, Lowdermilk concluded, "by the temperament of the people and their fatalistic philosophy."

But a "semi-feudal economy" was being reversed by Zionist land reclamation and industrial development, which had a "beneficent effect" on the local Arab population. The "thoroughgoing [Zionist] effort to restore the ancient fertility of the long-neglected soil," by applying "the principles of co-operation and soil conservation to the old Land of Israel," offered the "most remarkable" example of restoration that Lowdermilk had witnessed in his extensive travels through twenty-four countries.

Even "rural Palestine," Lowdermilk concluded, "is becoming less and less like Trans Jordan, Syria and Iraq and more like Denmark, Holland, and parts of the United States" (notably Southern California). Indeed, Zionist land development had exerted a magnetic pull on Arabs from Iraq, Syria, Trans-Jordan and the Arabian Desert, who came to Palestine in search of a better life (and eventually becoming "Palestinians"). But he cautioned that "Arab rule in Palestine would...put an abrupt end to the reclamation work now being carried on so splendidly" by the Zionists.

No less significant than the problem of land devastation was the striking absence of Palestinian national coherence; then, and for years afterward. Palestinian "identity" was a mix of Ottoman, Arab, Islamic, Christian, European, and local Palestinian influences. In their politics, social structure, land tenure and political and ideological trends Palestinian Arabs identified with Greater Syria and "the larger Arab people."

Even Columbia history professor Rashid Khalidi, an expert on Palestinian identity, has recognized that before World War I "Palestine" did not exist. During the Mandatory era internal Palestinian politics were dysfunctional. Leaders did not lead, nor could they mobilize public support or establish a Palestinian "state structure" or "representative institutions." Haj Amin al-Husseini, the Grand Mufti and recognized Palestinian leader, fled during the Arab revolt that began in 1936. Arriving in Nazi Germany in 1941, he achieved subsequent notoriety as Hitler's favorite Arab collaborator.

Shortly before the State of Israel was born, Arab historian Philip Hitti conceded: "There is no such thing as Palestine in history, absolutely not." By 1948, Khalidi concludes, Palestinians had "lost agency"—to the nascent Jewish state, neighboring Arab states, and international bodies. As late as 1964, when the PLO was founded (largely by Arab states to control their Palestinian brethren), "the very idea of 'Palestine,'" he suggests, "appeared to be in a grave, and perhaps in a terminal state."

Indeed, a Palestinian people with a distinctive identity and consciousness did not begin to emerge until the humiliating Arab defeat in the Six-Day war. Why was it, wondered Walid Shoebat from Bethlehem, "that on June 4th 1967 I was a Jordanian and overnight I became a Palestinian.... We considered ourselves Jordanian until the Jews returned to Jerusalem. Then all of a sudden we were Palestinians." With a fragile national identity, in a land that had never been inhabited by a (previously nonexistent) "Palestinian" people, West Bank Jordanian Arabs would soon become known as Palestinians.

Even Zuhair Muhsin, PLO military commander and member of the Executive Council, acknowledged: "There are no differences between Jordanians, Palestinians, Syrians and Lebanese. We are all part of one nation...the existence of a separate Palestinian identity serves only tactical purposes." The vision of a Palestinian state, he conceded, was merely "a new tool in the continuing battle against Israel."

That is hardly a recipe for nation building, but it may help to explain why Palestinians have plundered Jewish history to define themselves while engaging in persistent efforts to delegitimize Israel. A continuing theme in this campaign has been a twisted version (perhaps not unintentional) of Rev. Keith's aphorism about a land without a people for a people without a land—to which he added, in his Conclusion, a sharp reference to "those few" who "have but a slight hold on the land that is not theirs."

The distortion came from Edward Said, the renowned Columbia University literary scholar and passionate Palestinian advocate in exile who served in its National Council (the legislative body of the Palestine Liberation Organization). In *The Question of Palestine* (1979), Said wrote (erroneously) that Zionists had viewed Palestine as a land "without people." Altering Rev. Keith's observation by changing "a people" to "people," he invested the phrase with new meaning that inspired loyal acolytes to condemn Zionist "racism" and moral blindness, feeding the malevolent desire for the ethnic cleansing of Palestinians.

Ironically, Said imaginatively constructed his own "Palestinian" identity. Born during a brief family sojourn in Jerusalem to a Lebanese mother and Egyptian father (holding American citizenship), his boyhood was spent amid wealth and comfort in Cairo—until he moved to the United States as a teen-ager. Yet in his memoir *Out of Place* (1999), Said fondly recalled the "Jerusalem" boyhood (in Cairo) that molded his "Palestinian" identity.

What is most striking about Palestinian identity is its derivation from, and sustained grounding in, Jewish sources. Like other Middle Eastern Muslims, Palestinians claim Ishmael, Abraham's son by his servant Hagar, as the ancestral link to "their" patriarch Abraham. They have adopted the biblical Canaanites, displaced according to the biblical narrative by the conquering Israelites, as their own victimized ancestral people. Their insistent claim of a "right of return" to Israel for Palestinian refugees mirrors more than a century of Zionist yearning; it also emulates the Law of Return passed by the Knesset (1950) assuring to every Jew the right to immigrate to Israel.

In a grotesque inversion Palestinian teen-agers have compared themselves to Anne Frank, suffering from the "Holocaust" that Israelis have inflicted on them. In this mendacious historical travesty Palestinians have become the new "Jews," victimized by Israeli "Nazis." A year ago the *Mari Marvara* flotilla to Gaza was designed to replicate the rickety refugee ships, most famously the *Exodus*, that tried to bring desperate Jews to Palestine before and after World War II. It succeeded in casting the Israeli navy in the role of the malevolent British military forces that had turned Jewish refugees away from their promised land.

Recently an Israeli Arab Member of the Knesset (how many Jews are members of Arab parliaments?) introduced a bill to deny government funding to any group refusing to recognize that Israeli independence was a *naqba* (catastrophe) for Palestinians. Any resemblance between "*naqba* denial" and Holocaust denial is, of course, purely intentional (and surely preposterous).

But a people without its own national history must relentlessly plunder Jewish sources to persuade a gullible world audience that Palestinian victims are the rightful inheritors of Jewish traditions and land. So the Palestinians, in a fitting expropriation, cast themselves as Jacob, stealing Esau's birthright.

By now, Palestinians have updated the world's 2000 year-old "lethal obsession" with Jews. Like the ancient Romans, they seek to obliterate the Jewish name and historical presence from the biblical homeland. The Palestinian usurpation of Jewish identity is now widely applauded by nations that indifferently witnessed the annihilation of European Jewry. Gullible allies (including Jews) in trendy intellectual, academic and media circles, have made the very idea of a Jewish state anathema.

To be sure, there already is a Palestinian state—in Jordan (part of Mandatory "Palestine" until the partition of 1922), with a majority Palestinian population. There is another *de facto* Palestinian state in the Hamas fiefdom of Gaza. Yet another Palestinian state, wrapping itself in the mantle of Jewish history in the biblical Jewish homeland, would climax a brazen pattern of national identity theft—and confront the State of Israel with lethal danger.

III · Rewriting History

Encountering the past, historians invariably discover its power to shape the present. Engaging with the residue of evidence, our own values, and each other, we endlessly debate and define the meaning of then from our perspective now. My occasional forays into interpretive disagreements among historians have included commentary, not always favorable, on the practice of our craft. Whether we are inclined to affirm or challenge conventional wisdom about the past, the rigor of our analysis always deserves careful scrutiny.

As a young historian of freedom of speech in wartime my attention was drawn to the attribution to a president (endlessly reiterated over the years) of memorable words that he was quite unlikely to have spoken. Early and late in my career I was occasionally provoked by interpretations of the past that primarily served present political objectives (and, occasionally, fabricated self-images). A Santa Fe vacation alerted me to the historical construction of Pueblo "dream palaces" to express longings for an imagined idyllic past (whether in the Middle East or the American Southwest).

A touch of skeptical iconoclasm, I either instinctively understood or learned along the way, enables a historian to reconsider and even reset the terms of debate about the past and its consequences for the present. It has been reassuring (if occasionally dismaying) to discover that historians display the same human foibles as do those whose stories and yearnings we delight in telling and interpreting.

21 · Woodrow Wilson's "Prediction"

Half a century ago another American President wrestled with the cruel decision for peace or war. "He kept us out of war"—the successful campaign slogan of 1916—sounded increasingly hollow after Germany's resumption of unrestricted submarine warfare in February 1917. Woodrow Wilson's torment increased as the gap between hope and reality widened. The decision for war, which terminated Wilson's uncertainty, only deepened his anguish. The night before Wilson went to Congress to request a declaration of war, he summoned Frank Cobb, editor of the New York *World* and a presidential confidant, to the White House. Cobb arrived belatedly at one o'clock in the morning of April 2. Only the editor was present to hear the President justify his decision and reveal his fears for the future.

Cobb had never seen Wilson "so worn down"; indeed, Wilson admitted that "he'd never been so uncertain about anything in his life" as about the decision for war. Yet, by now, "he couldn't see any alternative...." Wilson asked: "What else can I do?" Cobb told him that there truly was no other choice. "Do you know what that means?" Wilson replied. War would "overturn the world we had known...." War standards would replace peace standards and a defeated Germany would suffer "a dictated peace, a victorious peace." For the United States the consequences would be no less serious. War "required illiberalism at home to reinforce the men at the front." "Once lead this people into war," Wilson predicted, "and they'll forget there ever was such a thing as tolerance. To fight you must be brutal and ruthless, and the spirit of ruthless brutality will enter into the very fibre of our national life, infecting Congress, the courts, the policeman on the beat, the man in the street." The President warned that "the Constitution would not survive" war, "that free speech and the right of assembly would go." Wilson even anticipated the course of his own political future: "the adulation certain to follow the certain victory, the derision and attack which would come with the deflation of excessive hopes and in the presence of world responsibility."

Wilson's prescience amazed Cobb, who subsequently described the President as "uncanny"—with "the whole panorama in his mind." Historians, too, have been impressed. From William Allen White in 1924 to William C. Bullitt in 1967, the Wilson-Cobb conversation, especially the "Once lead this people into

---

"Woodrow Wilson's 'Prediction' to Frank Cobb: Words Historians Should Doubt Ever Got Spoken," *Journal of American History* (December 1967), 608-16.

war..." portion, has wound its way into more than two dozen studies of Wilson, American intervention, or civil liberties in wartime. Both Wilson's admirers and his detractors have cited the conversation, as have his wife, a member of his cabinet, his current biographer, and authors of at least five standard textbooks on modern America. Wilson's forebodings—particularly his gloomy prognosis for civil liberties—are as embedded in American lore as is Lincoln's torment over desertion and disloyalty during the Civil War.

Historians have found Wilson's words irresistible for two reasons. First, to justify the decision for intervention. American participation in the war represented such a sharp break in the history of this nation that only especially compelling reasons could justify it. Wilson's remarks to Cobb present the most compelling reason of all: the absence of alternatives. Surely one cannot be condemned for doing what *must* be done. Although he anticipated the dire consequences, Wilson could not refuse to demand intervention because by April intervention was the sole remaining option. Or so historians have argued, citing Wilson's statements to Cobb as substantiation.

The other context for Wilson's prediction relates to the first, yet is distinct from it. The absence of alternatives notwithstanding, Wilson still must bear the onus of moral responsibility for demanding intervention. How much less onerous this is, however, when Wilson's suffering and sagacity receive emphasis. The image of a detached and calculating President, coolly weighing national self-interest and oblivious to the consequences of his acts, would hardly suffice. Wilson seems so human, and his plight so tragic, when his "mental agony," "turmoil," "horror of war," and "anguish" are stressed. This was "the better Wilson" speaking, the tormented President vainly seeking escape. And this was the President who knew beyond doubt how the world, his nation, and Wilson himself would suffer. Wilson "foresaw it all, down even to the bitter end." He made "a remarkable prediction of future events" which stands as "one of the most sagacious prophecies ever made by an American political leader...." This was indeed "uncanny perspective."

The Wilson-Cobb conversation fits neatly, then, into historical interpretations that justify, first, American intervention, and, second, the President's conduct during the final prewar hours. It could, of course, also sustain an antiwar interpretation. Wilson would then become the devil who foresaw war and did nothing to abate it. Yet, the preponderant weight of evidence indicates that however justifiable any of these interpretations may be, the Wilson-Cobb exchange should no longer be cited to substantiate them. The sources for the conversation, its content, the circumstances of its publication, and all that we know about Woodrow Wilson strongly suggest that the President never spoke the words so frequently attributed to him.

Historians invariably cite John L. Heaton's *Cobb of THE WORLD* as their source for Wilson's statement. Heaton, a colleague of Cobb on the *World*, published his volume of Cobb's editorials and speeches in 1924; in it appears the earliest printed version of the Wilson-Cobb conversation. Yet of all the historians who rely upon this source, only Samuel Eliot Morison and Henry Steele

Commager note that the recollection was not Cobb's directly but a remembrance by two of Cobb's associates of what Cobb said Wilson had said seven years earlier. The first published account, therefore, constituted hearsay evidence twice removed. And it did not appear until a considerable period of time had elapsed from the original conversation, a lapse that looms large considering that the Wilson-Cobb account runs to three pages—indeed a remarkable recollection of words spoken seven years before. Furthermore, when the account finally was published, both participants in the original conversation were dead. Cobb died in December 1923; Wilson died two months later; the Heaton volume appeared five months after the President's death, when neither of the principals could confirm its veracity.

Evidence of a different sort casts doubt on the alleged time of the Wilson-Cobb meeting. According to the original version, and to all subsequent secondary accounts but one, Cobb came to the White House early in the morning of April 2, 1917, just hours prior to Wilson's address to Congress. In the most recent volume of Arthur Link's biography of Wilson, however, the author, while quoting extensively from the conversation, suggests that it occurred on March 19, not during the night of April 1-2. "There is no evidence whatsoever," according to Link (who examined the White House appointment book), "that Cobb went to the White House" at the latter date. Of course, it is conceivable that such a meeting could have passed unrecorded. But it is also conceivable that the absence of documentation, in conjunction with other evidence, indicates that the words that presumably were spoken at a nonexistent meeting on April 2 never were spoken at all.

The very language of the original document raises doubts regarding its authenticity. It is so exact a statement of what actually transpired between 1917 and 1920 that one is almost forced to conclude that it was written after these years, not before. Two specific phrases confirm this impression. First, Wilson supposedly stated that the Allies "would have their way in the very thing America had hoped against and struggled against." It is as though Wilson had already attended the Versailles Conference and observed the fate of his pleas for "open covenants of peace, openly arrived at" and for a "peace without victory." Second, the expression "dictated peace" is attributed to Wilson. Not only does this constitute a remarkable prediction of events, it employs the precise language with which those events would be described—*after* they occurred. To believe that Wilson spoke thus in April 1917 is tantamount to believing that Franklin D. Roosevelt in 1939 could have referred to the circumstances of American involvement in World War II as "a date which will live in infamy."

It is always risky, and never susceptible to final proof, to argue that certain words attributed to a person were so incongruous as never to have been spoken. Yet Wilson's conversation with Cobb does run so completely counter to the President's documentable words and deeds that this line of argument may briefly be explored. Wilson, on at least two other occasions, did anticipate certain consequences of war for the United States. In a letter to Josephus Daniels he lamented the probability that with war, "The people we have unhorsed will inevitably come into the control of the country for we shall be dependent upon the steel, oil and financial magnates. They will run the nation." To Representative William C. Adamson, Wilson predicted such "disorganization of business..., profiteering run rampant, [and] robbery" that "it would require a generation to restore normal conditions." These statements clearly reveal Wilson's concern lest war undercut progressivism and restore displaced business titans to power. Only to Cobb does Wilson seem to have demonstrated concern for civil liberties.

In fact, the President's civil-liberties posture was emphatically antilibertarian, before and after American intervention. In 1915 Wilson spoke of naturalized Americans "who have poured the poison of disloyalty into the very arteries of our national life...." He urged: "Such creatures of passion, disloyalty, and anarchy must be crushed out." During the 1916 campaign he once again questioned the loyalty of foreign-born Americans. And in his Flag Day address of June 1917 Wilson warned: "Woe be to the man or group of men that seeks to stand in our way...." Wilson's wartime acts, of omission and commission, confirmed his warnings. Cobb, among others, located the primary source of Wilson's intolerance: the President's assumption that because he had presumably done everything possible to avoid war, the country would unite uncritically behind him. A unified nation, of course, would not confront civil-liberties issues. Wilson anticipated such unity and was, therefore, unable to tolerate either dissent or dissenters. Measured against his behavior and his prewar warnings, the notion of Wilson agonizing over the potential loss of freedom of speech and assembly seems less than plausible.

By far the most intriguing evidence, albeit circumstantial, for disputing the authenticity of the Wilson-Cobb exchange arises from the identity of those responsible for relating the incident to Heaton—not Cobb, as noted earlier, but two of his colleagues on the *World*. Their names, all but ignored by historians, were quite prominent in the postwar literary and theatrical world: Maxwell Anderson and Laurence Stallings, collaborators on the play *What Price Glory?*—a striking antiwar drama that "banished the romantic treatment of fighting that had prevailed in the American theatre after every previous war."

The war had scarred both Anderson and Stallings. Anderson, a pacifist, suffered dismissal from the faculty of Whittier College and from an editorial position on the San Francisco *Bulletin* because he opposed American intervention. Stallings suffered physical as well as emotional distress. Seriously wounded at Belleau Wood, he spent two years in and out of French and American hospitals before one of his legs was amputated. In 1924, a month before the premiere of *What Price Glory?*, Stallings published *Plumes*, a weary autobiographical novel revealing his retrospective disenchantment with efforts to make the world safe for democracy. Richard Plume (Stallings) returned from war "a broken fool" with a "terrible bitterness" consuming him. He felt compelled to read incessantly about the Allies' secret wartime agreements, "trying to face the fact that he threw himself away." War, Plume now knew, was "a mistake, a brutal and vicious dance directed by ghastly men. It was the tragedy of our lives that we had to be mutilated at the pleasure of dolts and fools."

In theatre as in fiction, Stallings asked: what price glory? The Anderson-Stallings play, which opened in New York on September 5, 1924, was considered "the last word in pacifism...." In a program note the director cautioned the audience: "In a theatre where war has been lied about, romantically, effectively—and in a city where the war play has usually mean sugary dissimulation—*What Price Glory* may seem bold." It seemed not only bold but raw; an abortive attempt was made to censor it. But however abrasive the play's language, its mood fit perfectly into the postwar ambience of disillusion and disavowal. Joseph Wood Krutch subsequently wrote: "only an audience for whom long-established ideological complexes involving patriotism, courage, and honor had completely disintegrated could have comprehended, much less accepted, the attitudes taken by the authors...." Such an audience empathized with Captain Flagg's reference to "that world-safe-for-democracy slush" and with Sergeant Quirt's reflection just before the curtain fell: "What a lot of God damn fools it takes to make a war!"

The summer of 1924 apparently marked a critical time of intellectual and emotional release for Stallings and Anderson, especially for Stallings. Within three months their play was produced, Stallings' *Plumes* was published, and their account of Wilson's conversation with Cobb first appeared in Heaton's book. These separate fragments of a single mood evidently gestated simultaneously; all were variations on the theme of revulsion at the cost of "glory." Flagg, Quirt, and Plume learned on the battlefield how exorbitant was the price. Woodrow Wilson, Stallings and Anderson seemed to say, knew of its exorbitance long before payment—but he still chose to pay. Wilson, once he ceased to be too proud to fight, became one of Plume's "ghastly men."

The Wilson-Cobb conversation, printed below in its entirety, reveals far more about 1924 than about 1917. The war, in Henry F. May's suggestive phrase, marked the end of American innocence. "We believed," Malcolm Cowley reminisced years later, "that we had fought for an empty cause,...that the world consisted of fools and scoundrels ruled by scoundrels and fools...." Maxwell Anderson and Laurence Stallings articulated the postwar sense of outrage against the apparent stupidity, brutality, and futility of the blundering generation that had waged war. Nowhere is the price of this tragic mistake stated more explicitly than in Woodrow Wilson's prediction—a "prediction" surely made in retrospect by Anderson and Stallings. A world overturned, death and destruction, a dictated peace, illiberalism, ruthless brutality, conformity, the loss of civil liberties—this was the true price of glory.

A Recollection.

PRESIDENT WILSON had a way of summoning Cobb to Washington. Cobb rarely spoke of these visits to the White House. Since Wilson's death two of Cobb's associates, Maxwell Anderson and Laurence Stallings, have written down their memory of his recollection of one such occasion which is history. Mr. Anderson remembers that something said in disparagement of Clemenceau gave the impetus to the revelation; Mr. Anderson continues:

" 'He was a tricky old bandit,' said Cobb, as the three of us entered his office. 'A tricky old bandit, but he knew the game. He was the most formidable person at Versailles when it came to a pinch. Lloyd George was a child beside him. W. W. knew it, and knew how to meet the old boy, but he was hampered by having ideals of justice and government. Clemenceau used to look at Wilson as if he were a new and disconcerting species. He thought Wilson had the Messiah complex.

" 'He was dead wrong about it though, and everybody who thinks Wilson didn't know his way about and didn't know what he was in for should have heard what he said about the war before he went in. Old W. W. knew his history. He knew what wars were fought for, and what they do to nations that wage them.

" 'The night before he asked Congress for a declaration of war against Germany he sent for me. I was late getting the message somehow and didn't reach the White House till 1 o'clock in the morning. "The old man" was waiting for me, sitting in his study with the typewriter on his table, where he used to type his own messages.

"'I'd never seen him so worn down. He looked as if he hadn't slept, and he said he hadn't. He said he was probably going before Congress the next day to ask a declaration of war, and he'd never been so uncertain about anything in his life as about that decision. For nights, he said, he'd been lying awake going over the whole situation; over the provocation given by Germany, over the probable feeling in the United States, over the consequences to the settlement and to the world at large if we entered the melee.

" 'He tapped some sheets before him and said that he had written a message and expected to go before Congress with it as it stood. He said he couldn't see any alternative, that he had tried every way he knew to avoid war. "I think I know what war means," he said, and he added that if there were any possibility of avoiding war he wanted to try it. "What else can I do?" he asked. "Is there anything else I can do?"

" 'I told him his hand had been forced by Germany, that so far as I could see we couldn't keep out.

" ' "Yes," he said, "but do you know what that means?" He said war would overturn the world we had known; that so long as we remained out there was a preponderance of neutrality, but that if we joined with the Allies the world would be off the peace basis and onto a war basis.

"It would mean that we should lose our heads along with the rest and stop weighing right and wrong. It would mean that a majority of people in this hemisphere would go war-mad, quit thinking and devote their energies to destruction. The President said a declaration of war would mean that Germany would be beaten and so badly beaten that there would be a dictated peace, a victorious peace.

" ' "It means," he said, "an attempt to reconstruct a peace-time civilization with war standards, and at the end of the war there will be no bystanders with sufficient power to influence the terms. There won't be any peace standards left to work with. There will be only war standards."

" 'The President said that such a basis was what the Allies thought they wanted, and that they would have their way in the very thing America had hoped against and struggled against. W. W. was uncanny that night. He had the whole panorama in his mind. He went on to say that so far as he knew he had considered every loophole of escape and as fast as they were discovered Germany deliberately blocked them with some new outrage.

" 'Then he began to talk about the consequences to the United States: He had no illusions about the fashion in which we were likely to fight the war.

" 'He said when a war got going it was just war and there weren't two kinds of it. It required illiberalism at home to reinforce the men at the front. We couldn't fight Germany and maintain the ideals of Government that all thinking men shared. He said we would try it but it would be too much for us.

" ' "Once lead this people into war," he said, "and they'll forget there ever was such a thing as tolerance. To fight you must be brutal and ruthless, and the spirit of ruthless brutality will enter into the very fibre of our national life, infecting Congress, the courts, the policeman on the beat, the man in the street." Conformity would be the only virtue, said the President, and every man who refused to conform would have to pay the penalty.

" 'He thought the Constitution would not survive it; that free speech and the right of assembly would go. He said a nation couldn't put its strength into a war and keep its head level; it had never been done.

" 'If there is any alternative, for God's sake, let's take it,' he exclaimed. Well I couldn't see any, and I told him so.' "

22 · New Deal, Old Deal, or Raw Deal

In a time of rampant social criticism, when American verities seem precarious, the past no less than the present falls under scrutiny. Indeed, past and present lose their very separateness. Present issues guide research into the past; historians call upon the past to speak to present needs; strident demands are heard for a "new" or "usable" past. Just as turn-of-the-century progressive ferment provided the setting for Charles A. Beard's reinterpretation of the Founding Fathers and the Depression elicited Matthew Josephson's discovery of the "robber barons," so current social issues promise to leave new eddies of historical revisionism in their wake. Revisionist historians, like automobile drivers, learn to keep one eye on the rearview mirror while the other scans the road ahead.

Given the focus of current protest—against racism, imperialism, liberalism, the power elite, bureaucratic centralization, and the very nature of corporate capitalism—it is understandable that the New Deal should become a prime target for revisionist fire. In a dual sense the particular achievements and failures of the Roosevelt administration become both compelling and galling. First, because it is so alluring to consider March 1933 as tabula rasa, after which New Dealers quickly dissipated the last best hope for a drastic restructuring of American society. And second, because presumably we are now reaping the noxious harvest of welfare capitalism whose seeds the New Dealers sowed three decades ago. As historian Irwin Unger has observed, "the New Deal is the immediate source of the liberal welfare state, and they [New Left critics] despise it as much as they do the flaccid, self-satisfied society that they hold is its direct descendant." Thus one critic complains: "Most of the time America is an ugly place to live in. All the 'reforms' only seem to have made it uglier. And more sophisticated in its evil.... In the long run, what did the New Deal do? Besides the Smith Act?" Another laments the reluctance of historians to discuss "in what way and to what extent the New Deal...contributed to the rise of the political, economic, and social conditions we are familiar with today." According to a third, the New Deal "launched the American welfare state, a brand new, large, ungainly infant, destined to survive all the hazards of childhood and a maladjusted adolescence, eventually to mature in the Great Society...."

The bill of grievances compiled by New Left critics against the New Deal

---

"New Deal, Old Deal or Raw Deal," *Journal of Southern History* (February 1969), 18-28, 30.

makes the Roosevelt administration seem more ominous even than the reign of George III, which prompted an earlier declaration of independence. Manifold causes impel the critics to their separation from previously favorable estimates of the New Deal. These include the absence of any philosophy of reform; the consequent failure of New Dealers even to attack, much less resolve, fundamental social problems; a commitment to the salvation of corporate capitalism; destruction of the Left; remoteness from popular authority and indifference to participatory democracy. Running through this jeremiad is the refrain made explicit by Paul Conkin: "The story of the New Deal is a sad story, the ever recurring story of what might have been."

Conkin, more than any of the critics with whom he is here associated, concedes that the New Deal initiated "some important modifications of the American economic system." Considering what might have been, however, its record was spotty and disappointing: "...no core of political principles, no clear economic philosophy, no new clarification of the dilemmas of liberal democracy" emerged from the New Deal. Without them, apparently, little else matters. Conkin is especially eager to smite the canard that the New Deal was pragmatic, or even experimental. "Above all," he writes, "Roosevelt was not a pragmatist." And experimentalism, Conkin adds, means "the advocacy, in terms of what is known, of a tentative solution, as comprehensive, as systematic, as consistent, as formally perfect as possible, and then as careful a testing of the tentative answer as circumstances permit...." The New Deal, Conkin complains, "denied the idea of experimentation—clear hypotheses and controlled verification."

The flaw in this model—as Conkin himself concedes—is that in politics circumstances do not very often permit careful tests of tentative answers. Because political leaders are not scientists, because people are not chemicals, and because life is not a test tube, laboratory metaphors are deceptive. Scientists are not necessarily compelled to dilute their experiments in order to complete them, nor must they submit their results to a national electorate for approval. In tearing the mantle of pragmatism from the shoulders of New Dealers, Conkin and others have only demonstrated the incompatibility of pragmatism, defined as a formal system of thought, with politics. By their definition, no political administration can be pragmatic; the term is without meaning in a political context. Instead of waving the "bloody shirt" of pragmatism, therefore, both defenders and critics of the New Deal would do well to pass beyond pragmatic shadows to substance.

Far more serious is the allegation that the New Deal failed to resolve, or even to attack, fundamental social problems. It is around this proposition that a cluster of New Left critics of the New Deal have directed their most concentrated assault. Lloyd C. Gardner asks: "How many of the society's fundamental problems had really been corrected, or even attacked? How real had the recovery been? How dangerous the path taken?" Howard Zinn suggests that the New Deal failed to solve the most fundamental problem confronting it: "how to bring the blessings of immense natural wealth and staggering productive potential to every person in the land." Barton J. Bernstein complains that "The New Deal failed to solve the problem of depression, it failed to raise the impoverished, it failed to redistribute income, it failed to extend equality and generally countenanced racial discrimination and segregation."

The premise upon which these criticisms rest is the impossibility of solutions to "fundamental problems" short of "a radically new economic equilibrium" and a "significant redistribution of power in American society...." Yet this is a slippery premise at best, with several concealed semantic traps. By definition, "fundamental" problems become those which the New Deal did not solve. A "radically new economic equilibrium" seems tantamount to any equilibrium that the New Deal failed to attain. And "significant redistribution of power" means any redistribution beyond the one actually achieved. Of course, if total repudiation of capitalism becomes the sole test by which to measure the New Deal, obviously it (like every preceding and subsequent administration) failed. But critics who apply this test should at least begin to indicate its relevance within the context of a political system whose voters and leaders have persistently refused to sanction the destruction of capitalism as a goal.

If any point short of total repudiation is acceptable, then the issue may be fairly joined. New Left critics concede a new legal framework for labor-management relations; new controls over banks, stock exchanges, and other institutions of private enterprise; social security; relief; public housing and public works; the restoration of jobs to at least half the jobless; legitimization of a new economic role for government; and a profound political and constitutional shake-up. Yet, according to Bernstein for example, "seemingly humane [reform] efforts" by New Dealers only "revealed the shortcomings of American liberalism." One is compelled to inquire: Did they seem humane because they were humane, in which case Bernstein's point is lost; or did they seem humane despite the fact that they were not humane, in which case we desperately need a new definition of "humane." Furthermore, against what standard of the thirties are liberalism's "shortcomings" measured? How fruitful is it to label New Deal efforts at slum clearance and public housing (or other reforms) as "faltering and shallow," when the point of reference for this judgment clearly is 1968, not 1938?

The subject of race relations, a pressing current concern but for many and legitimate reasons not a paramount New Deal issue, understandably attracts attention from New Left critics. Black Americans, Bernstein concedes, did receive (minimal) aid and (cautious) recognition. But Roosevelt should not be too quickly praised, for even if the results were commendable, bad reasons negate them. Rather than making color the basis of assistance, the New Deal dispensed aid on the basis of need. This distinction seemed less important to Negroes than to Bernstein, who uneasily balances his judgment that "the New Deal left intact the race relations of America" with the fact that it was able "to woo Negro leaders and even to court the masses." According to Conkin Negro support for the New Deal arose from the fact that Negroes were "politically purchased by relief or by the occasional concern of bureaucrats...." Unless one assumes, as Bernstein, Conkin, and others elsewhere assume, that the New Deal was so diabolically clever that it won the support of those whom it did not help, one must conclude that most black (and white) Americans found much in the New Deal to command their allegiance.

In addition to social welfare and race, labor relations can serve as a useful litmus test of the New Deal record. Surprisingly, New Left critics have little to say about the single most vital issue for Old Leftists. In manifold ways, the resolution of capital-labor discord represented the most enduring and compelling need in American public life. This vexing problem, with its serious economic, political, and constitutional ramifications, had lingered since the nation's earliest years as an industrial power. Without legal protection for the right to organize and bargain collectively, industrial workers were helpless in the face of concerted employer power. It was precisely this legal protection that the New Deal provided, albeit with reluctance in presidential circles.

The New Left critics demur, insisting *Plus ça change, plus c'est la même chose*. Bernstein concedes change but insists that its significance was merely "the institutionalization of larger interest groups into a new political economy.... It was not the industrial workers necessarily who were recognized, but their unions and leaders...." Brad Wiley, noting the forces of industrial unionism unleashed by New Deal laws, complains that the CIO merely "furthered the process of rationalization of the economy by disciplining the working class through containing the militancy of the workers, eliminating the threat of strikes, and generally mediating between the boss and 'his' workers." This line of argument, of course, creates a neat whipsaw effect. Whether the New Deal ignored labor or succored it, New Deal culpability is assured. Criticized for only slowly awakening to workers' grievances and aspirations, the New Deal is criticized equally strenuously for eradicating the major sources of their discontent.

Bernstein and Wiley carry their portable whipsaw one step further. Each feels compelled to note New Deal reforms, but neither will accept mere reform as sufficient. In fact, reform becomes destructive—more destructive, paradoxically, than failure to reform. According to Bernstein: "The liberal reforms of the New Deal did not transform the American system; they conserved and protected American corporate capitalism, *occasionally by absorbing parts of threatening programs*." Wiley maintains: "The New Deal's *recognition of potentially antagonistic social groups* served a conservative integrating purpose. If these groups could be led to cooperate with the dominant economic and political elite on the basis of the rules of corporate capitalism, any possibility that their demands for reform might begin to question fundamental property relations was eliminated."

What especially seems to perturb the New Left critics is the very willingness of the New Deal to absorb radical proposals into its own program. This might be interpreted to reveal both the viability of many radical demands and New Deal responsiveness to pressure from the Left. New Left critics have, however, taken a different sounding. Conkin observes sadly that Roosevelt's 1936 landslide "almost destroyed the political left in American politics, whether dogmatic fringe groups or the terribly honest and flexible American Socialist Party." Bernstein seems to regret New Deal assistance to the needy, because "Roosevelt's humane efforts also protected the established system: he sapped organized radicalism of its waning strength and of its potential constituency among the unorganized and discontented." Zinn notes the emergence of a plethora of protest groups and complains that "there was no political program around which these disparate groups could effectively unite. And many of them began to lose their thrust *when their demands were partially met.*"

Implicit in this critique is an assumption that the New Deal undercut radical reform. This assumption is highly questionable; at the very least it requires more documentation and less assertion. It is more than conceivable that a depression without the New Deal would have produced no reform at all. Such was the American experience between 1930 and 1932. The New Deal may well have made radical reform, to the extent that it existed, possible. We know that radicalism flourished more in the wake of New Deal reforms of 1933 and 1935 than in anticipation of them. A sense of possibilities, elicited by the Roosevelt administration, repeatedly galvanized the Left. Tocqueville's insight that endured evils become intolerable when avenues of escape are opened is especially relevant in this context. This certainly was true in labor-management relations: radicals launched their most successful forays from the legal fortifications erected under the National Industrial Recovery Act and the National Labor Relations Act. Radicals, like factory workers and sharecroppers, waged a revolution of rising expectations. The success (unintended, of course) of the New Deal in stimulating and even legitimizing radical ferment would seem to warrant more attention from New Left critics than it has received....

From the perspective of the 1960's, which for New Left critics provides the only relevant standard, one of the most serious of New Deal deficiencies was its alleged remoteness from sources of popular authority—four presidential and numerous congressional victories to the contrary notwithstanding. A curious ambivalence pervades New Left analysis of this issue. Wiley, for example, argues that New Deal centralizing tendencies served "to isolate government further from popular authority...." Concentration of power in executive agencies meant that policies were formulated and implemented "by Presidential advisers and...technicians, none of whom are ever directly answerable to the commonwealth they ostensibly serve." Zinn moves one step further to claim that "Only the aggrieved themselves can provide the motive power to create that new deal which neither FDR nor JFK nor LBJ gave us." Yet Zinn himself asserts that "the boldest programs" and "the largest expectations" came not from the aggrieved, but "from intellectuals not closely associated with the White House, from those whose ideological reach is not impaired by their clinking glasses with the mighty." New Deal half measures, Conkin concurs, were repudiated by "the more alienated, more sensitive, and more analytic intellectuals," who were "too honest and too clearheaded" to "master the soothing art of the fireside...."

Again, the categories are so neat and functional: the New Deal allegedly shunned participatory democracy, yet the most innovative alternatives came not from the demos but from a powerless intellectual elite. *Ipso facto,* intellectuals who held power were corrupted by it; intellectuals without power could only wallow in their own sensitivity and alienation. Conveniently, so long as they remained remote from power their ideas retained force and energy. But the moment they arrived in Washington to apply these forceful ideas energetically they were guilty of a sell-out. So loud was the noise of "clinking glasses" that serious intellectual discourse was obliterated. By definition, intellectual contributions could be made only by those who opted for purity over power.

Imprisoned by their assumption that the New Deal offered so little to so many, New Left critics find themselves hard-pressed to explain why the Roosevelt administration received such enthusiastic popular mandates. Bernstein proposes that "the marginal men trapped in hopelessness were seduced by rhetoric...." Conkin conjectures that downtrodden Negroes were "politically purchased." Again the whipsaw: Had marginal men *not* voted for Roosevelt, it would prove New Deal programmatic deficiencies. That they *did* vote for him indicates only the power of rhetoric—or relief. (It is revealing that Bernstein's application of the notion of rhetorical seduction does not extend to radicals like Huey Long or Father Coughlin, whose slogans, "Every Man a King" and "Social Justice," certainly were far more seductive—in the dictionary meaning of leading someone astray—than Roosevelt's program.) Since opposition to the New Deal is the only posture consistent with New Left interpretations of New Deal defects, support of the New Deal, in a somewhat patronizing fashion, becomes a measure of the folly of those who failed to appreciate where their true interests lay. Indeed, Conkin even argues that opponents "misconstrued the direction of the New Deal.... The enemies of the New Deal were wrong. They should have been friends." Rather than assume, as the evidence warrants, that enemies and friends of the New Deal realistically pursued legitimate conceptions of their own self-interest, New Left critics transform ardent admirers into "real" enemies and vigorous critics into misguided friends.

Perplexity mounts when one recalls Conkin's assertion regarding the New Deal as "a sad story...of what might have been." This refrain resounds throughout Conkin's essay: Roosevelt "might have" acted differently during the 1932-1933 interregnum; the administration "might have" encouraged recovery and "might have" restored confidence in 1933. "*If* Roosevelt had not, by 1936, turned in devastating fury upon business...*If* Roosevelt...had really turned toward increased federal direction and ownership. Or *if* the government... had pumped such enormous sums of borrowed money into the economy that it had to respond." But one sour note mars the crescendo. In his penultimate paragraph Conkin asserts: "The plausible alternatives to the New Deal are not easily suggested, particularly if one considers all the confining and limiting circumstances." The hypothesizing, then, was for naught; the critic has become tacit defender, leaving the New Deal imprisoned by circumstance and thereby implicitly exonerated for its deficiencies.

It should by now be apparent that the New Left critique of the New Deal—spirited, controversial, and provocative though it may be—is occasionally illogical and consistently ahistorical. This dour estimate is in no way intended as a blessing for all that the New Deal did or failed to do—or for all that its defenders have said or left unsaid about it. Nor, most emphatically, does it imply that all criticism of the New Deal is unwelcome, for the uniformly favorable treatment of the New Deal which has prevailed for two decades is indeed in need of revision. Rather, it is an assertion that the New Left critique is sterile because New Left critics have applied irrelevant standards and a protean vocabulary to reach a priori conclusions. It is hardly necessary for them to display surprise (or indignation) at their "discovery" that the New Deal saved capitalism and refused to abandon private property. No one has seriously doubted this; indeed, the New Deal received no mandate to do otherwise. Its Old Left critics were numerically overwhelmed by those who wanted little more than the reshuffling of an old deck. Its New Left critics are trying to win a verdict in the history books that was decisively rejected thirty years ago. Lloyd C. Gardner, referring to Roosevelt's defenders, has observed: "Any incongruities which turned up in the legend of the New Deal were carefully tucked away in chapters called 'Behind the Mask,' where human errors and failings all became part of the 'enigma' that was Franklin Roosevelt." Yet it is equally true that Roosevelt's detractors have applied to the New Deal ex post facto standards of judgment that would render every administration since Washington's equally culpable. It is, in fact, the search for culpability rather than the quest for understanding that looms as the most prominent—and characteristic—defect of the New Left critique.

Howard Zinn, for example, would have historians "consider present needs at the expense, if necessary, of old attachments." If these were the sole alternatives, Zinn's position would have more to recommend it. But they are not. The historian who is a partisan for or against the present deprives himself of the insights that only come after he permits the present to frame his questions and insists that the past alone provide his answers—on *its* terms, not his. If it is understandable that the interest of historians in the abolitionists should be rekindled in an era of intensive civil rights activity, it would nonetheless be a betrayal of the historian's function to berate ante-bellum egalitarians for pursuing *their* goals and tactics rather than those of the freedom riders and black nationalists of the 1960's. Similarly, while generations of New Deal historians predictably will be guided by the questions and methodology of *their* present, their evaluations of the New Deal will remain suspect so long as they judge New Dealers harshly (or indeed kindly) for misbehaving in the thirties according to the gospel of the New Left in the sixties. Historians blessed with twenty-twenty hindsight who flail their forebears for lacking twenty-twenty foresight are themselves plagued by myopia. If men in public life today are imprisoned by New Deal categories and solutions, it is they who are the proper targets of criticism, not those who innovated so successfully thirty-five years ago that their program set the terms of political discourse not only for their generation but for succeeding ones....

Such absolute moral judgments can neither be proved nor disproved; hence their appeal. Furthermore, they are quite irrelevant to historical analysis if history is to remain distinct from propaganda for or against current policies.

This is not to insist, however, that the New Deal (or any era) be measured only against its past. Although the configurations of the future were not, and could not have been, even dimly perceptible in the 1930's, historians retain the freedom, denied to contemporaries, to measure an era against both its subsequent and its antecedent developments. But historians who concentrate exclusively on either, as the New Left critics have done, take an implicit vow to write one-dimensional history. They repudiate the subtle interaction of the historical past and the historian's present for the sharp thrust of current political protest. Historians of the post-New Deal era, along with Paul Conkin, may properly maintain that "The United States has neither moved beyond it [the New Deal] nor searched for valid alternatives." This fact will disappoint New Left critics, and others, but it is incumbent upon them to recognize that the onus of responsibility devolves upon those who have governed since 1941, not upon the New Dealers. Even historiographical victories cannot be won against the wrong enemy in the wrong place at the wrong time.

23 · Means and Ends in the 1960s

Of the making of books about the fabled 1960s, there is no likely end in sight. Long after the cascade of self-celebratory memoirs has finally subsided and the last Baby Boomer passes from the scene, historians will still be analyzing the enduring impact of that turbulent decade. For the foreseeable future, the sixties are likely to retain their significance as one of the crucial turning points in American history, their consequences vigorously disputed and endlessly debated.

It is not too soon, however, to offer a provisional hypothesis: their substantial achievements notwithstanding, the conspicuous failure of Sixties activists and their defenders to comprehend the necessity of linking presumptively noble ends—participatory democracy, racial equality, academic reform, anti-imperialism—to honorable means ultimately unraveled much of their efforts and turned the nation against them. Despite significant breakthroughs in race and gender relations, and the retraction of American power that ended the Vietnam War, the conservative counter-revolution against the major achievements of the sixties still gathers momentum nearly half a century later.

To be sure, sixties rebels confronted formidable obstacles: entrenched racism (and sexism), academic rigidity, and unyielding anti-Communism. They encountered violence in the South and police brutality wherever they assaulted the bastions of authority, whether at Berkeley or Columbia, or in Chicago or Los Angeles. These endless confrontations raised serious questions about the legitimacy of authority in vital American institutions. But that is not the only measure of protest and rebellion. Those who challenge authority must know that the legitimacy of their own actions will be placed under scrutiny.

It all began, ironically, in the 1950s, that notoriously "placid" decade. The emergence of Martin Luther King, Jr. in Montgomery, Alabama, as the leader of a nascent civil rights movement infused the struggle for racial equality with moral urgency and (it is worth remembering) religious passion. A young, unknown, untested minister, apparently committed at the outset (as Coretta Scott King conceded) merely to "a more humane form of segregation," King nonetheless understood that disobedience, if it was to be translated into freedom and equality, must remain non-violent. Rallying his followers, he put them on notice that pursuit of a worthy cause was insufficient. No less important was how that

---

"Means and Ends in the 1960s," *Society* (Sept.-Oct. 2005), 9-13.

cause was pursued. Through this narrow opening—the legitimacy, even purity, of means required to overthrow the evil of racism—a civil rights movement was born that transformed the nation.

The wave of spontaneous local sit-in protests that began in Greensboro, North Carolina, in 1960, followed by the Freedom Rides that carried the struggle for racial equality across state lines a year later, remained faithful to non-violence. Even as the protesters encountered the violent fury of hostile racists, they never relented in their commitment. King declined to participate in the Freedom Rides, but he articulated their underlying principle of non-violent resistance. "Our conscience tells us that the law is wrong and we must resist," he told Attorney General Robert F. Kennedy, "but we have a moral obligation to accept the penalty." Non-violence, King insisted, must be "moral, legal and peaceful."

Already, however, the cutting edge of the civil rights movement was encountering criticism over its professed fidelity to non-violent means. "We would be nonviolent, absolutely nonviolent," James Farmer, leader of the CORE-sponsored Freedom Rides insisted, "and we would accept the consequences of our actions." But Farmer also knew that he could count on white racists in the deep South to respond violently to the riders of integrated buses, the better to elicit public sympathy for the Freedom Riders' cause. *The New York Times*, which had supported King's non-violent strategy, backed away from the Freedom Riders, asserting: "Non-violence that deliberately provokes violence is a logical contradiction." Who, then, bore responsibility for racial violence: those who defended segregation, or those who confronted it?

The stage was set for Birmingham. In the spring of 1963, Rev. Fred Shuttlesworth, seeking "some different type of confrontation," invited King to join him in Project "C," an effort to desegregate local department stores. In Birmingham, King wrestled with difficult choices. Local black leaders resented his presence, and a court injunction prohibited mass demonstrations. Just days after Commissioner of Public Safety Bull Connor called out his police dogs, bringing worldwide notoriety to Birmingham, King decided to disobey the injunction, lead a march, and go to jail.

There, in response to the criticism of religious leaders for his "unwise and untimely" action, he wrote the letter that fully articulated his philosophy of non-violent civil disobedience. Non-violent action, he conceded, "seeks to create such a crisis and foster such a tension that a community which has constantly refused to negotiate is forced to confront the issue." King continued: "We know through painful experience that freedom is never voluntarily given by the oppressor; it must be demanded by the oppressed." The crux of the issue, King acknowledged, was "our willingness to break laws." For a movement that arguably depended upon the rule of law, as enunciated by the Supreme Court in *Brown v. Board of Education*, "it may seem paradoxical for us consciously to break laws." But, King continued: "The answer lies in the fact that there are two types of laws: just and unjust…. One has not only a legal but a moral responsibility to obey just laws. Conversely, one has a moral responsibility to disobey unjust laws."

But who decides? In this instance, at least, King decided: "I can urge men to obey the 1954 decision of the Supreme Court, for it is morally right; and I can urge them to disobey segregation ordinances, for they are morally wrong." Indeed, King insisted: "it is wrong to urge an individual to cease his efforts to gain his basic constitutional rights because the quest may precipitate violence." Conceding that "it is wrong to use immoral means to attain moral ends," he defended the morality of the non-violent means that the movement had chosen.

But with protest flagging, King shared the concern of local ministers Wyatt Walker and James Bevel that the press and public were losing interest in Birmingham. A new and dynamic strategy was required for a breakthrough. Bevel and Walker made the fateful decision to mobilize black children in mass demonstrations. Some black adults opposed the use of their children as shock troops in confrontations with Bull Connor and his police dogs. King was hesitant. But as Walker subsequently explained, in justification: "I had to do what had to be done. At times I would accommodate or alter my morality for the sake of getting a job done.... I felt I had no choice. I wasn't dealing with a moral situation when I dealt with a Bull Connor. We did with design precipitate crises, crucial crises in order to expose what the black community was up against."

King, too, had come to appreciate the importance—even necessity—of provocation to illuminate the reality of racism and discrimination. "We are merely bringing to the surface the tension that has always been at the heart of the problem," he asserted. Demonstrations "may be peaceful and nonviolent, but you make people inflict violence on you, so you precipitate violence." With such provocation, however, were "the means we use" still "as pure as the ends we seek," as King had pledged in his letter from the Birmingham jail?

The next year, Mississippi Freedom Summer highlighted this question with tragic consequences. Bob Moses and Dave Dennis, who coordinated the challenge to the most entrenched racist society anywhere in the nation, made the fateful decision to invite Northern white college students to participate. As Dennis explained to journalist Howell Raines: "It's sorta cold, so I'm gonna just tell you what my feeling was about it. We knew that if we had brought in a thousand blacks, the country would have watched them slaughtered without doing anything about it." Instead, "We made sure that we had the children, sons and daughters, of some very powerful people in this country.... If there were gonna take some deaths to do it, the death of a white college student would bring on more attention to what was going on than for a black college student getting it. That's cold, but that was also in another sense speaking the language of this country." Pressed by Raines to justify the decision that cost the life of Andrew Goodman, along with Michael Schwerner and James Chaney, while transforming Freedom Summer into an enduring symbol of courageous struggle against intransigent racism, Dennis responded: "It was something that had to be done.... We were in a war."

New Movements of Social Change

Any lingering commitment to the morality of means, already ominously frayed in Alabama and Mississippi, completely unraveled with the turn to Black Power. In the urban North in the spring of 1964, Malcolm X posed a choice between "the ballot or the bullet." Predicting an imminent explosion between the races, he warned of the new black American "who just doesn't intend to turn the other cheek any longer." In a sharp rebuke to the Civil Rights Movement under King's leadership, Malcolm explained: "We want freedom *now*, but we're not going to get it saying 'We Shall Overcome.' We've got to fight until we overcome...."

In the South, Stokely Carmichael, newly elected president of the Student Non-Violent Coordinating Committee (SNCC) in 1966, terminated its bi-racial commitment, declaring that "whites' role in the movement has now ended." Dismissing white participants as colonizers, and insisting that black freedom depended on black power, he founded the Black Panther Party. That same year, on the West Coast, Huey Newton and Bobby Seale founded their own Black Panthers in Oakland, with its armed "black self-defense groups that are dedicated to defending our black community from racist police oppression and brutality." Before long, a group of armed Panthers, their array of guns conspicuously on display, made their way into the state capitol in Sacramento. So it was, within a decade after the beginning of the nonviolent movement in Montgomery, that the struggle had swung decisively toward Malcolm's slogan: "any means necessary."

The student movement experienced a similar trajectory. The New Left was born at Port Huron in 1960, where Students for a Democratic Society pledged itself to freedom, equality, and "a democracy of individual participation." As troubled as its founders were by racial bigotry and Cold War threats of nuclear annihilation, they still yearned for change within a framework of identifiably liberal values. They might denounce "the hypocrisy of American ideals," but their pursuit of freedom and equality, at least rhetorically, was located well within those very ideals. Perhaps their boldest assertion was the claim, quite unimaginable to college graduates just a few years earlier, that universities offered "a potential base...in a movement of social change."

Port Huron theory became stark reality at Berkeley in 1964. Emboldened by their civil rights activism, students challenged university restrictions banning on-campus solicitation for off-campus political causes. The very name of their Free Speech Movement suggested a commitment to fundamental First Amendment values. As student leader Jackie Goldberg explained, they were prepared to risk everything—education, jobs, careers—because "we believed in American values": the Constitution, democracy, individual rights. It did not take long, however, before the Free Speech Movement confronted precisely the problem of means and ends that was beginning to torment the civil rights movement.

It was one thing to surround a police car for thirty-two hours to protest the arrest of a movement leader (who, ironically, was not even a student). Immobilized by students, the police car became a spontaneous open-air forum for the expression of a wide range of views. Climbing on the roof to speak, students politely removed their shoes out of respect for police property. But when the university administration failed to respond with sufficient alacrity to their demands, students raised the ante. In the stirring words of Free Speech Movement leader Mario Savio: "There's a time when the operation of the machine becomes so odious, makes you so sick at heart, that you can't take part, you can't even tacitly take part. And you've got to put your bodies upon the gears and upon the wheels, upon the levers, upon all the apparatus and you've got to make it stop."

It was a compelling, yet disturbing, call for action. But who decides when it is time to shut down the "machine": anyone who claims to be "sick at heart"? On that occasion, seven hundred students who were determined to "create a confrontation" and "force a response" from President Clark Kerr occupied Sproul Hall, the administrative center of the university. There they remained—talking, singing, studying and dancing—until police dragged them out of the building. With the faculty supporting their struggle against "autocratic and powerful minority rule," students won back the rights to set up their tables, distribute literature, and solicit funds.

But as the Vietnam War came more sharply into focus, protest at Berkeley spiraled into massive civil disobedience. When thousands of students surged into downtown Oakland in an attempt to shut down an Army induction center, civil disobedience erupted into random violence. As students put their bodies upon the gears of the "machine" (trashing cars and property along the way), they began their own journey from prudent constitutionalism to violent protest, and ultimately even to armed rebellion.

Making Revolution

By 1968-69, the student protest scenario was endlessly repeated, with local variations. At Columbia and Cornell, two major battlegrounds, the animating issues remained race and the Vietnam War. At Columbia, protest quickly evolved from civil disobedience to "barricaded resistance" to university authority. Condemning university "exploitation of the community and her support for the government's imperialist policies," and feeling "*caught in this 'system,'*" students seized Low Library, where the president's office was located, along with several other University buildings.

A euphoric student activist recalled believing at the time: "Maybe we were going to make the revolution." But a more prudent history professor, whose papers and book manuscript were burned during the uprising, knew that the students "were totally divorced from reality." When New York City police swarmed through the buildings to pummel, evict, and arrest their occupiers, students confronted the counter-revolutionary consequences of their illegal acts.

At Cornell, a year later, black students seized Willard Straight Hall to express their demands for a Black Studies department. Fearing a retaliatory raid by conservative white students, they made the logical, but nonetheless shocking, revolutionary decision: they smuggled in guns. After an agreement was negotiated for their departure, with weapons conspicuously displayed, black student leader Tom Jones told a packed student convocation that "our blood would not be the only blood that was shed if the university took a hard line." His dire warning that the university had "three hours to live" produced the abject capitulation of the administration, which authorized a Black Studies department and issued a sweeping amnesty. Years later, Jones, by then a bank director and Cornell trustee, conceded: "This might have been done at a price that was too high."

The price was high indeed. From SDS (Students for a Democratic Society) extremists who led provocative and violent protests in Chicago during and after the Democratic convention of 1968 emerged the Weathermen, determined to "bring the war home" to Americans through random acts of violence. In a tragic twist of irony, they became their own victims, in the home of their choosing. A Weathermen cell in New York City converted a townhouse on West 11th Street, owned by the parents of one of its members, into a bomb factory, where three members of the group blew themselves up while preparing an attack against soldiers at Fort Dix.

To Bill Ayres, who went into hiding with accomplice Bernardine Dohrn after his girlfriend was killed in the explosion, "being illegal didn't strike us as a great obstacle." As fugitives, they conducted an underground guerrilla campaign, placing bombs in the Capitol and the Pentagon, among other chosen sites. Ayers subsequently conceded that "some of it was undoubtedly misguided, but in no way does it measure up to the crimes that were committed by this country, when you look at what the United States unleashed against Vietnam." Indeed, his primary regret was that "we didn't find ways to put a more serious obstacle into the path of this onrushing machine of destruction."

After a decade in hiding Ayres finally resurfaced in 1980, living in relative obscurity as a professor of education at the University of Illinois, Chicago. In his memoir, *Fugitive Days*, he would fondly recall: "Everything was absolutely ideal on the day I bombed the Pentagon. The sky was blue. The birds were singing. And the bastards were finally going to get what was coming to them." Interviewed by a beguiled *New York Times* reporter, Ayres added: "I don't regret setting bombs. I feel we didn't do enough." With uncanny (if unplanned) timing, the *Times* printed the Ayers interview on the morning of September 11, 2001.

Among Ayers's associates in the Weather Underground (as the Weathermen had renamed itself to avoid allegations of sexism), Kathy Boudin, who escaped from the Greenwich Village bomb-factory explosion, served twenty-two years in prison for second-degree murder in the killing of two policemen and a security guard during a Brink's robbery. (She was paroled in 2003.) David Gilbert, the father of her son (who was raised by Ayres and Dohrn), is serving seventy-five years to life for his role in the robbery and murders. Susan Rosenberg, implicated in the Brink's hold-up, was sentenced to fifty-eight years in prison for illegal weapons possession (including 740 pounds of explosives). Her prison term was commuted in the waning hours of Bill Clinton's presidency.

Is there, in the end, ideological continuity, reinforced by moral obtuseness, linking the Free Speech Movement and its spin-offs to the Weathermen? From Mario Savio's impassioned plea to stop the Berkeley "machine," reinforced by Malcolm X's demand for "any means necessary" to secure the rights of black Americans, to the underground acts of violence, not to say terror, committed by the Weathermen, there was an alarming disregard for the morality of means. Comprising a small minority of the protesters who rallied to the civil rights, university reform, and anti-war causes during the sixties, they nonetheless came to define the final agenda of protest. By the end of the decade, without public support and with their leaders dead, or in hiding and hounded by the FBI, only the shattered remnants of a protest movement remained.

Lasting Consequences

Did the slippery slope of moral flaccidity begin with the decision in Birmingham to use children to provoke violence (non-violently, to be sure), the better to attract national attention and a response from the Kennedy administration? Was it already in place when Dave Dennis and Bob Moses decided that the purposes of Mississippi Freedom Summer would best be served by placing Northern white students at risk of their lives? The trajectory of Students for a Democratic Society, which began with the Port Huron proclamation of participatory democracy and ended in spasms of violent street rampages, self-destruction, and murder, serves as an ominous paradigm.

Can moral ends, even those as noble as free speech, equality, democracy, and peace, nonetheless be inexorably corrupted by the immoral means chosen by their self-proclaimed defenders? Even by philosopher Martin Buber's moral test—commit no more injustice than is necessary—the unequivocal answer from the sixties is Yes. Certainly those who challenged the status quo of authority and conformity created new possibilities for change in ossified sectors of American society—whether in race and gender relations, academic institutions, or Cold War policy. But as Baby Boomers mounted the barricades to the battle cry of "any means necessary," putting their bodies on the gears of the machines of power that they had come to detest, they contributed to the crisis of legitimate authority that plunged the nation into prolonged turmoil. Its political and cultural ramifications still reverberate through American society.

By 1980, two presidents had gained office by running against sixties rebels. Between them they forged a new Republican majority that grows stronger with each passing election. Campaigning in 1968 to preserve "law and order," Richard Nixon warned that "the deterioration of respect for the rule of law all across America" was directly attributable "to the spread of the corrosive doctrine that every citizen possesses an inherent right to decide for himself which laws to disobey and when to disobey them." (To be sure, Nixon tried to justify his own illegal Watergate activities by citing as precedents the illegal student activities that he so vehemently condemned.) Two years later, Governor Ronald

Reagan of California spoke with evident outrage when he told a delegation of Berkeley faculty: "It all began when you didn't say No to students who believed they could break laws in the name of social protest." Nearly twenty years later, when Bill Clinton lied under oath to a grand jury to preserve his presidency, he vividly illustrated the corruption of means that was a legacy of the 1960s. Who, after all, better personified sixties culture—in all of its denials, circumlocutions, evasions, and tortured justifications for irresponsibility—than the first Baby Boomer president, also the first president in more than a century to be impeached?

The sixties are long gone, but the struggle over their meaning endures. For Bill Ayres, battered by the post-9/11 criticism that his memoir provoked, *Fugitive Days* was merely an attempt to explore "the intricate relationships between social justice, commitment, and resistance." For journalist Studs Terkel, Ayers's book was "a deeply moving elegy to all those young dreamers who tried to live decently in an indecent world." But dreams, we know, can become nightmares—especially when noble ends are undermined by corrupt means. Sociologist Alan Wolfe properly condemns the American left for "its fatal attraction" to the notion that worthy ends can justify reprehensible means. As a new generation of college students, children of the Baby Boomers, ponders these troubling legacies, it is revealing to see what lessons they can learn from what political scientist James Miller has aptly called the "overpowering moral hubris" of their parents' generation.

In the opening meeting of a course I teach on the sixties, I always ask students to write down one question that they hope to have answered during our time together. Explanations for assassinations and curiosity about the counterculture still rank high on their lists. But mega-questions of meaning occasionally intrude. Last year, a puzzled student wondered: "Why are the issues of the 60s still with us?" Queried another: "to what extent have the 60s been glorified by the Baby Boomer generation?" And another: "Why did the 60s end with the revival of conservatism?"

Just days after the recent presidential election, Daniel Henninger wrote in *The Wall Street Journal*, "The color-coding of the 2004 election began around 1965," when the generation of John Kerry, Al Gore, and the Clintons emerged as the best, brightest, and most idealistic in our history. (Anyone who doubts their claim need only ask them, or their avid followers.) But their children seem increasingly skeptical. Some of them are coming to understand that the answers to their compelling questions have much to do with the relationship of means and ends. If the prim morality of the fifties repels them they seem ready to relinquish the distorted romantic images of the sixties that they have imbibed with their parents' lattes.

24 · Thomas Friedman's Israel

Israel is a Rorschach test for American Jews. As an alluring symbol of Jewish authenticity, it has promised compensation for deficiencies in American Jewish life. But once reality in the Jewish state failed to confirm the throbbing fantasies of liberal Jews, they expressed their disillusionment with reflexive predictions of Israel's moral demise. Since 1977, when the election of Menachem Begin punctured some favorite liberal notions about the Jewish state, Israel has come to qualify as the latest "God That Failed"—the role formerly played by the Soviet Union in the Thirties and the United States in the Sixties. In the conventional cliché the once heroic Israeli David, as played by Paul Newman in *Exodus*, now is a menacing Goliath, the deformed progeny of Ariel Sharon and Meir Kahane. These days, "Hatikvah" sounds like a mournful dirge for what might have been.

Thomas L. Friedman's *From Beirut to Jerusalem* reiterates the familiar lament about the moral decline and fall of the Jewish state. That surely helps to explain its rapid ascent on the Best Seller list. Indeed, the book is likely to inflate this distortion precisely because Friedman brings to his task the impeccable credentials that are splashed across the dustjacket: "Two-time Pulitzer Prize-winning correspondent of *The New York Times*." Widely hailed—especially by journalists who share his bias—as the book to read about the Middle East, it has far more to say about the disillusionment of American Jewish liberals, like Friedman, whose fantasies about Israel have been frustrated by reality. His story contains few surprises. But its subtext, the subjective bias concealed beneath journalistic objectivity, gives the book a certain distressing fascination. At the very least, it explains how a liberal Jew from the American heartland, with a penchant for "evenhandedness" designed to cast Israel as a typical Middle Eastern crazy land, can persuade himself that "Israel and Lebanon, Jerusalem and Beirut, had more in common than I could have dreamed."

Friedman's dreams about Israel began on June 6, 1967, when Walter Cronkite, of all people, introduced the Minnesota youngster to "my Jewish identity." Until the Six-Day War, Friedman was a "three-day-a-year Jew," on Rosh Hashanah and Yom Kippur. Raised in "a rather typical middle-class American Jewish family," he believed in "a Judaism without land," or, for that matter, religion. He experienced only boredom or embarrassment from five

---

"Thomas Friedman's Israel," *With Friends Like These: The Jewish Critics of Israel* (1993), 59-74.

years of Hebrew school and summer camp, and his bar mitzvah. A victorious Israel, however, "made me feel different about myself as a Jew." Throughout high school, he wore Israel as "a badge of pride"; his vicarious identification was so strong, even "insufferable," that he relinquished his consuming dream of becoming a professional golfer.

Not yet thirty when the *Times* sent him to Beirut in 1982 (after a preliminary assignment for UPI), he divided a decade between Lebanon and Israel during the turbulent era that began with the Lebanese civil war and ended with the Arab *Intifada*. Friedman enjoyed the distinction of being the journalist selected to break the "old unwritten rule" at the *Times* of never allowing a Jew to report from Jerusalem. As Friedman tells it, his Jewish pride endured until September 1982, when it suddenly turned to shame. Sabra and Shatila, he writes, were "something of a personal crisis for me. The Israel I met on the outskirts of Beirut was not the heroic Israel I had been taught to identify with." Illusion and infatuation turned into outrage. Friedman, "boiling with anger," determined to "nail Begin and Sharon" and to "help get rid of them," wrote the four-page *Times* article that won his first Pulitzer. One week later, in an exclusive interview with the Israeli commanding officer in Lebanon, Friedman's rage was unabated. Banging his fist and shouting, he demanded an explanation for Israeli conduct. "But what I was really saying, in a very selfish way, was 'How could you do this to me, you bastards? I always thought you were different. I always thought *we* were different.'" The next day, Friedman "buried" the officer on page one of the *Times*, and "along with him every illusion I ever held about the Jewish state."

Thus the myth of Thomas Friedman's disillusionment was born, to be widely propounded after publication to propel his book up the Best Seller list. His "personal crisis," as the once "heroic" Israel stripped his "illusion" away, is by now an all too familiar cliché among leftist Jews who delight in presenting themselves as anguished innocents. Friedman, abetted by credulous colleagues who have swallowed his autobiographical pronouncements whole, has created a myth of personal disillusionment with Israel that is designed to lend credibility to his indictment of the Jewish state and, not incidentally, to conceal its ideological sources. As he writes, and endlessly reiterated in post-publication interviews, his is the story of "a Jew who was raised on…all the myths about Israel, who goes to Jerusalem in the 1980s and discovers that it isn't the summer camp of his youth." His gullible interviewers have embellished the tale. One of them, breathlessly anticipating Friedman's third Pulitzer Prize, listened deferentially to Friedman recount his "much deeper identification with Israel" after the Six-Day War, as the Jewish state became "a symbol of my own identity." Friedman's faith in Israel's moral rectitude endured, he claimed, until his "experiences as a reporter" in the Middle East undermined it fifteen years later. Then, according to still another interviewer fascinated by his lost "illusion," Friedman experienced "a remarkable transformation," indeed "a personal crisis." He watched "an Israel he had deeply believed in while in high school and college recede from gilded, heroic mythology to the shadows of bleak reality."

In fact, Friedman invented at least the timing of his conversion story, while remaining silent about the indisputable evidence of his own political bias that long antedated his professional career—and may, indeed, help to explain it. If he actually did plunge into a Gethsemene of crisis and transformation, it occurred well before he went to the Middle East as a reporter. Friedman's adolescent infatuation with Israel was distinguished by its brevity. By the time he graduated from Brandeis University in 1975, he had already identified himself with the Palestinian national cause, with apologies for PLO terrorism, and with the single organization so reflexively critical of Israel that it quickly became a pariah group within the American Jewish community.

During his final year at Brandeis, after returning from a summer of study in Cairo, Friedman belonged to the steering committee of a self-styled "Middle East Peace Group." It vigorously opposed the mounting storm of protest among American Jews (to be expressed in a "Rally Against Terror") over Yasir Arafat's impending appearance before the United Nations General Assembly. In November 1974, literally on the eve of Arafat's infamous declaration that "Zionism is racist," delivered while brandishing a pistol on his hip, the Peace Group published a statement. Co-signed by Friedman, it supported "Palestinian self-determination," the standard euphemism for a Palestinian state in the Land of Israel. It discounted repeated acts of PLO terror against Jews as "clearly not representative of the diverse elements of the Palestinian people." (No evidence of such diversity was cited, as though even its existence would matter to Jewish victims.) The Group joined Breira, already notorious for its endorsement of Palestinian aspirations and for the blame it placed on the United States and Israel for Middle East instability, in urging "a more meaningful and constructive approach" than protesting against Arafat or the PLO.

The Middle East Peace Group, co-steered by Friedman, continued to profess its "concern" for Israel by criticizing American "military and political elites" for reinforcing the strategic alliance with Israel. It cited a "Jewish liberal tradition [sic]" for its conspicuously New Left agenda: "the reordering of American domestic priorities." Among all the impediments to peace in the Middle East, not the least of which was unrelenting Arab hostility to the very existence of a Jewish state (expressed only a year earlier in the Yom Kippur War), Friedman's group could only locate the "dangers of U.S. power as a tool for forging peace." Since such absurdities were largely confined to an irrelevant academic precinct in Waltham, Massachusetts, there was no need for anyone but steering-committee members to take them seriously.

Friedman pursued graduate study at Oxford. "I decided to study with the masters of Middle Eastern Studies—the British." (British academics, like British Foreign Service officers, were hardly renowned for their sympathetic, scholarly interpretations of Israel.) There Friedman wrote his first newspaper articles and discovered his "calling as a Middle East correspondent." Nowhere does Friedman note, however, that when he arrived in the Middle East as a reporter, he had a well formed political ideology in place, with little sympathy for Israel within it. If he had a conversion experience, it had occurred long before—certainly no later than his senior year at Brandeis nearly a decade earlier.

Similarly, Friedman neglects to indicate that when he "buried" the Israeli officer in the *Times*, he simultaneously buried any claim to journalistic objectivity. Confessing that he was not "professionally detached" at the very moment when he wrote the articles that brought him professional recognition (what does that say about those journalists who bestow Pulitzer Prizes upon each other?), he concedes that "an 'objective' journalist is not supposed to have such emotions." But Friedman is nonetheless certain that "they made me a better reporter." Mercifully, readers are spared the process of self-exculpation that led him to this preposterous conclusion. Those with fewer illusions, either about Israel or about journalists, may be less persuaded by Friedman's claim.

In one of his most self-incriminating self-revelations (among several possibilities), Friedman describes the ruthless PLO pressure upon all journalists in Lebanon to heed the Arafat line—or else. Even if Friedman was already predisposed in that direction, as his Brandeis manifesto might suggest, it still must have been disconcerting to learn that the PLO was displeased with his dispatches. Indeed, Friedman (like any sensible person) "lay awake in my bed the whole night worrying that someone was going to burst in and blow my brains all over the wall." Hardly an unreasonable fear (although he is retrospectively inclined to downplay it by trivializing Arafat as the "gipper" and a "teflon guerrilla"). The next day, Friedman was advised by an Arafat spokesman "to do a little better in the future." Sabra and Shatila eased the task of compliance.

Friedman's anger at the Jewish state, perhaps fired by some remnant of adolescent passion—whether for or against Israel would be hard to say—virtually determined his Israeli sources. His discomfort with Israel was exceeded only by theirs. In Lebanon, his favorite military source was an American-born, Israeli captain who "knew a Vietnam when he saw one." Once Friedman reached Israel he was drawn, like a duck to water, to American immigrants, beset by suffocating idealism and guilty moralism, and to Israeli leftists, for whom the world ended when Likud came to power. Conspicuous among them was David Hartman, a Brooklyn-born, liberal Orthodox rabbi, whose endowed institute in Jerusalem has become a fashionable oasis for American academics yearning to discover Talmudic sources for their Jewish guilt. Not that Hartman has uninteresting things to say about Israel, nor, surely, did he lack skill in cultivating the *Times* as his international pulpit. But Hartman, joined by some other Friedman favorites—West Bank analyst Meron Benvenisti, political theorist Yaron Ezrahi, and Internist for Peace Laura Blumenfeld (Friedman's researcher and translator)—represent merely a cross-section of the Israeli opinion that flourishes within the narrow intellectual corridor that connects Mt. Scopus to Dizengoff Street. The Israelis—an overwhelming majority—who live in such places as Qiryat Shemona or Arad, outside his favored precincts, seem unworthy of Friedman's attention.

Friedman's preferred sources are tortured by their own utopian myths about Israel and Judaism; doubtless, this is why he prefers them. They are certain that "something had gone terribly wrong" in the Jewish state (as Hartman had earlier explained to Friedman's predecessor, David Shipler). They provide

Friedman with certifiably Israeli (best of all, in Hartman's case, Orthodox rabbinical) pegs on which to hang his critical judgments, without having to identify them as his own. For a dose of Israeli normality, Friedman turns to Zeev Chafets, another American-born journalist, whose cynical whimsy, delivered over drinks at the Bonanza Café in Tel Aviv, all but reduces Israel to a series of one-liners. By the end of his book, to document his assertion that Israel has become "a source of confusion" for American Jews (as it surely is for him), Friedman cites that renowned authority on Jewish angst, Woody Allen, whose *Times* Op-ed at the beginning of the *Intifada* will surely endure as a classic statement of self-pity among American Jews who identify as Jews only in order to criticize Israel when it embarrasses them.

Although Friedman once imagined that he was "more Middle East than Minnesota," his frame of reference always is "the Minnesota boy still in me." He retains the "innocent can-do optimism," based upon an "almost childlike belief that every problem has a solution, that people will respond to reason, and that the future can triumph over the past"—concepts which must flourish in Minnesota fairgrounds and country clubs. The Middle East, to Friedman's despair, is stubbornly "primordial" and "tribal," a place where, in such un-American ways, "the past had buried the future." Friedman seems altogether oblivious to the notion that Jews are endlessly instructed to remember their past, which serves both textually and liturgically to connect them, through time, to their shared history and destiny. Israel, after all, makes no sense without some comprehension of the historical memories, both ancient and modern, that lie at its core.

Friedman invariably dates creation from his own awakening in 1967. But historical amnesia is a debilitating handicap, leading to predictable distortions. Friedman diminishes, indeed virtually ignores, the unceasing Arab terror against Jews that long antedated 1967—part of the seamless web of Arab violence connecting past to present. Palestinian nationalism, he imagines, was "a direct result of the Israeli occupation"—a statement certain to cause the Grand Mufti, Yasir Arafat's inspiration and relative, to turn over in his grave. If it took Israel, after 1967, to "provoke Palestinians in the West Bank and Gaza into fully asserting their own distinctive identities," one wonders precisely what the Palestinians were asserting, with knives and guns, in 1929, again between 1936-1939, and during 1947-48. Even after 1967, when Palestinian assertion took a form that Friedman acknowledges—bombs in supermarkets, buses, cinemas, planes, public squares, and synagogues, punctuated by hijackings and murdered hostages—he can only comprehend that ruthless terror as "a continual poke in the ribs," presumably a minor annoyance which nonetheless "really got to the Israelis."

With the *Intifada*, Friedman suggests, there finally was a Palestinian "people"—so, of course, Israel, "through its repressive and humiliating treatment," deserves the dubious credit for creating it. The fact that the *Intifada* is merely the most recent Palestinian assault, in a continuing eighty-year history of Arab violence against Jews, escapes Friedman altogether. Transplanting the American Sixties—his own golden age—to the Middle East, he transforms stones and Molotov cocktails into "a new method of resistance—massive, relatively non-lethal civil disobedience." (What, after all, is more likely to elicit liberal guilt on behalf of Palestinians than their equation with civil-rights demonstrators demanding constitutional rights?) But what Friedman variously calls "civil disobedience," "massive non-lethal civil disobedience" (since non-violent just won't work), and "non-lethal civil disobedience" are nothing but euphemisms for violence. The stones, to Friedman, are merely symbols bearing a political message. The Palestinians are only trying to signal to Israelis their readiness "to live next door to them, if they would only vacate the territories and allow a Palestinian state to emerge there."

To be sure, the Palestinians never said so. Friedman concedes that whenever he asked them why they threw stones, "they did not reply by quoting Martin Luther King Jr." He recounts his dialogue with a Palestinian prisoner who, asked the question, candidly replied, "Because I didn't have a grenade." What does the *Intifada* mean, Friedman inquired. He was told: "We want our land back." Which land? "The land the Jews took in 1948"—not only Hebron and Shechem, or Jericho and Ramallah, but Haifa and Jaffa, Lod and Ramle. The Palestinians, according to Friedman's prisoner, want not to become Israel's good neighbor next door, but to obliterate the Jewish state.

Friedman is oblivious to the message. Even when a symbol, curiously resembling a stone, came smashing through his car window in Jerusalem, Friedman knew that "the Palestinian wasn't aiming at us specifically"—only presumably, at abstract Jews. His young daughter doubtless will be relieved to learn, some day, that the "lasting scar" to her psyche is also merely symbolic. Friedman might have better distinguished between symbols and stones had he not been so determined to evade his own identity as a Jew, in a part of the world where it could hardly be more consequential. When Lebanese, responding to his "Mediterranean features," would ask if he was of Arab origin, Friedman invariably replied, "I'm American. One hundred percent." Pressed further, he would only answer "Romanian!" Little wonder that "the gap between who I was and who many people assumed I was" created constant "tension inside my gut"—and, one suspects, in his journalism. His worst apprehension, understandably, was that he might be unmasked—as a Jew. Here again, he does not care to explore the implications of his deception for his objectivity.

It comes as no surprise, given his credulity toward Palestinians, that Friedman is incomprehending of Israeli mistrust of the PLO. Even after Palestinians have told him, explicitly, that they want a state from the Jordan to the Mediterranean, he wonders why Israelis are not persuaded by Arafat's ambiguous messages of peaceful co-existence. Why did they not respond more enthusiastically after the Palestinian National Council, in December 1988, "in very convoluted language, conditionally accepted UN Resolutions 242 and 338 and the 1947 partition plan—thus implying a recognition of Israel within its pre-1967 boundaries"? He seems surprised that Israelis—duly skeptical of a convolution based on a condition resting on an implication, punctuated by still another Arafat evasion—did not rush to embrace the PLO leader.

All of which, inevitably, raises the nagging issue of media bias. Friedman does not ignore the problem, and he even came—remarkably slowly, to be sure—to perceive it. His epiphany apparently occurred in London, while reading *The International Herald Tribune*. There he discovered that a front-page, four-column photo of an Israeli soldier collaring a Palestinian youngster during a routine security check merited only two small paragraphs on an inside page, although the picture virtually obliterated the story of that day's human carnage in the Iran-Iraq war. This "lack of proportion" actually startled Friedman—in March 1988, after nine years in the Middle East and his own rather substantial contributions to media disproportionality. He grudgingly concedes that "the spotlight on Israel has been so glaring at times that it has totally distorted people's ability to make sense of the Palestinian-Israeli conflict." To Friedman, however, the spotlight is only bright, not blinding; it distorts perception, but not reality; and then occasionally, not persistently.

Even so, Friedman is puzzled. What, aside from the obvious newsworthiness of "brutal and stupid" Israeli behavior, constantly thrusts Israel to the front page? After turning to Hartman and Ezrahi for their cosmic explanations of good and evil, morality and hope, messianism and biblical paradigms, Friedman attributes "this unique double dimension" (also known as an ordinary double standard) to "the historical and religious movements to which Israel is connected in Western eyes." The Bible, after all, is "the main lens through which Western man looks at himself and at the world. The Jews—the ancient Israelites—are the main characters in this biblical super story." Therefore, "what the West expected from the Jews of the past, it expects from Israel today." All journalists really want is for Israel to fulfill its biblical promise of justice and morality. Media anonymity for Israel would signify "that something very essential in Israel's character and the character of the Jewish people has died." Conveniently, the more unfairly Israel is scrutinized, the better it is for Jewish morality!

One lengthy example, among many in Friedman's book, demonstrates the absurdity of this analysis. The subject is Israeli military justice—actually, injustice. Friedman minutely recounts the Israeli policy of administrative detention (the incarceration of security suspects for six months without trial), and assorted due-process violations, with every Palestinian allegation taken at face value. Friedman, of course, sees through this "pretense of law," a prime example of the "moral double book keeping" that accounts for the "self-delusions" of Israelis. Only at the end of his long moral homily does he note, in a brief aside, that most of the convicted Palestinians actually "were guilty of planning or carrying out violent attacks against Israeli civilians." He then concedes that Israel's laws and courts indeed "created a restraining legal culture" on the arbitrary exercise of authority, precisely as laws and courts are designed to do. Furthermore, Israelis were fighting against "a community that itself was not playing by any rules." So the Israeli "legal veneer," dismissed with a Friedman sneer, "wasn't entirely a sham" after all. It just might have been instructive for Friedman to have examined the Palestinian rule of law, under which approximately one of every ten Palestinian deaths during the *Intifada* (by the summer of 1989, one in two) has resulted from a Palestinian "trial" (with what attention to Miranda warnings and Fifth Amendment guarantees can only be imagined), followed by summary execution. Unlike Israel, which does not permit capital punishment, the Palestinian legal system seems unable to tolerate anything less. There are, alas, no Palestinian "super stories" to warrant such critical scrutiny.

The issue of media bias, like Banquo's ghost, hovers over Friedman's book. The evidence for it that he provides, both advertently and inadvertently, amply sustains the most incriminating denunciations of what Professor Edward Alexander has aptly labeled "The Journalists' War Against Israel." Why were Sabra and Shatila "front-page news for weeks," when Israelis were indirectly involved, while the far more direct Lebanese involvement in the slaughter of four times as many Palestinians in those very camps, just a few years later, was all but ignored? One reason, of course, is that the *Times* had Tom Friedman "boiling with anger" about Israel and determined to "get rid" of its democratically elected leaders. Another might have something to do with the *Times*' own prolonged Jewish identity crisis. For decades, its publishers never wanted the paper to appear "too Jewish." They succeeded admirably. Anti-Zionism was a fundamental precept of *Times* editorial policy. Reporters named Abraham were given by-lines with their initials only. The documented Nazi slaughter of tens and hundreds of thousands of Jews was consigned, early on, to the inner pages, where it competed for space with stories of hijacked truckloads of coffee in New Jersey. Unlike the *Intifada*, the Warsaw Ghetto uprising was only sporadically reported; verified descriptions of Auschwitz did not make the front page. If Bible super stories make Jews such endlessly fascinating subjects, as Friedman claims, one is left to wonder why the media were so conspicuously silent during the Holocaust. Could it be that Bible stories, irrelevant when Jews are murdered by the millions, become compelling only when Jews act in ways that make liberal journalists queasy?

Friedman concludes his book, all too appropriately, with a quotation from Mark Twain's *The Innocents Abroad*. Friedman's innocent illusions about the Middle East, along with his golf clubs, always accompanied him on his journey. From his first moments outside Lebanon, when Israeli security officers "refused to believe that anyone could be arriving from Hobbes's jungle carrying a set of Wilson Staffs on his shoulder," Friedman always brought his American baggage with him. (As he wrote: "You can't come to a hockey game and expect to play by the rules of touch football; Middle East diplomacy is a contact sport.") Boasting of the success and comfort of American Jews, he retained the undiminished fantasy that the United States "has much to offer the Middle East" that could lessen its obsessive preoccupation with martyrs and messiahs. Precisely what? "Optimism," "truth," and, judging by Friedman's priorities, a healthy dose of recreational sports....

It is a fair guess that without the pervasive bias against Israel for which the media are renowned—inflating even the most mindless distortion into an eternal truth, Friedman's book would have sunk like a stone to the bottom of the well-stocked pool of anti-Israel polemics. Indeed, Friedman virtually disqualified himself, in public, as even a remotely objective analyst. Back in 1985, after the Shi'ite hijacking of a TWA airliner, he vigorously attacked Israel (on Israeli radio) for not releasing the 700 terrorists whose freedom the hijackers were demanding. Israel's refusal, he claimed, "certainly contributed to the hijacking" (as, certainly, a victim's body contributes to rape or homicide)....For sheer vulgarity, in the guise of evenhandedness, such characterizations of Israel are exceeded only by Friedman's own description of the Jewish state, in his book, as "Yad Vashem with an air force."

As for the "old unwritten rule" at the *Times* about not sending a Jew to Jerusalem—presumably lest his Zionist sympathies interfere with objective reporting—that, too, is a myth that can be exploded by ten minutes of investigative journalism. During the 1929 Arab riots in Palestine, the slaughter of more than one hundred Jews in Hebron and Jerusalem produced a stream of *Times* articles as hostile to the Zionists as they were indifferent to Jewish victims. The correspondent who wrote them, Joseph Levy, might as well have been Thomas Friedman's earlier incarnation. An American Jew, conversant in Arabic and Hebrew, he had spent years in Beirut before coming to Jerusalem, where he wrote for the *Times*, even conceding that if his efforts toppled the Zionist administration, so much the better. So the *Times* was needlessly concerned, half a century later, about sending another Jewish reporter to Jerusalem. In 1984, as in 1929, the assignment of a liberal Jewish journalist to the Holy Land virtually assured that the struggle for a Jewish national home would be insidiously undermined as part of "all the news that's fit to print." But who remembers Joseph Levy?

As for Thomas Friedman, perhaps it is sufficient to note that although you can take a nice Jewish boy out of Minnesota, you can't take Minnesota out of the boy. Many American illusions, Friedman's among them, have shattered on the reality that the Middle East is not the Middle West. Until that truth sinks in, however, journalists are likely to continue to bestow their most prestigious prizes upon colleagues who reiterate the current demonology about the Middle East, invariably at the expense of Israel. Thomas Friedman may remain a likely candidate for such awards. But his book suggests that in reality, if not in his own self-created mythology, journalism carried him further along the same path of ideological partisanship that he chose as an undergraduate—that of fellow traveler of the most ruthless and relentless enemies of Israel.

25 · Edward Said's Silence

Since 1967, there has been no more impassioned and articulate advocate of the Palestinian national cause, nor a sharper critic of Israel, than Edward W. Said, University Professor of English and Comparative Literature at Columbia University and, between 1977 and 1991, a member of the Palestine National Council.

From Said's uncompromising premise that Zionism always was a colonial and racist movement, it followed that "a largely European people" would come to Palestine, "pretend that it was empty of inhabitants, conquer it by force, and drive out 70 percent of its inhabitants." Israel, he has charged, was "the first theocratic state in the Middle East." Its laws exemplify "monotheistic xenophobia, exclusivism, and intolerance." In Said's indictment, Israel's crimes against the Palestinians have ranged from colonial exploitation, at the very least, to virulent ethnic cleansing.

Nothing has given more emotional bite to Said's jeremiads against Israel than his palpable personal identification with Palestinian victims and refugees. With passionate reiteration, Said has proclaimed his "sense of belonging to the Palestinian people" and displayed his "pain at their sufferings and defeats." For, as he said in an interview several years ago, "I am a Palestinian who was born in Jerusalem and was forced as a result of the 1948 Catastrophe to live in exile, in the same way as many hundreds of thousands of Palestinians were." In 1948, he wrote, "my entire family became refugees from Palestine." He has repeatedly conflated his life as "a Palestinian in exile" with "a condition that...includes the largest part of the Palestinian population."

Ever since Said returned to Jerusalem in 1992, for the first time in 45 years, the poignancy of his exilic narrative has deepened. Later that year, he noted succinctly: "I was born, in November 1935, in Talbiya, then a mostly new and prosperous Arab quarter of Jerusalem. By the end of 1947, just months before Talbiya fell to Jewish forces, I'd left with my family for Cairo." In a recent essay in *The New York Review of Books*, excerpted from his new memoir, *Out of Place*, he referred to the "wrenching, tearing, sorrowful loss [of Palestine] as exemplified in so many distorted lives, including mine."

Yet these various strands of Said's autobiographical narrative, as compelling as they are, raise some troubling questions of veracity. There is the clever

"Edward Said's Silence," *Congress Monthly* (Nov.-Dec. 1999), 12-14.

insinuation, which turns out to be false, that between 1935 and 1947 Said lived with his family in Jerusalem. And if the Said family left Jerusalem in 1947, as Said recounts, precisely how could they have been forced into exile "as a result of the 1948 Catastrophe"?

Edward Said's oft-told tale of his Jerusalem boyhood, his lost home, and his dispossession has now been exposed as a self-constructed myth—to put it most charitably. Writing in the September issue of *Commentary*, Justus Reid Weiner, a scholar in residence at the Jerusalem Center for Public Affairs and formerly a lawyer in the Israeli Justice Ministry, has virtually demolished Said's autobiographical claims which, upon Weiner's careful scrutiny, turned out to be "a tissue of falsehoods."

Edward Said was indeed born in Jerusalem in 1935. The Saids were there because they had decided that one "hospital disaster" in Egypt (the earlier death of an infant son) was quite enough. But on Edward's birth certificate, his parents identified Cairo as their permanent address, which it remained until his teenage years. Throughout his boyhood, Edward Said's immediate family—his parents, sisters, retinue of servants, and Said himself—resided in Cairo, where his father owned a lucrative office supply business.

The Said family "home" ("my beautiful old house") in the elegant Talbieh neighborhood of Jerusalem, it turns out, never was "his" house, nor had it ever been owned by his parents. (Title to the house, Weiner learned, had passed from Edward Said's grandfather to his aunt and her children.) Nor was that all. One could hardly invent a more poetically-just refutation of Said's claim of dispossession by the victorious Israelis than Weiner's discovery that the philosopher Martin Buber, who rented an apartment in the Said house, had actually been expelled from *his* Jerusalem home by none other than Said's aunt.

Indeed, at nearly every crucial point in Said's published accounts of his Jerusalem boyhood, Weiner has found substantial contradictory evidence. Said's father had lived in Egypt since 1926, and his mother moved there after their wedding. Cairo was "where Edward Said in fact grew up." The Said family hardly departed from Jerusalem as "refugees." Late in 1947, as intercommunal violence accelerated between Arabs, Jews, and the British Mandatory authorities, they left an increasingly volatile situation on their own volition to return to their home in Cairo. Said's anguished claim that "I lost—and my family lost its property and rights in 1948" in Jerusalem, it turns out, more accurately describes the family plight in Cairo. There revolutionary supporters of Gamal Abdel Nasser destroyed the family business in 1952 and subsequently nationalized Said family property.

In sum, Weiner concludes, Edward Said's "parable of Palestinian identity," ostensibly forged in the suffering inflicted by Israelis on his family and his people, is nothing more than "an artful lie; a skillful lie; above all a very useful and by now widely accepted lie—but a lie." Said may insist that the highest task of the intellectual is "to speak the truth, as plainly, directly, and as honestly as possible." But Weiner's evidence suggests that Said has preferred to invent memories of his "Jerusalem" boyhood, the better to align himself with Palestinian refugees whose dismal fate he never came close to sharing.

Edward Said, for so long an academic superstar and an icon on the Left for his sophisticated, and politically charged, cultural criticism (especially in *Orientalism* and *Culture and Imperialism*), has now been recast as a cultural symbol of a rather different sort. Rather than speak truth to power, it seems that he has spun a web of half-truths and untruths in service of the political cause that he belatedly embraced after the crushing Arab defeat in the Six Day War.

Could it be that Said's outpouring of Palestinian nationalist zeal after 1967 was driven by guilt over the premature departure of his family from Jerusalem twenty years earlier? With the decisive struggle over Palestine looming on the horizon in December 1947, it had been, to say the least, a rather conspicuous abandonment by the Said family of the Palestinian people in their time of gravest peril. What better filial retribution for the abject betrayal of Palestinians by the father than the fierce Palestinian ardor of the son?

If guilt over parental abandonment of the Palestinian people did not drive Said's carefully constructed Palestinian identity, what did? His newly-published memoir, *Out of Place*, is quite suggestive. It demonstrates, in language of genuine anguish, the deep and pervasive identity confusion that permeated Edward Said's immediate family. Although many members of the extended clan lived in Palestine, his parents' identity—who they were, where they lived, and where their allegiance was grounded—was anything but Palestinian, except by the accident of birth. Like parents, like son.

We are told that Edward Said's father "never much liked" Palestine. Born in Jerusalem, which "he hated," he had left as a teenager in 1911 for the United States, where he became an American citizen. Here he lived for ten years, long enough to claim forever after that America was "his country." Returning to Jerusalem in 1920, he relocated within a decade to Cairo, where his business and family life were subsequently grounded.

Edward Said's mother, born in Nazareth, was sent to boarding school and junior college in Beirut by her father, a Baptist minister who had been born in Safed and lived for a time in Texas. With her marriage to Wadie Said, she was "wrenched from a happy life in Beirut" to relocate to Cairo, where she lived for the next 20 years, returning to Lebanon, her true exilic home, shortly before her death.

Given the scrambled identities of his parents, "Edward" (as he invariably refers to himself to signify his discomfort with his "foolishly English name") grew up understandably confused about his own "exceptionally complicated background." Because the family was exceedingly affluent, it could afford annual three-month summer respites from the brutal Cairo heat in the hills of Lebanon. There were also visits to Jerusalem, which Said himself describes as "off-and-on sojourns in Palestine." The Saids may have been occasional sojourners in Palestine during Edward's boyhood, but Wadie and Hilda Said had left it behind for the greener pastures of opportunity in Egypt long before 1947.

Based on abundant evidence in his own memoir, Palestine hardly was, as Edward still claims, the place "I grew up in." If his memoir clarifies anything, it is that the Saids lived as wandering Arabs in the Middle East. Never at home anywhere, they invariably returned to their preferred "native environments" in Cairo and Lebanon. Palestine did not become Edward's "home" until long after it no longer was possible for him to return for yet another visit.

Israelis have endlessly tormented themselves with the question "Who Is a Jew?" It seems only appropriate, therefore, that Edward Said should leave us wondering, "Who Is a Palestinian?" His memoir is a lengthy, often tortured, meditation on his own convoluted encounter with precisely this question. It suggests that a declaration of "Palestinian" identity became irresistible once the Arab states suffered their humiliating defeat and the West, held hostage to the terror of Yasir Arafat, adopted the Palestinians as their favorite victims. But if Arafat (who was born in Cairo) and Said (who grew up in Cairo) personify the Palestinian cause, it may indicate that the more tenuous the connection to Palestine, the more fervent the affirmation of Palestinian identity.

In certain academic precincts, these days, every written text becomes merely another subjective "narrative" to be deconstructed at the readers' pleasure. The search for objective reality, for "truth," is airily dismissed, with evident embarrassment at the very idea, as camouflage for "hegemony" and domination. As Said himself writes, in the opening words of a first chapter of his memoir, "All families invent their parents and children."

After reading *Out of Place*, nothing seems more invented than Said's own Palestinian identity narrative. As compelling as it may be in service of the Palestinian national cause—and, not incidentally, in elevating Said's own international reputation as an intellectual-in-exile—it deserves to be read, like so many contemporary narratives of recovered memory, as a largely mythological construct.

Yet old narratives, however contrived they may be, die hard if they are repeated often enough. Consider some 30 compelling family photographs in *Out of Place*. These include Edward with his mother in the Mena House gardens in Cairo, Edward with his father on the beach at Alexandria, Edward with his family at the Giza pyramids, and Edward with his sister Rosy in Gezira Preparatory School uniforms on their Cairo apartment terrace. Only one of them, however, has been deemed worthy of reprinting. Both the *New York Review of Books*, when it published an excerpt from Said's memoir, and the *New York Times*, to illustrate its review, chose to display the photograph of Edward and his sister Rosy "in traditional Palestinian dress, Jerusalem, 1941."

It is, undeniably, a fetching childhood photograph. Rosy, silver bangles on her wrists, wears a beautifully embroidered dress. Edward, age 6, wears a long robe; his head is wrapped in a *keffiya*. It may or may not be significant, as a portent of future Palestinian proclivities, that Edward's right hand rests on the handle of a knife tucked into his belt, while his left hand holds a pistol. This "traditional Palestinian" photo certainly affirms the mythological narrative of Edward Said. But the Gezira prep school picture of young Edward, wearing his double-breasted school blazer, neatly-pressed shorts, and knee socks, is a far more faithful depiction of his most un-Palestinian boyhood in Cairo.

Edward Said has now lived in the United States for nearly 50 years. It is, however, but one more place where he has felt out of place, not home. Yet here, burdened by "the unsettled sense of many identities" and "the deeply disorganized state of my real history and origins," he finally reinvented himself as a Palestinian after the Six Day War. Then, for the first time, he experienced (as he writes in his *New York Review* excerpt) the "wrenching, tearing, sorrowful loss [of Palestine] as exemplified in so many distorted lives, including mine..."

The rest is not only history but, as Weiner convincingly demonstrates, mythology shading into mendacity. How ironically appropriate it is that Professor Said, so fond of deconstructing "narratives" written by others, should now have his own autobiographical "narrative" similarly shredded. More astonishing, perhaps, is Said's most uncharacteristic silence since Weiner's *Commentary* article appeared. From so eloquent and outspoken a man, so firmly committed to truth-telling, only this, in a *New York Review* footnote: "I speak, in this article and in my forthcoming memoir, only of my family as being refugees, not myself."

Edward Said, memoirist, meet the Edward Said who, in 1995, told an interviewer for *Al-Arabi*: "I am a Palestinian who...was forced as a result of the 1948 Catastrophe to live in exile, in the same way as many hundreds of thousands of Palestinians were." Regarding this critical autobiographical contradiction, upon which the entire edifice of his personal identification with the plight of Palestinians has rested, nothing speaks more eloquently than the sound of Edward Said's silence.

26 · The Corruption of Historians

Historians, like accountants, have been much in the news lately—for all the wrong reasons. Just as accountants are expected to get their numbers straight, historians are expected to get their facts and footnotes straight. The very least that professional integrity requires is honesty. For historians, this not only demands as accurate a rendition of the past as they can reconstruct, with fidelity to evidence that invariably is complex and even contradictory, but accurate citation of sources and, perhaps above all, rigorous self-scrutiny and truthful self-representation.

There is no firm of historians whose collapse can rival the recent demise of Arthur Andersen. But in their own individual ways, Joseph Ellis, Stephen Ambrose, Michael Bellesiles and Doris Kearns Goodwin have committed serious breeches of professional integrity—ranging from classroom dishonesty through plagiarism to outright fraud—that might even make an accountant blush. Within the past year, a litany of scandals has implicated two academic luminaries (Ellis and Ambrose), an aspiring star (Bellesiles), and a popular biographer (Goodwin). They have strayed so far from conventional norms of professional truth-telling as to embarrass all but the most cynical disciples of Clio.

It began during the summer of 2001, when the Boston *Globe* broke the Ellis story. Ellis, a highly esteemed historian, had within five years won both a National Book Award and a Pulitzer Prize. But in his Mt. Holyoke course on the history of the United States and Vietnam, Ellis had virtually transformed himself into James Thurber's Walter Mitty. He had regaled his students with tales—all fanciful—about his war-time military service as platoon leader, paratrooper, and staff member to General Westmoreland. He claimed to have been in My Lai shortly before the notorious massacre there. As one of his students recalled "That really left an impression on me and the class."

Not only had Ellis "served" in Vietnam while actually pursuing his Ph.D. at Yale and teaching at West Point, but he had "returned" to the United States disillusioned with the war effort. He was "the veteran who came back and participated in the antiwar movement," another student remembered. Ellis further burnished his heroic image with a claim of civil-rights activism; and, perhaps to prove that he was just a normal all-American boy, he even invented a game-winning touchdown in high school to leave Mt. Holyoke students agog at his

"The Corruption of Historians," *Society* (Nov.-Dec. 2002), 38-43.

range of heroic manly exploits.

The immediate response from the Mt. Holyoke administration to the *Globe* revelations was a mixture of denial and evasion. President Joanne V. Creighton wondered "what public interest the *Globe* is trying to serve through a story of this nature." An interest in truth seems never to have crossed her mind. The dean of faculty, who occupied the position that Ellis himself had held between 1980-90, sounded eager to exculpate his predecessor: "There's an element of great teaching that's theatre." Ellis, he noted, "has been a star, our star" ever since coming to the college in 1972. Clearly, Ellis's light was still shining brightly over the Pioneer Valley. It took historian David Garrow of Emory, another Pulitzer prize winner, to remind everyone that "knowingly being dishonest in class is... an act of moral turpitude" every bit as serious as dishonest writing.

As the Ellis story unfolded, it generated attention considerably beyond the pristine precincts of Mt. Holyoke. A number of certifiably real Vietnam War veterans expressed their outrage with "Fightin' Joe Ellis," whose pilfering of their own traumatic experiences gave new and distressing meaning to the concept of plagiarism. Ellis's uncanny ability to play both sides of the war, by offering military "service" and anti-war "recantation," rubbed even more salt in veterans' wounds that were still raw after more than thirty years.

In real life, as in his fantasies, Ellis had not been hesitant to employ history as a weapon to advance his preferred political causes. As a signatory (among 400 others) to "Historians in Defense of the Constitution," Ellis had urged Americans not to support the impeachment of President Clinton. Indeed, Ellis offered DNA evidence in support of the claim that Jefferson had fathered a child from an illicit relationship with his slave Sally Hemings. Ellis apparently saw Jefferson as a "character witness" for Clinton, welcome proof that "the primal urge has a most distinguished presidential pedigree."...

In the end, Ellis's punishment for knowingly lying to his students seemed less than draconian. Required to relinquish his course on the United States and Vietnam, he was also suspended for a year without pay. Not long after his suspension began, Ellis reportedly signed a $500,000 contract for a new book about George Washington, who, of course, could never tell a lie—at least according to the historically dubious account of his hagiographer, Parson Weems. Whether Ellis has rid himself of the curious attribute that he had assigned to Jefferson—his "internal ability to generate multiple versions of the truth"—remains to be seen.

Ellis, *Time* noted, is "one of the most widely read historians not named Stephen Ambrose." An appropriate introduction, indeed, to Ambrose himself, who has been accused of repeated acts of plagiarism in his recent work. Ambrose had made himself *sui generis* among American historians for his entrepreneurial zeal and the frenetic productivity that accompanied it. Author of twenty books in thirty years, and six best-sellers since 1994, he had long since left behind serious scholarship for $40,000 lecture fees, private planes, and presentation of himself as "the best selling author who served as historical consultant on

Spielberg's *Saving Private Ryan*."...

Early in January 2002, *The New York Times*, *The Weekly Standard*, and *Forbes* ran stories within days of each other documenting rampant plagiarism in his current best seller, *The Wild Blue*. It contained entire passages lifted from historian Thomas Childers's *Wings of Morning*, published six years earlier. Suddenly, there was a flurry of similar allegations about other Ambrose books. Joseph Balkoski, author of *Beyond the Beachhead*, read Ambrose's *Citizen Soldiers* and discovered that "The writing seemed very familiar, and much to my astonishment, it was my own." (Ambrose, it should be noted, had candidly acknowledged that he "stole material profitably and shamelessly" from Balkoski's book.) Author Sam Anson found passages from his own *Exile: The Unquiet Oblivion of Richard Nixon* in Ambrose's *Ruin and Recovery*. Other Ambrose books also fell under a cloud of suspicion over plagiarism.

Writing in *The Weekly Standard*, Fred Barnes presented parallel columns of text lifted by Ambrose from the Childers book. Such lugubrious sentences as these, for example, could hardly have occurred to two authors independently: "The bombardier, navigator and nose turret gunner were forced to squat down, almost on hands and knees, and sidle up to their stations through the nose wheel of the ship." Or: "The gunner climbed into the ball, pulled the hatch closed and was then lowered into position." Indeed, as Nicholas Confessore demonstrated, Ambrose not only incorporated the words of others in his books, but he was "an efficient and unabashed recycler of his own work."

Ambrose seemed not in the slightest chagrined, to say nothing of repentant, for his dereliction of professional responsibility. He defended his approach to *The New York Times* as entirely suitable for the creation of lively narratives for the enjoyment of ordinary people. "I tell stories," he explained."I am not writing a Ph.D. dissertation." His job, as he elaborated on another occasion, "is to explain, illustrate, inform and entertain."

There could be no quarreling with the entertainment that Ambrose provided. As even Childers conceded, "Veterans love him." One veteran asked, "So what if he plagiarized? Everyone plagiarizes to some extent." They cared as little about plagiarism as did Ambrose's publisher, Simon & Schuster, whose spokeswoman blithely proclaimed: "This doesn't affect his status as an important and original historian."

As far back as his very first meeting with Eisenhower, Ambrose seems to have grasped his lucrative potential: "I was filled with awe and reverence, all of that. But the emotion I felt above all was opportunity." For beneath Eisenhower and the other generals, as Ambrose came to realize, were the grunt soldiers and airmen whose voluminous oral history recollections could be converted into his own private pot of gold. Ambrose made his fortune telling war veterans what they most wanted to hear, in their own words, about bygone days of glory when they were very young and brave.

Beneath the radar screen of fame and fortune, but well within the parameters of scholarly notoriety, emerged Michael Bellesiles, professor of history at Emory University. His *Arming America*, published in 2000 by Knopf, had garnered rave reviews from professional and journalistic stalwarts such as Edmund Morgan in *The New York Review of Books*, Gary Wills in *The New York Times*, and, most euphorically, Jackson Lears in *The New Republic*, who praised his "debunking counter-narrative" and its "exhaustive research." It also won the prestigious Bancroft Prize awarded by Columbia University.

Bellesiles's message was undeniably appealing to the liberal academic community. He presented a convincing rebuke to the ingrained assumption of contemporary political conservatives that colonial Americans, accustomed to a culture of guns, had written the Second Amendment into the Constitution to protect the right of all Americans to bear arms. Challenging the accepted wisdom that guns had been widely owned in colonial America, Bellesiles offered an array of statistical data, ostensibly drawn from probate records and census returns, that made him, according to historian Michael Zuckerman, "the NRA's worst nightmare." Indeed, Bellesiles sharply criticized the NRA in his Introduction.

But the accuracy of Bellesiles's findings, and even the very existence of his sources, was challenged with devastating results. Indeed, his "exhaustive" research quickly exhausted scholars who tried to replicate it. According to Professor James Lindgren of Northwestern University Law School, "his errors in using sources are dramatic and go to the heart of his book's argument." Professor Don Hickey of Wayne State College (Neb.), who had peer-reviewed his earlier work, alleged that Bellesiles "misread, misused, and perhaps even fabricated some of his evidence." Professor Robert Churchill, writing in *Reviews in American History*, charged that Bellesiles had "mischaracterized, misrepresented, and sometimes grossly misinterpreted" the language of original sources to document his claim of gun scarcity in colonial America.

As it turned out, Bellesiles claimed to have examined records in San Francisco Superior Court that had been destroyed by fire in the 1906 earthquake. He was discovered to have examined nonexistent Rhode Island wills, altered the evidence available from Vermont probate records, and counted as old or broken guns not so identified in census records. When challenged to produce his notes, Bellesiles claimed that they had all been destroyed by a flood in his Emory office. True to form, he misdated the flood and falsely claimed that he was out of the country when it happened.

His account of the flood was labeled "fantastic" by a scholar who ingeniously tried to replicate on his own pads of paper the water damage that Bellesiles claimed to have obliterated his evidence. His research methodology was scathingly shredded as fraudulent in the *William & Mary Quarterly*, the preeminent colonial history journal, where he was accused of "repeatedly misquoting, distorting, falsifying, or perhaps even deliberately inventing evidence." His data were variously described as "incredible," "meaningless," "nonsense," and "mathematically improbable or impossible."

Months after the initial criticism had surfaced, Bellesiles was advised by his chairman to respond to his critics, which he did quite unpersuasively in the newsletter of the Organization of American Historians. Emory finally announced the formation of a faculty committee to investigate his work; that led, in turn, to the appointment of an outside examining committee. The result, according to David Skinner in *The Weekly Standard*, has been the "persistent avoidance of coming to any conclusion." Nor did Columbia display eagerness to reconsider its Bancroft prize award. The prize judges, supplied with critiques of the shoddy scholarship they had so generously rewarded, could only manage to decline comment.

Measured against Bellesiles, or even Ambrose, Doris Kearns Goodwin, who is not a trained historian but a popular biographer and frequent television commentator, seems almost innocent in the simplicity of her dishonesty. Like Ambrose, she retained a team of research assistants who conveniently relieved her of the task of doing her own work. Like him, also, she had appropriated the words of others without bothering to enclose them within quotation marks. Indeed, it was revealed that back in 1987, Simon & Schuster had paid damages to author Lynne McTaggart, from whose book (among others) Goodwin had plagiarized in her *The Fitzgeralds and the Kennedys*.

A subsequent Pulitzer-prize winner, and frequent guest on Jim Lehrer's *NewsHour*, Ms. Goodwin had become a media darling, with her enthusiasms ranging from the Kennedys and Roosevelts to the Boston Red Sox. When the allegations of plagiarism broke last spring, she used her appearance on Today to cite "mechanical problems on this one book." Then she accepted the verdict of her husband that she had done "nothing really wrong."

It was husband Richard Goodwin, however, who was wrong. Not only had Ms. Goodwin lifted as many as fifty phrases from McTaggart's biography of Kathleen Kennedy; she acknowledged (belatedly) that her research assistants had also found passages copied from other books. The problem, she claimed at first, was "having taken hand-written notes on the books"—something most historians have done for years without committing plagiarism. She subsequently blamed "the mechanical process of checking things," which "was not as sophisticated as it should have been." In sum, Ms. Goodwin, like Ambrose, had cut ethical corners in her rush to publication.

Yet, as Martin Arnold observed in the *Times*, both of them got off rather easily. Their books were still stocked and sold, while their publishers made the necessary excuses and apologies to protect their authors, investments and profits. Certainly Ms. Goodwin was a difficult plagiarist to dislike. Whether it was because she is a woman, or a nice person, or simply well connected in journalistic circles, especially in Boston, she was most vigorously defended.

Thomas Oliphant, Goodwin's *NewsHour* colleague and Boston *Globe* columnist, referred to her plagiarism as merely a "screw-up." Sociologist Amitai Etzioni, writing in the *Globe*, condemned the "witch-hunt" against her and pleaded for her repentance to be honored. Laurence Tribe of the Harvard Law School, a fellow liberal Democrat from Cambridge, maintained that her "inadequate sourcing dispute" did not detract from her role as "a distinguished historian." Dorothy Rabinowitz of *The Wall Street Journal* pilloried "the legions of the self-righteous now sitting in judgment on her."

The larger issue, however, is not who is the nicer plagiarist but how historical truth is to be protected from abuse, whether for money and fame, or from political partisanship. It is hardly confined to technique or technology, as both Ambrose and Goodwin claimed. For Ambrose, computers made cutting and pasting too easy; for Goodwin, however, notes made in longhand caused her difficulty. But assembly-line publication, as Martin Arnold suggested, is better suited to the production of toasters than books. And neither Ambrose nor Goodwin seemed to be in control of their own assembly lines. Nor was it merely a problem with the hired help; Bellesiles, after all, did his own "research."And even a most accomplished scholar, such as Ellis, was tempted into fictionalizing his own past in the classroom to burnish his image among students.

Yet once the dust of scandal settled, little seemed to have changed. Ellis, presumably invigorated by his sabbatical year and enriched by the publisher's largesse that accompanied it, is likely to return to his position of academic privilege at Mt. Holyoke, there to be admired by new generations of students. Ambrose and Goodwin will surely continue to publish and prosper. For Bellesiles, it is still too soon to say anything other than that no scholar with such dubious professional credibility has been given so many opportunities to explain and defend himself to so little benefit.

As information about these transgressions accumulated, I found myself alternately bemused and outraged. Like Ellis, I have taught American history for thirty-plus years at an elite women's college in Massachusetts; like him, also, I have long taught a course on the 1960s. And I am always aware, as Ellis surely was, that my students have an irrepressible interest in locating me within the events that we analyze together. How old is he, really? Is his beard a give-away? Where was he then? Was that him among the civil-rights demonstrators in the South, the student protesters at Berkeley, or the anti-war activists who marched on Washington?

Carefully disguising my past (and present) politics behind a Socratic screen, I have always waited until the last day of class to reveal the mundane truth: like the overwhelming majority of young Americans who came of age in the Fifties, as I did, or even in the Sixties (as many of the parents of my students did), I was a spectator, not a participant. Already past my adolescent prime at the time of the Sixties rebellions, I had been trained to learn by watching, not by doing. In the interest of full disclosure, I (truthfully) recount my pilgrimage in 1957 to Montgomery to hear Rev. Martin Luther King, Jr. preach a sermon at his Dexter Avenue church, and my belated presence at the fringes of two anti-war rallies a decade later. But although students are easily enthralled even by such meager reminiscences, it seems much too long ago, and much too little, to matter very much.

I am neither ashamed nor proud of who I was then. It was just who I was. I never felt even the slightest temptation to embellish my life for self-vindication or for the titillation of my students. Indeed, the brightest among them now seem increasingly suspicious, if not overtly hostile, toward the enduring romanticization of Sixties activism, for which they have little affection. They may have had enough of Baby Boomers who, nearly forty years later, still laud the range of excesses that were committed in the names of freedom and justice.

As a teacher of modern American history, I can easily comprehend the yearning for money and fame that must have driven Ambrose and Goodwin. Indeed, when I first entered the history profession, back in the mid-Sixties, I discovered to my dismay that all those slightly sleazy entrepreneurial types who I had hoped to avoid by rejecting a career in my father's business were already swarming through academe, angling for job offers, promotions and book contracts if they were young, and...editing multi-volume series of other people's work and scrambling for endowed chairs if they were nearing forty-five.

A decade into my professional life, I had the unexpected good luck to experience a sudden, and mercifully brief, elevation to what passes for academic stardom. After my book was reviewed on the front page of *The New York Times Book Review* (by Alan Dershowitz, who even then was already a celebrity), I watched myself instantly become commodified to suit the voracious needs of others. Suddenly I was certified by editors and TV hosts for a *Times* op-ed, an article in *Harper's*, and appearances with law-school deans who smoothly used my presence to proclaim, at some length, their own high-mindedness. The fickle spotlight of media attention, with the discomfort that accompanied my fifteen minutes of fame, quickly returned me to the task of writing books, not selling them.

But I must confess that I, too, once used my wife's editorial skills, along with my daughter's zeal for checking footnotes, to propel a manuscript toward publication. Even now, I often rely upon my son, an accomplished professional historian, to sharpen my prose and to alert me to trendy scholarship that I might otherwise miss. But plagiarism, for which I would instantly flunk any student, is something else. And, although Bellesiles and I both won the same professional prize at an early stage of our careers, I have never been tempted to invent or falsify evidence in the service of a personal or political agenda.

Personal impulses and lapses aside, can such professional corruption be historicized? Can we, that is, explain its recent proliferation by locating it in the context of time and culture? To be sure, four examples (or three, excluding Goodwin, who is not professionally trained as a historian) are a minuscule sample of a large, and largely honorable, profession. Indeed, if professional historians must be chastised, it is far likelier—as anyone who attends professional meetings or reads professional journals can attest—to be for their stodginess than for their flamboyant disregard of ethical proprieties.

Yet historians, like other professionals, have experienced the inevitable moral coarsening that can accompany the pursuit of fame and fortune, or tenure, in modern America. Just a century ago, Louis D. Brandeis, in some anguish, asked whether law was a profession or a business. If the answer was not already depressingly evident, he probably would not have asked. Of late, doctors, and now accountants, have confronted the same question. It just took historians a bit longer to get there, perhaps because the financial incentives for teaching and scholarship were so meager for so long.

Once the professional boondoggles—fellowships, travel grants, publisher's advances, lecture stipends, bidding wars, consulting fees, even celebrity status—beckoned, historians (who are, more or less, like other people) eagerly succumbed. The rise from rags to riches, after all, is so genuinely an American success story that it is unreasonable to expect historians, who know more about it than most, to exempt themselves. It is easy to forget, until it is too late, that the self-made man who, like Jay Gatsby (or Joseph Ellis?), emerges from a web of deception is likely to destroy himself along the way.

Beyond the corruption of money is the moral relativism that has penetrated academic precincts. Ever since the 1960s, when it became permissible to reject authority in order to pursue noble ends with corrupt means, American society has floundered in the backwash of moral contingency. Now everything is "socially constructed," invariably according to the endlessly regurgitated categories of race and gender. No longer are there bedrock truths, only personal choices. Unwanted criticism is quickly dismissed as inappropriately "judgmental." As history has disintegrated from factual authenticity into mere "narrative," the past has all but lost its authority to instruct. What, then, is there to anchor scholars—or anyone else—to norms of ethical behavior when the very notion of "norms" is obsolete?

Enter Bill Clinton, the political personification of these broader social trends. If the moral sleaziness of the Clinton years pushed conservatives over the edge, the Clinton impeachment process did the same for liberals. Led by Sean Wilentz (who lectured members of the Judiciary Committee on their Constitutional responsibilities as though they were his Princeton undergraduates), liberal historians rallied behind their maligned president. Wilentz, joined by Arthur Schlesinger, Jr. and C. Vann Woodward, sponsored "Historians in Defense of the Constitution," the petition signed by four hundred historians including Ellis, Ambrose, and Goodwin.

This may explain the alacrity with which conservative commentators pounced on the Fallen Four historians for their ethical improprieties. (Although Bellesiles was not a signatory, his attack on the NRA in the guise of exploring the original intent of the framers of the Second Amendment certainly qualified him for the liberal hall of shame.) It was payback time for Clinton defenders, for liberal historians whose own ethical lapses were placed on public display not long after their leader departed from Washington....

How gratifying it would be, after all these sordid disclosures, to discover that honesty still matters, even in academic circles. Yet it is precisely scholars who are the keepers of our national memory, whose writings and teachings instruct Americans about our past, who have so cavalierly traduced their responsibility to tell the truth. The corruption of historians, in the end, expresses the corruption of the very society whose "narrative" of dishonesty now implicates them.

27 · American Holy Land

From their earliest encounters with Pueblo Indians in New Mexico Territory, Anglo-American visitors chose biblical images to express their sense of wonder and enchantment. Instantly and reflexively, they tapped into the deepest source of American self-understanding: here, surely, was the last lingering remnant of the newly promised land, the biblical homeland in America. During more than two centuries of settlement, the yearning for an Edenic garden of new possibilities had propelled Americans in their relentless migrations westward. Late in the nineteenth century, the pueblos of the Southwest inspired the last best hope of return to the wellspring of American distinctiveness as a chosen people.

Even before the first Puritans set sail from England, the Hebrew Bible had begun to frame the American experience. In his farewell sermon to the intrepid English adventurers who were departing for America, Rev. John Cotton identified the Puritans' journey with the exodus of the Israelites from Egypt. On board the *Arbella*, John Winthrop reassured his uneasy companions that "the God of Israel is among us." Certain that they comprised a holy community, the new Israel, the Puritans arrived in the "howling wilderness" of Massachusetts Bay, a "desert" that must be transformed into "a land of milk and honey." As Puritan ministers incessantly instructed their congregations, "The Historie of the Old Testament is Example to us." Accordingly, "*Jerusalem* was, *New England* is, they were, you are God's own, God's covenant people." Cotton Mather succinctly proclaimed: "You may see an Israel in America."

In the New England wilderness, Edenic fantasies of biblical antiquity quickly yielded to the harsh realities of hunger, disease, and war. But the dream of a promised land for God's newly chosen people endured for centuries—and, for many Americans, arguably still does. In time, even before factories and railroads spewed the fire and smoke of progress upon the bucolic American landscape, old dreams were relocated to new frontiers further west. Driven relentlessly by their quest for personal salvation, whether they defined it in spiritual or material terms, Americans remained faithful to their special mission. Indeed, as literary historian Richard Slotkin has written, "to a people nourished on the lore of the Puritans,...the association of anything American with the biblical Promised Land and Chosen People was virtually self-evident." From the earliest

---

Explorers in Eden: Pueblo Indians and the Promised Land (2006), 1-14.

colonial settlement, "a special relationship" with the land of the Bible was an article of American belief: biblical metaphors, endlessly reiterated, "explained the United States as a new Israel, a New World promised land."

During the struggle for national independence, biblical metaphors were refurbished to suit revolutionary purposes. As Israel was remade from a holy community into "a commonwealth of liberty," George Washington became the American Moses, sent by God to deliver "the posterity of Jacob" from the "worse than Egyptian bondage of Great Britain." King George III, predictably, was variously compared to Pharaoh and Haman. Americans were reassured that "the star which rose from Judah lights our skies." When the revolutionary struggle faltered, a New Haven minister blamed the people for their own unrighteousness, which led them to "act over the same stupid vile part that the Children of Israel did in the wilderness." With independence assured, biblical parallels were even more stridently asserted. Just as David had prevailed in his struggle against Goliath, so "by a series of providential wonders have the Americans emerged from oppression and risen to liberty and independence." The Constitution was the "covenant" that secured divine favor for the new nation. As a "heavenly charter of liberty," according to Harvard president Samuel Langdon, it indicated that "God hath...taken us under his special care, as he did his ancient covenant people."

Biblical allusions came easily to the Founding Fathers. For the new national seal, Benjamin Franklin suggested Moses lifting his arms to divide the Red Sea, while Thomas Jefferson proposed the children of Israel in the wilderness, following pillars of cloud and fire. In his response to inaugural felicitations from the Hebrew Congregation of Savannah, President George Washington expressed his belief that the same God who had liberated the Israelites from their Egyptian oppressors had once again demonstrated his "providential agency...in establishing these United States as an independent nation."

Biblical metaphors and Holy Land references were sufficiently ingrained in American consciousness to reemerge episodically throughout the nineteenth century. The Mormons understood themselves as a covenant people, spiritually descended from the Israelites, whose journey through the wilderness was replicated in their own cross-country trek. Finally settled in their American Zion in Utah, they instantly recognized the resemblance of the Great Salt Lake to the Dead Sea. The Mormon town of Moab affirmed the geographical connection (just as Canaan in Connecticut and Salem in Massachusetts had done for previous generations of Americans). The Mormons hardly were unique in their reliance upon biblical typologies. African-American slaves found in the Exodus narrative a powerful source of inspiration in their struggle for freedom. Identifying themselves as a chosen people, they assumed divine favor in their journey toward emancipation. So, too, Mordechai Noah decided to build his biblical commonwealth of Ararat in upstate New York, while John C. Fremont described California as "the modern Canaan, a land 'flowing with milk and honey.'" And why not? As Herman Melville wrote evocatively: "We Americans are the peculiar chosen people—the Israel of our time."

After the Civil War, however, amid the turbulence of social change in an emerging urban industrial society, biblical analogies seemed increasingly tenuous. Cities and factories could not fit easily into a biblical paradigm, nor did hordes of new immigrants inspire confidence in a chosen American people. Religious orthodoxy began to yield to principles of modern criticism and scientific truth. Yet just when biblical imagery had begun to fade, travel abroad became more feasible, affordable, and safe, enabling Western visitors seeking exotic adventure and spiritual rejuvenation to visit the actual Holy Land. They were often disappointed. Mark Twain found it difficult to retain his sense of humor in so "desolate and unlovely" an outpost of the Ottoman Empire as Palestine, a land of "poverty, dirt, and disease," where ubiquitous beggars and lepers, eager for handouts, testified to the modern degradation of once sacred space. But Christian tourists to Palestine could still experience tremors of connection from their contact with an ancient, if sadly corrupted, incarnation of themselves. Travelers, observed a French visitor, "can always find in the retarded races" of the East "the living types of disappeared societies." After all, as Dr. Samuel Johnson suggested, "almost all that sets us above savages"—religion, law, the arts—came from the shores of the Mediterranean.

No matter how bleak Palestine might be in contemporary reality, it remained a "homeland of imagination" for Western visitors, stimulating nostalgic yearning for the "spirituality, wisdom, contemplative life, metaphysics, and emotion" of biblical antiquity. With the increasing popularity of photography in the second half of the nineteenth century, tourists could easily transform holy sites and local inhabitants into "the living traces of biblical times" to be preserved on film for showing and sharing. Three-dimensional stereographic images brought the Holy Land to Americans at home, stoking their yearning for holy places and images. In sporadic outbursts of "geopiety," elaborate replicas of Holy Land sites were constructed for public entertainment.

By the 1870s, Jerusalem and Bethlehem had become favored venues for Holy Land photography. Christian pilgrims along the Via Dolorosa, Orthodox Jews at the "Wailing" Wall, Arab street life in the Old City souk, and Bedouin nomads riding camels were familiar images. Rachel's Tomb competed in popularity with the Tower of David and the Church of the Holy Sepulcher as attractions for the photographer's lens. The renowned Bonfils Studio in Jerusalem popularized an emerging staple of Holy Land imagery: Arab women with their clay pots aesthetically displayed, lovingly touched, or gracefully balanced on their heads. To anyone familiar with the biblical narrative, these images instantly evoked Rebecca, so compelling a symbol of the innocence and purity of antiquity now irretrievably lost amid the poverty and squalor of Ottoman Palestine. Might the United States, "where freedom has fashioned a nation that is a suitable heir to the Holy Land," be an even more appropriate repository for biblical fantasies than the Holy Land itself?

So it was, far from Palestine, at twilight on a September evening in 1879, that Frank Hamilton Cushing, member of an expedition sponsored by the U.S.

Bureau of Ethnology to gather information about the Indians of the Southwest, arrived on horseback at the edge of Zuni Pueblo in western New Mexico. His gaze was riveted by the sight of women emerging from the well, "a picturesque sight, as, with stately step and fine carriage they followed one another up into the evening light, balancing their great shining water-jars on their heads." As he watched, the focus of his reverie sharpened: "A little passageway through the gardens, between two adobe walls to our right, led down rude steps into the well, which, dug deeply in the sands, had been walled up with rocks, like the Pools of Palestine."

For this awestruck twenty-two-year-old explorer, it was a stark moment of cultural encounter: a young man descended from the venerable Cushing family of New England that traced its origins in America to the pioneering settlers, extracting from virtually his first contact with the native peoples of the Southwest an instant evocation of the Bible and Holy Land imagery. Cushing's account of his introduction to Zuni, published in *Century Illustrated Monthly Magazine*, was accompanied by an evocative sketch of the pastoral scene that he described.

In the lush foreground, three women, two with water-jars on their heads, emerge from reeds by the well. A small flock of goats grazes nearby. Behind them, in the distance, is Zuni Pueblo, an enclosed village accessible only through a narrow gate. The drawing, entitled "Pool of Zuni and Water-Carriers," invites comparison to those sketched by David Roberts or William H. Bartlett, artists whose languid depictions of Holy Land scenes stoked the nostalgia of nineteenth-century Anglo-Americans for the spiritual nourishment of sacred antiquity.

Cushing's encounter at Zuni revived the faded dream of America as an Edenic paradise, ancient Israel renewed. If not in the teeming cities and fiery factories of the East, then in the pueblos of the Southwest, among native tribes of whom most Americans were completely oblivious, might the biblical promise to the American people still flicker? Indeed, for the next sixty years an intriguing cohort of American explorers would discover in the pueblos, or imagine there, the deep spiritual allure of biblical antiquity converging with American history. Among the Pueblo Indians, they found an elixir for their discontent with the world of modernity they yearned to escape, a source of inspiration for their Edenic fantasies of regeneration....

Cushing imagined that he had entered a time warp in Zuni, a community governed by tradition and custom expressed in sacred rituals unchanged for centuries. In these religious ceremonies, Cushing observed, "the Zunian throws off everything foreign," retaining only what was indigenous to the tribe. Like so many of the Anglo explorers who followed him to the Southwest, Cushing failed to comprehend how much of indigenous Pueblo culture had been penetrated and transformed by Spanish conquistadores and missionaries during nearly three centuries of occupation. He could imagine that he was the first Westerner since Cabeza de Vaca to gaze upon these pristine communities, so isolated from modernity that they might even inspire dreams of return to an imagined biblical past. Yet Cushing had barely arrived before he perceived the vulnerability of

Pueblo culture. "My anxiety would not be so great were there not a probability that I am among the last who will ever witness all this in its purity," he explained to his supervisor at the Smithsonian Institution. "The proposed advent of the Rail Road next fall, will, with its foreign inflow, introduce all sorts of innovations."

Indeed, Cushing had arrived in Zuni when the Southwest was on the cusp of discovery, exploration, and development by Anglo Americans. Within another year, precisely as he anticipated, the Atchison Topeka & Santa Fe Railroad cut across New Mexico, inexorably linking the pueblos to the new economy and society of Gilded Age America. Before the century ended, Pueblo Indians were discovered and popularized as inspirational and marketable symbols of "America's ancient, unspoiled past" a past whose spiritual antecedents were located in the Bible. In Zuni and Acoma, in Taos and Laguna, and in the Hopi pueblos of Walpi and Oraibi in northeastern Arizona, time had apparently stood still for centuries. Here was the world of premodern virtue—with self-contained villages, sacred rituals, self-reliant farmers, and skilled craftspeople—doomed to imminent oblivion by the relentless materialism of an encroaching urban industrial society. "As exemplars of a natural life thought to be pure and unchanging," historian Philip Deloria writes, "Indians were among the most important symbols used to critique the modern." Especially in the pueblos, they were invested with the power to evoke "a nostalgic past more authentic and often more desirable than the anxious present."

The Zuni of Cushing's imagination, historian Eliza McFeely has observed, was "frozen in time, caught in a moment before contact with the culture of the United States changed it forever." But the arrival of the railroad, a streamlined symbol of the new American industrial colossus, destroyed the imagined purity of Pueblo culture. Reaching Gallup, just north of Zuni, in 1882, it brought a "foreign inflow" to the pueblos. Many of these new visitors, like Cushing himself, were eagerly in pursuit of that elusive "lost moment in the American past" before modernity intruded. But Cushing understood, better than most, that their very presence—and, by implication, his own—would relegate it to oblivion.

The discovery or, more precisely, creation of the Southwest as an American Eden was the spontaneous response of many people at a particular historical moment. In the 1880s, Americans were conspicuously ambivalent about modernity, every bit as unsettled as they were inspired by its machine-made wonders. Amid late Victorian optimism about the new industrial society, there were "undercurrents of doubt and despair" among the members of older professional elites with reason to fear their own diminishing power in the new world of industrial tycoons, political bosses, and foreign-speaking immigrants. Many educated, middle-class Easterners, predominantly Protestant males, felt squeezed by concentrations of economic and political power, and demographic changes, over which they had no control. Confronting what historian T. J. Jackson Lears has aptly called "a crisis of cultural authority," these "antimodern dissenters" searched in memory and geography for alternatives to modernity, taking refuge in the past, in exotic lands, and among native peoples.

The American Southwest, and the Pueblo Indians who lived there, could satisfy these yearnings. Here was an unexplored land, the last vast "empty" space within American continental boundaries, inhabited by peaceful tribes who lived completely isolated from modernity, enclosed by languages and rituals that only a handful of Anglo-Americans had ever encountered, no less penetrated. An American aesthetic sensibility that was sufficiently eclectic toward the end of the nineteenth century to embrace Gothic architecture, Japanese art, Buddhist spirituality, and artisan craftsmanship—indeed almost anything that expressed what Lears calls "the healing wholeness of primitive myth"—could not help but be enchanted by Pueblo Indians. They seemed to retain precisely what many Americans had lost and wished desperately to recapture: the (imagined) organic unity, spiritual wholeness, and moral integrity of premodern society.

Just a few years after Cushing visited Zuni, the "barren magnificence" of New Mexico evoked for writer Susan Wallace (whose *The Land of the Pueblos* became an early compendium of Pueblo lore) "the land once the glory of all lands," biblical Palestine. There was "much," she insisted, "to remind us of Bible pictures; the low adobe houses, the flocks with the herdsmen coming to drink at the shallow stream, the clambering goats in scanty pastures high up the rocks." In the arid Southwestern desert, she saw abandoned villages that reminded her of "the desolation of Zion." Pueblo men, she observed, used farming tools that resembled "the oriental implement in the days of Moses." Like Cushing and Baxter, she was captivated by women "carrying water-jars on head or shoulder, like maidens of Palestine." In these Pueblo women, Wallace saw "the veiled face of the gentle Rebecca."

But a "deep sense of foreboding" afflicted many Americans at the end of the nineteenth century. As Frederick Jackson Turner declared at the Chicago Exposition in 1893, reading a paper that redefined the writing of American history for decades to come, the frontier—and with it the meaning of the American experience as a promised land—had vanished. Modernity and "progress" meant that the promise of a second chance on the Western frontier, the shimmering possibility that lay at the core of the American dream ever since the earliest settlements, was gone forever. From John Winthrop's vision of the "City on a Hill" to Turner's lament over the closing of the frontier, Americans—and those who aspired to become Americans—had been prepared to leave their homes to strike out for new, and seemingly limitless, possibilities. As long as there had been virgin land to explore, to conquer, to settle, and to develop, that dream endured. Until the 1890s, Americans had never confronted geographical boundaries that closed off the timeless future of hope and possibility. Now, with evident uneasiness, they did.

Like the closing of the frontier that Turner popularized, the "vanishing" American Indian was a staple of *fin de siècle* nostalgia. In the Southwest, photographers and artists discovered a new "Eden," a place of extraordinary beauty where Pueblo Indians lived as Americans imagined their own spiritual ancestors had lived, in an Arcadian golden age before modernity intruded. As a Taos artist explained, "the manners and customs and style of architecture are the same today that they were before Christ was born. They offer the painter a subject as full of the fundamental qualities of life as did the Holy Land of long ago." Pueblo Indians wrapped in blankets were even more artistically evocative than Arabs wearing *keffiyas*, and easily interchangeable with them.

To those Americans for whom progress meant decline—whether defined as the loss of community to urban sprawl and anomie, or the submission of workers to factory discipline—Pueblo culture offered an enticing leap backward in time, a return to what was indigenously "American," in a place settled long before the first colonists reached New England and the inexorable corruption of "civilization" began. Longing for a recoverable past, Americans would discover in the Southwest "a special American precinct—the nation's exotic, the faraway nearby." Pueblo Indians, still untouched by modernity, epitomized the primitive virtues that have always retained their appeal to overcivilized peoples. "It is through communication with the primitives of past and present, and with our own primitive possibilities," writes Eric R. Wolf nostalgically, "that we can create an image, a vision, a sense of a life once led by all men and still lived by some, a life richer and more intricately human than their own."

Unlike the Plains Indians, those "noble savages" whose defeat in battle and confinement to reservations served the greater glory of American manifest destiny, Pueblo Indians were perceived as settled and pastoral, law-abiding, and self-governing—a gentle people who remained "devotees of peace and order." They were promoted to a receptive public as "Indians who are neither poor nor naked; Indians who feed themselves and ask no favors of Washington; Indians who have been at peace for two centuries and fixed residents for perhaps a millennium; Indians who were farmers and irrigators and six story house builders before a New World had been beaten through the thick skull of the Old. They had nearly a hundred republics in America centuries before the American Republic was conceived." Reviving the promise of American life, they seemed even more genuinely American than modern Americans themselves. Might they become a vital source of American rejuvenation, even salvation?

Visitors encountered the Pueblo peoples through the lenses of their own fanciful projections. A provincial American might experience a pueblo "as foreign of atmosphere as Egypt is," where even horses treading grain resembled "the unmuzzled oxen of Scripture." And "Rebecca at her well was not a fairer sight, we fancied, than some of those Indian maidens in their picturesque pueblo dress." To Anglo men, the appeal of Pueblo culture might be found in the clarity of its gender divisions at a time when the "proper" roles for men and women in American industrial society had become problematic and contested. In the pueblos, wrote Charles Francis Saunders, "the old-fashioned partition of life's labors between male and female is as it was in the days of the ancients." In an era of heightened gender fluidity, it could be reassuring to discover a place where men worked in the fields and women baked bread, where men hunted for meat and women cooked it, where men built homes and women plastered them, where women were potters and weavers while men were free to be men.

Early photographs of the Southwest conveyed these stereotypical images to Americans who were just beginning to perceive the world through the camera eye. That land, as Christopher Lyman wrote in his study of the photography of Edward S. Curtis, was "the Garden of Eden which many wanted to believe existed, a magnificent panorama of 'views' seldom marred by the mundanities of everyday life." Curtis was pre-eminent, but hardly alone, in transmitting Edenic vistas through his camera. Other contemporary photographers shared his sense of an Indian population verging on imminent disappearance, whose lives must be preserved—at least on film—lest they be forever lost. "In a remarkably short time," warned Frank A. Rinehart (who learned his photographic technique with William Henry Jackson, perhaps the foremost Western landscape photographer of his time), "education and civilization will stamp out the feathers, beads and paint—the sign language, the dancing—and the Indian of the past will live but in memory and pictures."

In what has come to be identified by contemporary scholars as the "construction" of the Southwest—from a barren desert wasteland into a major tourist attraction—the intrusive Santa Fe Railroad found an eager partner. Fred Harvey was an immigrant from England whose business acumen, perhaps more than anything else, stimulated public interest in the Southwest and its native peoples. By the end of the century, his aesthetic vision and entrepreneurial genius had all but transformed the Southwest into the last repository of American promise, an Edenic paradise populated with indigenous Americans whose lives exemplified the lost virtues of premodern America. "Inventing" the Southwest as a marketable commodity for tourists, Harvey introduced Pueblo Indians to eager American travelers and propelled native crafts—and the women who made them—to national attention.

An emerging urban middle class, with money to spend, leisure to enjoy, and cultural ambitions to satisfy, embraced rail travel to newly accessible exotic places. Once the Santa Fe Railroad opened isolated pueblo villages to the outside world, the Fred Harvey Company did the rest, enticing travelers with comfortable accommodations, quality food, and attentive service. It shrewdly capitalized on the growing popularity of the arts and crafts movement, with its emphasis on human creativity rather than machine-made products, to make Indian crafts both desirable and accessible to American consumers and collectors. The Fred Harvey Company and the Santa Fe Railroad cultivated relations with an expanding circle of artists in Santa Fe and Taos who were eager for freedom from traditional aesthetic constraints and promoted tourism with paintings of the natural beauty of the region and its exotic native inhabitants.

As the Fred Harvey Company stimulated the burgeoning ethnic arts and crafts markets of the Southwest, pueblo dwellers confronted the inexorable commercialization of their culture. As tourism to New Mexico increased in popularity, "exotic but docile Indians proved profitable." Lorenzo Hubbell, owner of a trading post at the gateway to the Hopi pueblos in northeastern Arizona, brought the potter Nampeyo to Harvey in 1904 to demonstrate her talent. Harvey installed her in his Grand Canyon lodge, where she gained national renown as the most artistically creative Hopi potter. The convergence of craft and commerce, native artisan and Anglo merchant, inaugurated the successful marketing of the Southwest, which has flourished ever since.

After World War I, for an array of cultural and personal reasons, women began to discover the possibilities of self-redefinition in the Southwest. Amid postwar disillusionment with American society and deepening feminist consciousness, women dramatically transformed the pueblos from places of missionary and teaching opportunity into feminist utopian communities. Pueblos attracted Anglo women, especially from the East Coast, who were seeking to elude the class and gender constraints of their upbringing, while gaining recognition for their intellectual abilities, cultural sensitivity, and entrepreneurial skills. They, too, used Pueblo culture as a projection screen for their own yearnings and struggles.

Elsie Clews Parsons, an outspoken feminist and anti-war pacifist, was attracted to anthropology as an instrument of social reform and personal liberation. She would abandon New York, she told her husband, for "Negroes and Indians." Especially Indians, she conceded, for the "tangle and fusion" of cultures in the Southwest intrigued her. Accompanied by Professor Franz Boas of Columbia University, the foremost American anthropologist of the early twentieth century, Parsons journeyed to the Southwest. Their experiences blazed a trail for a cohort of Boas's most talented female graduate students—including Ruth Benedict, Ruth Bunzel, and Esther Schiff—whose landmark studies emerged from their pueblo fieldwork. Their efforts to elude the constraints of family, gender, and culture made the distant and remote Southwest—with its natural splendor, tri-cultural (Native, Spanish and Anglo) population, and matrilineal patterns of pueblo life—uniquely appealing to young professional women coming of age in the postwar era.

Aspiring anthropologists were not the only women to become enthralled with Pueblo Indians. Mabel Dodge, born into a wealthy Buffalo family that prepared her for high society, marriage, and motherhood, had rebelled at an early age to redefine herself as a New Woman. After a seven-year sojourn abroad, she returned to the United States in 1912 to discover the sordid ugliness of American capitalism. Retreating to her Fifth Avenue townhouse, where she hosted her famous salon, she attracted disaffected artists and intellectuals who shared her despair about American society. In 1917, shortly after she married Maurice Sterne, a medium predicted that she would soon find herself surrounded by Indians.

In the Southwest, where she was drawn to the "quietude and nobility and wisdom" of the Pueblo Indians, she imagined "a garden of Eden, inhabited by an unfallen tribe of men and women." Taos represented her last, best hope to escape the torments and constraints of modern civilization. There she was attracted to Tony Luhan, a Taos Indian who looked "like a Biblical figure." The religion of white people, Tony told her, was machinery; but the religion of Indians was "Life." Choosing life, Mabel settled in Taos with Tony, immodestly offering herself as a model of "cultural renewal for the dying Anglo civilization." There she would live out her life as a "tourist" in "the Garden of Eden," generously supported by her trust fund and eagerly sharing the allure of the Southwest with legions of disaffected visitors from various decaying precincts of Western society.

Amid the hard times of the 1930s, Edenic fantasies about the pueblos began to wane. Ruth Benedict's *Patterns of Culture*, based upon her research in Zuni, was published in 1934 to rave reviews. Georgia O'Keeffe painted the Southwestern landscape, and Laura Gilpin photographed Pueblo Indians. But utopian dreams were deflated by the grim realities of the Great Depression, when fewer Americans could afford the luxury of travel. An Indian arts and crafts movement remained centered in Santa Fe and Taos, but the Fred Harvey Company, like other businesses, fell on hard times. The romance of the pueblos faded.

In recent years, however, the pueblos have attracted attention from a new generation of feminist scholars. Whether studying their predecessors who did fieldwork in the Southwest, exploring the "construction" of the Southwest by rapacious American business interests, or analyzing the "fetishization" of Pueblo women by patriarchal photographers, artists, and salesmen, these scholars have restored the pueblos to a conspicuous place in the literary imagination. "Something about the Southwest," writes one of them, has "attracted independent, unconventional women." The Southwest offered "sexual and intellectual freedom" that could not be found elsewhere in the United States, and a strategic vantage point for cultural criticism. For these academic women, working with Pueblo Indians provides "an escape from mainstream society and an active political statement."

Ever since Cushing's arrival in Zuni first provoked interest in Pueblo Indians, explorers and visitors have brought their own cultural assumptions—along with their personal frustrations, aspirations, and yearnings—to the Southwest. Largely oblivious to the deep penetration of Spanish culture in the pueblos, they imagined a pristine people untouched by foreign influences. For many of them, Pueblo Indians symbolized the last, best opportunity to discover, if not actually preserve, something indigenous and vital in American life—or, at least, in their own lives—before the inexorable corruption of "civilization" destroyed it forever. Longing for an unrecoverable past, or a revitalized future, they discovered in the Southwest new possibilities, for their nation and for themselves, that could not be found elsewhere in the United States. In their imaginations—whether framed by the Bible, their frustrations with American society, or their own gendered aspirations—Pueblo Indians became inspirational symbols of personal salvation and cultural redemption.

From the moment when Cushing's exploits first captivated the American public, Southwestern pueblos offered an enticing alternative to modernity—the Garden in its innocent purity, just before the corrupting intrusion of the Machine. Determined to explore, understand, document, market, or merely encounter Pueblo culture before it disappeared forever, adventuresome Americans who went to the Southwest have much to tell us still, not only about Pueblo Indians but about themselves—and who we are as a people.

IV · Reflections

I joined the Wellesley College faculty in 1970. Two years later I visited Israel for the first time. The unexpected conjunction of these two experiences was formative. Four decades at Wellesley, punctuated by frequent visits to Israel (including two year-long sabbaticals in Jerusalem), not only provoked sustained self-reflection about my Jewish identity but, along the way, profoundly transformed it.

As a Jewish male I always remained an outsider to Wellesley's female and traditionally Christian (now fashionably multicultural) ethos. But my marginality inadvertently accelerated my self-definition as a Jew. Confronting entrenched, if usually discreet and polite, anti-Semitism, I encountered administrators and colleagues whose discomfort with Jews (and, occasionally, overt hostility toward them) was evident. My Jewish colleagues, with few exceptions, were distinguished by their silence amid the anti-Semitism that surrounded them. They enhanced my understanding of the question posed by the great sage Hillel: "If I am not for myself, who will be for me?"

If Wellesley left me out, Israel drew me in. I was too much the American outsider ever to embrace Israeli culture. But my encounters in Israel with Jewish history, Jewish life, and unapologetic Jews encouraged me to retrace the formative journeys of my people: through the Sinai desert to the mountain of revelation; to Jericho and through the Judean wilderness to Jerusalem; to the burial tombs of the biblical patriarchs and matriarchs in Hebron; to the Temple Mount and Western Wall; and within shtetl neighborhoods where I encountered the ghosts of my own ancestors. In Israel a wandering American Jew finally returned home.

Brief personal reflections, including a tribute to the desks that were my constant writing companions and my valedictory to teaching, conclude this volume. Relinquishing my academic position after forty-six years of teaching was not difficult; it was time. But I knew that I would miss students whose eagerness to question, to think, and to learn had preserved the cherished legacy that I had inherited from my own teachers.

28 · Jacob's Voices

Jacob, my grandfather, came to visit when I was four years old. I still remember his austere gentleness. He sat, silent and erect, in the sunlit front room of our modest apartment in a two-family house in Forest Hills. Although his words and gestures quickly evaporated, my vivid memory of Jacob endured. Occasionally, I reminded my father of his father's visit—an implicit plea, surely, for Jacob to return. But Jacob never came again.

Whenever I asked about Jacob, my father seemed bemused. Each time, with a touch of impatience, he would remind me that Jacob had died thirteen years before I was born. That silenced me until—months or even years later—I tried again. My father never understood my insistence upon a visit that could not have occurred. And I remained puzzled, and hurt, by his denial of an encounter that was deeply etched in my memory.

My father and I were both right. Jacob may have died long before he came to see me, but his visit was as real as anything in my childhood. It simply made no sense to me that my own grandfather, after whom I was named, would vanish forever before we even met. I made my peace with adult reality, but I refused to relinquish the wish for Jacob that my memory of his visit so wistfully expressed.

I might have asked my grandmother Minnie, Jacob's widow, about my absent grandfather. As a young boy I knew her slightly from our occasional visits to Pittsburgh (an overnight train ride from New York) during the last years of her life. By then, she was a tiny, wrinkled woman, her white hair pulled back into a tight bun. Once we stayed in her small apartment, where she spoke to me incomprehensibly in Yiddish. The next time, after she had moved in with my father's brother and his family, she was completely withdrawn, a spectral presence burdened by age, memory, and sorrow. We viewed each other warily and silently. The last time, in a nursing home after her leg had been amputated, I was too terrified for anything but a glimpse of her, by then a tiny, broken bird, staring soundlessly, awaiting the imminent end.

Like my grandparents, all my elderly American aunts and uncles were immigrants from Russia or Romania. The women, vivacious and ample, wore their long hair in elaborately braided buns and cooked the same indigestible dinners. The men, stolid and bald, always seemed most relaxed in their suspenders, suit jackets, and watch chains. Their names, like their overstuffed, airless apart-

---

Jacob's Voices: Reflections of a Wandering American Jew (1996, 2010), 1-3, 10-13, 15, 22-26.

ments, were virtually identical. Anna and Sam, who owned a small drug store in Philadelphia, were known by the family name "Winokur," to distinguish them from her brother Sam, whose sister Annette, with her husband Morris, owned a small laundry on West 111th Street, literally in the shadow of the massive St. John's Cathedral. Looming across Amsterdam Avenue, it was a forbidding fortress of Christianity which, in my childhood imagination, menaced our entire family.

Not only were my relatives generationally distant; they were culturally foreign. Just how foreign I learned during a shared moment of family trauma, late in World War II. My mother's brother had just been drafted into the army. Our extended family gathered in my grandmother's living room in Philadelphia to lament his fate. (And, I subsequently learned, to berate the Christian neighbors whose irritation with his draft-exempt status had prompted the local draft board to reassess his deferment.) After some hushed conversation over tea, brewed in the Russian samovar that was the family icon of my childhood, my grandmother and her sisters, spontaneously returning to the Odessa they had left behind as young girls, suddenly burst into tears and began to shriek and wail in Yiddish.

I was stunned by their outpouring. I had never seen adults cry. The few cryptic Yiddish expressions I knew were reserved to conceal privileged information from my ears, or to admonish an intrusive relative to leave me alone. This outburst was extraordinary, an expression of primal fear as though my uncle was about to be impressed into the czar's army. No less startling than their volubility was my parents' controlled silence. A generation further along in the Americanization process, they stoically accepted what provoked terror in their elders, still haunted by old country fears. The language of silence, like Yiddish, had meanings that I could not yet fathom.

There was an apt childhood metaphor for the barrier that separated my family from our Jewish origins in Eastern Europe. It was our living-room wall, which we shared with neighbors in the adjacent apartment. In our small building in Queens, where we moved when I was five, voices always carried through walls and across the narrow courtyard. I knew the downstairs voice of maternal supervision, always shrill, admonishing my friend or his sister for their transgressions, real or imagined. And the courtyard voice, a soprano of aspiring culture, incessantly trilling musical scales in pursuit of operatic stardom. But the voice on the other side of our living room wall was unmistakably Jewish. I heard it constantly throughout my childhood. Splendidly cantorial, it was vibrant with words I did not understand and with melodies I could not elude.

I rarely saw our neighbor, Cantor Gorsky, a plump, cleanshaven, middle-aged man who, like my father, always wore a fedora. But I often heard him. Several afternoons each week, while I did my homework on the other side of the wall, he prepared neighborhood boys for their bar mitzvahs. I was a captive audience, inadvertently learning the *Haftarah* blessings long before it was my turn to cross the boundary that separated us.

Although the Sabbath bride never visited our family, Cantor Gorsky hovered nearby every Friday night. Nothing changed in our home, but Cantor Gorsky was an audible presence at our dinner table. His disembodied voice recited *kiddush* over our glasses of water; said the *motzi* over our whole wheat bread; and welcomed the Sabbath with song and prayer that resounded through our little dinette. It seemed perfectly normal to hear Cantor Gorsky sing while my parents conversed, their words and his melodies floating past me in American and Jewish orbits of sound....

After seven years of silent auditing, I finally crossed the barrier that separated Cantor Gorsky's apartment from ours. How strange it felt to be sitting on the other side of the wall, in the presence of the magisterial voice that I had heard for so long. I assumed that our curious relationship was shared. But Cantor Gorsky seemed oblivious. I was merely another boy in the endless procession of students who came to him to be taught what they did not want to learn. For all of us, normal life was suspended during our year with him. It was not quite as bad as orthodonture, but it was not appreciably better.

I felt overwhelmed by Cantor Gorsky's mastery of this mysterious Jewish world of language and ritual that I was now expected to enter. But why this ordeal, so vital yet so irrelevant? I could not begin to understand that the mixed message answered itself. This rite of passage to adult membership in the community of Jews was, in my family circle, the exit from Judaism. It was as though my parents had learned a garbled version of the traditional prayer that released the father of a bar mitzvah boy from responsibility for his son's deeds and misdeeds. In their American rendition, the bar mitzvah released the son from any further obligation to be a Jew. Cantor Gorsky presided over our transition to Americanism: he certified us as Jews as we departed from Judaism.

My bar mitzvah, elaborately choreographed by my parents, emphatically affirmed the contradiction. During Friday evening and Saturday morning services, the Jewish religious formalities were observed. Cantor Gorsky had prepared me well. My flawless singing, in a voice as yet unchanged, was matched only by my ignorance of what it all meant, or why I was doing it. Indeed, it was the only time in my life that my parents and I ever sat together in a synagogue. I am certain that my father was proud of me but on this subject, as on so many others, he could not easily articulate his feelings.

Shortly before my momentous day, however, he had accompanied me on a remarkable journey to the Lower East Side. It was as close to ritual as he ever came. Although the Lower East Side was no longer *the* authentic Jewish residential neighborhood of New York, stores along Hester and Essex Streets were still stocked with prayer books and ceremonial objects. We walked by them, gingerly navigating our way around barrels filled with pickles and shmaltz herring. To my astonishment, my father knew exactly where to take me to buy my blue and white *tallit* and my satin *yarmulka*. It was the only boyhood glimpse I ever had of the world of his childhood, and the only intimation that he still knew where to find it....

The boundaries of my childhood world seldom extended very far beyond the subway line that linked Queens to Manhattan. Pittsburgh, where my father's family lived, was remote. But Philadelphia, where my adoring maternal grandmother owned a small drug store and soda fountain, was paradise. There, my deepest cravings were sated. Early in the morning, I raced downstairs to help her open the store, where I was permitted to sell penny candy to envious neighborhood children. At the end of the day, my reward was an ice-cream soda made to my own recipe. My granny was the source of my sweetest childhood nourishment; ice cream was the least of it.

We also traveled occasionally to Brooklyn or the Bronx. But these neighborhoods, to say nothing of my father's relatives, aroused my mother's snobbery. She preferred vacations in Atlantic City with hotels, restaurants, and hired help (the more obsequious the better). Once we even joined the extended Greenberg family in Long Branch, where, during an hour of unmitigated euphoria, my cousins and I chased fly balls that Hank hit to us, while visions of his instant recognition of my fielding skills (sadly, quite limited) danced in my head.

A different realm of fantasy, one with rustic New England charm, was provided by my mother's cousin. Jen, a free spirit in her college days in Madison (where she had met her husband Karl), was the family bohemian. Old photos revealed her scantily clothed in diaphanous gowns (in the fashion of Isadora Duncan), dancing with her girl friends in the sylvan woods along the shore of Lake Mendota. I yearned for that freedom, and more.

When I met them, Jen and Karl were struggling to realize his vision of owning an old-fashioned country store in New England. They had purchased a ramshackle eighteenth-century farmhouse near Great Barrington, which they renovated during weekend visits from Brooklyn. It astonished me that anyone in our family would choose to live outside of the city, especially in a house at the bottom of a dirt road by a stream, nestled in the Berkshire hills. There was even a dog, a bouncy terrier named Val. No one I knew owned a dog, or even a cat. Among my friends, confined as we all were to small apartments, the limited possibilities were defined by tropical fish and turtles....

But it was Forest Hills, for the most part, that defined the cultural boundaries of my world. We lived at the end of a long block of attached row houses, in a low apartment building with perhaps thirty other families. Ours were the only apartments in a neighborhood of private homes, bounded by the aristocratic West Side Tennis Club at one end and the Forest Hills Jewish Center at the other. The adjacent streets were alphabetically arranged, with an English lilt: Dartmouth, Exeter, Fleet, Groton, and Harrow. Our neighbors, Cantor Gorsky excepted, were remarkably like us, in transit from immigrant Judaism to American respectability....

Some of my camp friends attended Horace Mann, a fine private school in Riverdale, and it seemed quite logical to me that I should enjoy the advantages of summer camp—boys and sports—the year around. I persuaded my parents that their dreams for my college education and my dreams for a career with the New York Knicks both hinged upon my transfer there.

I was eager, yet so apprehensive. There I was, a boy from the backwoods of Queens for whom serious reading meant John R. Tunis or *Life* magazine, about to enter an institution of tradition and culture. The imposing grey stone buildings with their arched enclosures and leaded glass windows evoked the same awed anxiety that once made me so uneasy in St. Patrick's Cathedral. Perhaps I sensed how a secular shrine of learning like Horace Mann might compound the dilemmas of acculturation that tormented second-generation American Jewish families like ours.

Horace Mann vigorously asserted its own diluted version of muscular Christianity. Headmasters named Tillinghast and Gratwick and teachers named Williams, Briggs, Farrington, and Crandall, were assigned to instruct six hundred boys named Cohen, Levine, Bernstein, Goldberg, and Rosenthal in the civilized virtues required for adult success. (A few Christian students, mostly the sons of Columbia faculty who recognized a good education when they saw it, comprised the minority at the periphery of each class.) As Jews, we knew that we were the real minority, lacking the proper certification for the Gentile world that enticed us. Horace Mann lured us beyond the invisible ghetto walls that still enclosed our parents, funneling us toward the next gateway to status and privilege: the Ivy League.

The school, as my best friend there subsequently entitled his book about the Boy Scout movement, truly was a "character factory." To be sure, we studied history, literature, math, and science in a rigorous regimen that began at 8:30 A.M. and did not end, at least for the athletes among us, until nightfall. But that was the least of it. As our senior yearbook declared portentously, "We entered Horace Mann as boys," and "we hope to graduate as men." As we ascended to masculine maturity, we carefully emulated English public-school students. Dr. Gratwick was the "Headmaster," not the principal (and, with all three buttons of his jacket always buttoned, he certainly looked the part); teachers were addressed as "Sir," not Mr. (unless they were "Coach"); I was not a tenth-grader, but a Fourth Former. The message—rigor shapes character, assuring excellence—was unambiguous.

For the first time, I had friends who took books more seriously than baseball. They jolted me from my torpid indifference toward disciplined study and rigorous learning. Indeed, it was quickly evident that I had joined a class of superstars, whose achievements at Horace Mann were merely the prelude to adult distinction: the serious newspaper editor serving his apprenticeship for a Pulitzer Prize; the flamboyant class president who won acclaim as an art curator and icon of pop culture; the wry intellectual who became a New Yorker writer; two talented artists, one an accomplished sculptor and the other a whimsical cartoonist; to say nothing of those honored as "leaders of leaders," who have carved out successful careers in law and medicine.

Even our endless disagreements about the respective merits of Duke Snider, Mickey Mantle, and Willie Mays did not detract from the high seriousness of our common endeavor. (Here, after all, was Talmudic exegesis with an adolescent American accent.) We came to Horace Mann to absorb an intellectual tradition that we respected, the more so since it was not yet ours. It seemed only natural that Christians should teach Jews, for they surely knew what we must learn. Our teachers, to their everlasting credit, were neither arrogant nor patronizing, even at their most terrifying. Indeed, they made it possible for us to imagine that we might leave behind the grubby world of wholesale.

Our grandparents had struggled to speak English; our parents did not attend college. We were expected to transcend their limitations, and we did. There we were, in Wednesday morning assemblies, exuberantly singing "Men of Harlech" while joyously affirming someone else's culture. So many nice Jewish boys from New York, proudly identifying with "Saxon spearmen, Saxon bowmen"! Once Judaism was irrelevant, anything was possible. Religion, according to our school newspaper, merely expressed "minor differences of custom" among people otherwise undifferentiated.

To a teenager who had learned at an early age that Judaism was an impediment to the good things in American life, Horace Mann was perfect. How many places were there, after all, for Jewish boys to affirm their identity among other Jews while simultaneously evading it? But the promised transformation was, for me, incomplete. For graduation, we were instructed to wear a dark (blue or gray) suit, which I had not owned since my bar mitzvah. It was too much to expect my parents to buy one for the occasion, so I never asked. Instead, I bore the shame of wearing an unmatched jacket and trousers. Rather forlornly, I hoped that navy blue mixed with charcoal gray would not testify too conspicuously to my inadequacies.

29 · American Jew

I am an American Jew. That has recently become a more problematic identity. Buffeted by conflict between my country and my people, the American and Jewish sides of my self are less compatible than ever. Simultaneously, the hostility that Israel has elicited from disaffected American Jews is profoundly disturbing. If a house divided cannot stand, the plight of a house divided and besieged is even more ominous. That leaves me in a quandary: must diaspora Jews wander endlessly, uprooted not only from their country but from their own people?

Unlike most Jews I know, I cannot reflexively or unconditionally assert that my only loyalty is to the United States. Nor, in the effete way that German Jews once resolved the issue by evading it (claiming that they were Germans of the Mosaic persuasion), can I rest comfortably with the assertion that I am an American whose religion is Judaism. It is not merely a matter of national affiliation and religious identity, as reassuring as that distinction might be to most Jews, and as quickly as that claim might silence most critics. It is more complex than that.

I am an American Jew, not a Jewish American. That is, I am a citizen of the United States but I belong to the Jewish people. It is, bluntly, a matter of competing—if not yet actively conflicting—loyalties. Usually they are compatible. Under stress, however, the link between them is fragile. It may be ready to snap.

Anatomically, the distinction is easy to describe: my body is in the United States; my heart and soul are in Jerusalem. It is a paradoxical contortion, for whenever I am in Israel I am identified as an American (if not as an Anglo-Saxon). Israelis tend to be impatient with the diaspora dialectics of Jews who profess their Zionist commitments from privileged American sanctuaries. But American Jews, by definition, are not Israelis; there are secular and religious dimensions of life in Israel that can easily instil discomfort among Jews of varying diaspora persuasions. A certain kind of Jewish state, after all, may contradict a Jewish state of mind that has been refined by a century in the American promised land.

In Israel I must always deal with the flip side of American suspicion about my ultimate loyalty: Israeli perplexity. If I am a Jew, I have often been asked, why do I not make Israel my home? Even after a year in Jerusalem (which feels

---

"American Jew," *Judaism* (Summer 1983), 263-66.

more like home than any place I have ever lived in), and many visits to Israel (the only place that inverts my normal anxiety about leaving "home" and my eagerness to return), I still have not formulated a satisfactory response. Because, I answer without conviction, I live in the United States.

Life in the United States is not difficult for Jews. For some it is still the golden land; for most it is, unquestionably, home. It is not that easy for me. Must I, therefore, in the memorable warning of the Sixties, love it or leave it? Suppose I cannot love it; and suppose, for a variety of reasons, I do not (at least, not yet) choose to leave it. Can I possibly be an American Jew on terms that will satisfy the Christian majority, persistently demanding affirmations of loyalty, the Jewish minority, usually all too eager to provide those affirmations, and me?

The dilemma is sharp. To affirm my undivided loyalty as an American I must occasionally suppress my competing allegiance as a Jew, attached by the deepest bonds of historical identity to my people. During my lifetime, Germans, Poles, Romanians, Hungarians, Czechs, and so many others, to say nothing of Israelis, have had to die as Jews. Why, then, should I not choose to live like one? In the diaspora I must comply, if only tacitly, with someone else's calendar, cultural norms, definitions of civility and propriety, enticements to my children, and benign (or maligned) insensitivities to Jewish concerns. When I affirm my deepest loyalty to the Jewish people, I subject myself to accusations of dual loyalty that invariably have served as the pretext for virulent anti-Semitism. There are those who would be delighted to discover that their suspicions of divided loyalty are confirmed. Most Jews would be appalled to have them acknowledged by another Jew. So be it.

If that were the only problem, *dayenu*. It is not only the latent conflict between my country and my people that leaves me uneasy, but the blatant bitterness among Jews. The flight of fellow Jews from Israel, at least in the mandarin academic circles that I inhabit, threatens to become a spiritual *yeridah* of considerable proportions. But the alleged need for moral redemption in Israel, a dubious proposition at best, is unlikely to be satisfied because American Jews denounce its government and impugn its moral credibility before a delighted Christian audience. Surely, as recent history amply demonstrates, there are more than enough people predisposed to condemn Israel without Jews clamoring to lead the chorus of public denunciation. The ferocious criticism that followed the Israeli invasion of Lebanon severely damaged some fundamental principles of trust among Jews. We are conditioned to expect the worst from everyone else, so we seldom are surprised by outrageous double standards that convict Jews of crimes for which others are instantly exonerated. There is cause for concern, however, when Jews internalize the indictments of their most hostile critics and race to distance themselves from their own people.

It is still painful to recall last summer and fall when American Jews, unrestrained in their public denunciation of Israel, accused it of everything from moral suicide to brutal genocide. Whether they were only engaged in agonized soul-searching, as they claimed, or experiencing a massive failure of nerve as

Jews under intense pressure, remains unclear. (But it is possible, as one Israeli observed, that "the only Jews in America frightened by Begin's policies are frightened American Jews.") Undeniably, the level of Jewish suffering was intense, and appropriately so. But to encounter so many self-appointed Jewish judges of Israeli morality, some of whom could not even make moral distinctions between the Israeli army and the PLO for their own children, is to contemplate a sorrowful chapter in modern Jewish history. Not one without precedent, however: in 70 C.E., while the zealots in Jerusalem fought the Romans, Jews also fought each other until nothing was left, except Masada, to fight about....

If the Jewish people is not destroyed by internecine warfare (which, after all, it has survived throughout its history), there always remains the possibility that it will be destroyed by others. As the double standard of Western judgment (which always finds Israel morally culpable) sharpens, silent accommodation loses its appeal. It was easy for Americans, perched on nightly news broadcasts and editorial boards, to denounce Israel. It was not the American border, after all, that was located a few kilometers from a heavily armed enemy. But if my government should act in ways that harm my people, it harms me because I belong to them...

I do not wish to feed anti-Semitism or heighten anxiety among those American Jews who instinctively flock to Uncle Sam for protection. But if I must choose, I will choose as a Jew. That choice will not erase the anomalies; it will merely shift their burden more comfortably. During two thousand years in exile, Jews recited "Next year in Jerusalem" with sorrow and yearning. In 1948, and more decisively in 1967, yearning merged with fulfillment. Now I can touch the Western Wall, this year in Jerusalem. When I do, I touch the entire history of my people: our dispersion and our return. Because I am an American citizen I can also choose to live here. I appreciate that choice, but I will not pretend that it precludes other commitments, other loyalties.

For the moment, it is my choice to identify with the historical experience of my segment of the Jewish people, dispersed in exile. I am not disloyal to my country. But I will remain loyal to my people, remembering "*Kol Yehudim mispakhah ahat.*" I am no longer persuaded by the trade-off, now almost two hundred years old, that defines "enlightenment" and "emancipation": in return for promises of civil equality and individual rights, Jews were expected to relinquish their claims for political autonomy and to compress Judaism into a religion. But it may not suffice to be an individual with a Jewish (religious) identity: a Jew at home, perhaps, but surely an American on the street. The historical essence of the Jewish people has always been, and remains, a collective communal identity. So, if American push comes to shove against Israel, with American Jews shoving as hard as anyone, I must consider whether I will dissolve my dual loyalties. How could I not immerse myself, unequivocally, in the shared collective fate of my people?

30 · A Community of Jewish Memory

In the gathering dusk of a late October afternoon, not long before sunset and the beginning of the Jewish Sabbath, I joined a seemingly endless stream of Jews flowing downhill from Kiryat Arba into Hebron. Men and boys in white shirts and dark trousers and women and girls wearing long-sleeved blouses and ankle-length skirts walked together separately, animatedly talking and gesturing. We passed through parallel lines of Israeli soldiers, in combat readiness, stationed ten yards apart as far ahead as we could see. At intervals by the side of the road, military vehicles, their red lights flashing like lighthouses, demarcated our safe path.

As the road flattened at the bottom of the hill, it turned past abandoned stone houses, many in advanced stages of disrepair. Shops were shuttered closed, their metal gates locked. Hebron seemed desolate, deserted, abandoned. On rooftops and behind the remnants of walls, soldiers watched impassively as we passed. Occasionally, greetings of "Shabbat Shalom" were exchanged.

Rounding a bend, we approached a broad plaza, dense with people, dominated by the massive rectangular enclosure of *Me'arat HaMachpelah*. Its graceful twin minarets loomed high above the ancient Herodion walls. At the far end of the plaza, we were funneled through security gates where soldiers calling out "*neshek*? *neshek*?" checked for weapons. Climbing a flight of stone steps, we wound our way through a labyrinth of hallways, past antechambers and an open courtyard, into a massive hall. In its center, large marble cenotaphs with dark horizontal stripes marked the burial tombs of Isaac and Rebekah.

Beneath the high vaulted ceiling, facing the elegantly carved ancient wooden *minbar* at one end of the room, I was engulfed by scores of dark-bearded men wearing large white knitted *kippot*. A cluster of rabbinical elders, in black coats and round-rimmed black hats, conversed separately among themselves. Everything seemed starkly black or white, without any intermediate shading or subtlety. It mirrored Hebron itself, where divisions are stark and clear—Israeli or Palestinian, Jew or Muslim, friend or enemy.

In one corner of Isaac Hall, men revolved in a large circle, with hands on each other's shoulders. Their rhythmic, wordless chants reverberated off the ancient stone walls while their circle opened and closed as newcomers joined. After a prolonged moment of self-conscious hesitation, I joined them, drawn

---

Hebron Jews: Memory and Conflict in the Land of Israel (2009), 189-96.

into the circle of Jewish memory that we had come to Hebron to celebrate. The next morning, the Torah reading would recount in careful detail Abraham's purchase of a burial cave for Sarah, ever since antiquity believed to be located here, beneath us, at this very spot.

That night in our crowded yeshiva dormitory, too restless for sleep, I had flashbacks to my own persistent fascination with Hebron. It began in 1972, during my first visit to Israel with twenty other Jewish academics. Our group leader, Yehuda Rosenman, was a Polish Holocaust survivor with the passionate conviction that encounters with the real Israel could mitigate conventional academic responses—ranging from sardonic indifference to overt hostility—to the Jewish state. Our typical tourist itinerary took us from Tel Aviv to northern Galilee, from Safed to Jerusalem, and then to the Dead Sea and the fortress ruins at Masada.

The next day, we visited Hebron. A meeting had been arranged with Mayor al-Ja'bari, the canny political survivor who had accommodated himself to the British before 1948, the Kingdom of Jordan until 1967, and the State of Israel since the Six-Day War. It was unclear why we were meeting with him but not with any of the Jewish settlers who had recently moved into nearby Kiryat Arba. I knew little about Hebron or its place in Jewish history. Indeed, like the child at the Passover Seder, I did not even know how to ask.

As our bus wound through the narrow streets of Hebron, we passed Beit Hadassah. Two Israeli soldiers stood guard laconically on the footbridge outside the entrance. It seemed puzzling that we did not pause at the only identifiably Jewish building, if now empty, on our route. A moment later, I caught a glimpse of the enormous rectangular stone enclosure, topped by towering twin minarets, that our guide Tuvia explained marked the burial caves of the patriarchs and matriarchs of the Jewish people. Once again, we did not stop. What fragments of Jewish history, I briefly wondered, were concealed within the walls of these buildings? My curiosity about Hebron increased as Mayor al-Ja'bari, surrounded by deferential acolytes, deftly evaded questions about Arab-Jewish relations, past or present. Impatiently, Tuvia prompted me, "Ask him about the role of his family in 1929." I did not grasp the implications of the question, but I asked nonetheless. The mayor's mumbled reply was inaudible.

A decade later, I returned to Hebron, this time with a friendly Arab antiquities dealer from the Old City of Jerusalem who had offered to take me on a guided tour of the Machpelah shrine. Ibrahim's generous invitation, coming from a participant in Kathleen Kenyon's landmark archaeological excavations in Jericho, was irresistible. Accompanied by my teenaged son and daughter, we left familiar Israel behind to encounter Arab Hebron, where by now handfuls of Jews lived in Beit Hadassah.

The casbah, where a bustling outdoor market filled a narrow street in the center of the city, was simultaneously fascinating and foreboding. Within its deep shadows, the market stalls were barely illuminated by narrow shafts of sunlight. It teemed with Arab shoppers and echoed with merchants' entreaties. Most of the men wore *keffiyehs*, threadbare jackets, and loose, baggy trousers.

An occasional woman, with only her eyes visible behind her *niqba*, darted past the fruit and vegetable stalls. Scattered through the casbah were pairs of Israeli soldiers on patrol. I knew that an Israeli yeshiva student recently had his throat cut and bled to death in this market and that six Jews—the target of Palestinian terrorist fury over the renewed Jewish presence in the city—had been murdered outside Beit Hadassah. As intruders in Muslim space, I wondered who would protect us—Ibrahim, Israeli soldiers, Arabs, anyone—if we confronted danger.

As we climbed the steps to Machpelah, the discomforting scrutiny of Israeli soldiers made me realize that Ibrahim's presence put us on the wrong side of our Jewish identities. Our American passports testified to our nationality, but I knew that they concealed more than they revealed. Feeling uncomfortably like a spy, I wanted the soldiers to know that while our guide was Arab, my children and I were Jews. In Hebron, I realized, there was no middle ground.

Perhaps because Hebron seemed so impenetrable, it became ever more alluring. I wondered what could explain the fierce determination of Jews to live in such a hostile and dangerous place where so many of their predecessors had been brutally murdered. Would such a closed community welcome an inquisitive outsider who wanted answers to questions still unformed? Although I planned an early return, I was repeatedly thwarted. Once the city was closed for security reasons; another trip was canceled by a blizzard, and still another for Ramadan. Hebron seemed to possess myriad ways to insulate itself from inquisitive strangers.

Finally, with the intervention of a politically influential colleague of an Israeli friend, I had my opportunity. Early one bleak December morning, an army colonel and his driver pulled up to my Jerusalem apartment. An hour later, we were welcomed into the Kiryat Arba home of a young Israeli woman from Kentucky who graciously provided coffee and conversation. Miriam offered no grand ideology to explain her presence in Kiryat Arba, only that this was the Jewish homeland and her family belonged here, and, in any event, life was now less complicated for her than it had been while growing up as a Jewish girl in Louisville.

Her apartment was small; the living room also served as the nursery for her young infant, who slept in a nearby crib. Classical music played softly; one wall was lined with books, interspersed with photographs of prominent rabbis whom she identified for my military escort. By then I could recognize Rabbi Kook, the inspirational chief rabbi of Palestine during the Mandatory period. Many Jewish settlers, I had learned, were galvanized into activism by his son's prophetic call, a month before the Six-Day War, to remember biblical Hebron.

Our conversational pleasantries were interrupted by the blustery arrival of Rabbi Eliezer Waldman, head of the Kiryat Arba yeshiva and one of the influential leaders in rebuilding the Hebron Jewish community. Stocky, gray bearded, and voluble, he unexpectedly turned out to be my religious Zionist Other. Born in 1936 in Palestine shortly after his family left Czechoslovakia, he had grown up in the ultra-Orthodox enclave of Williamsburg in Brooklyn. Born in Philadelphia the same year, I grew up in the assimilated middle-class

Jewish respectability of Forest Hills in Queens. While Rabbi Waldman studied Hebrew texts at the Flatbush Yeshiva, I studied American history and literature at the Horace Mann School. When he returned to Israel to learn in a Bnei Akiva yeshiva, I set out for college in Oberlin, Ohio. At every crucial marker of Jewish identity, aspiration, experience, and commitment, our paths had diverged.

Rabbi Waldman passionately and unequivocally asserted his religious-nationalist principles. If there were illegal Jewish settlements anywhere, he suggested in response to my first question about Hebron, they were to be found in Boston and New York, not in the Land of Israel. Here, no Jewish settlement could be considered illegal. In Hebron, after all, new settlers were merely reclaiming property abandoned in 1929 that rightfully belonged to the Jewish community. A Jewish settlement in Judea or Samaria was no less legitimate than Israel itself, which Rabbi Waldman pointedly identified as the largest Jewish settlement in the Middle East.

I questioned and Rabbi Waldman answered for nearly an hour, until the colonel's driver interrupted to inform us that we must return to Jerusalem ahead of an approaching blizzard. There would be no opportunity that day to visit Hebron. During our drive, the colonel and I discovered that each of us had a grandparent who had grown up in the tiny Romanian *shtetl* of Piatra Neumts. As so often happened in Israel, I felt circles closing and links connecting.

Not long afterward, I returned to participate in another academic seminar, this one focusing on competing definitions of Jewish identity. Some pointed observations from an eclectic array of speakers illuminated the relationship between religion and nationalism in Jewish tradition. A renegade Hebrew University professor reminded us, "Israel is the national expression of attachment to land based on a religious source." A yeshiva student added, "Judaism is defined by Torah, people and land." And a Maronite priest suggested, "Jewish identity is formed by the link between the Jewish people and the Land of Israel within the framework of the Bible."

While we mulled over the implications of these observations, stunning news broke across Israel. More than two dozen Jewish settlers, including several from Hebron and Kiryat Arba, had been arrested for belonging to an underground group that had planted explosives beneath the cars of Arab mayors and Arab buses, killed three students at the Hebron Islamic College in retaliation for the murder of a yeshiva student in Hebron, and, most astonishingly, developed a plan to destroy the mosques on the Temple Mount in Jerusalem. Instantly, the morality, to say nothing of the political wisdom, of Jewish settlement in Judea and Samaria came under withering nationwide scrutiny.

After the seminar concluded, I returned to Kiryat Arba to renew contact with Rabbi Waldman. Here, if anywhere, the arrests had hit with stunning impact. The target of scathing criticism from outsiders and palpable self-scrutiny within the settler community, the Underground called into question the legitimacy of the entire settlement movement. Seated at a table in his study, the rabbi carefully differentiated between "understanding" the settlers' actions and "justifying" them. Indeed, when consulted about the Temple Mount plan, he had insisted, "Nothing would hurt us more. Rebuilding the Temple is a Godly matter." Yet the Temple Mount, he noted bitterly, is "the only place in the world where Jews cannot pray." The Israeli government, he added, "puts us to shame." It was not enough for settlers to be told by Defense Minister Moshe Arens that "you are *halutzim* [pioneers]; you must suffer." If the government would not protect them, Rabbi Waldman asserted, it should remove them.

The next morning, I read a newspaper article by Elyakim Haetzni, a Kiryat Arba lawyer and another founder of the Hebron community. He sharply condemned "the religious deviation" of attempting to hasten the arrival of the Messiah with guns and dynamite. In the Land of Israel, Arabs may be *gerim* (strangers), just as Jews once were strangers in Egypt, but their lives must be protected. He excoriated rabbis who had failed to admonish their followers, "Thou shall not kill."

The spiritual challenge to secular Zionism posed by religious settlers and the murderous actions of extremists among them raised fundamental questions about the identity of the Jewish state and the future of the settlement movement. Hebron was at the epicenter of this acrimonious struggle. To secular liberal Israelis, as daily newspaper reports incessantly revealed, the Hebron Jewish community symbolized everything they despised about the settler movement: its religious zeal and arrogant assertion that it was the rightful inheritor of Zionist tradition. Headlines suggested that the intense debate over the future of the settlements might determine whether Israel was truly a Jewish state—or merely a state of Jews.

Some months later, during another sabbatical year in Israel, I once again set out to visit Hebron. By then, the West Bank had become a virtual war zone, with frequent Palestinian attacks on Israeli vehicles and their occupants. Driving south from Jerusalem, my guide Dov maintained close radio contact with settler security headquarters. His car had protective plastic windows, and his pistol was in the glove compartment. Perhaps to ease the tension, Dov told the apocryphal story about Henry Kissinger after his term as secretary of state had ended. In his new job as manager of a zoo, he had finally discovered how to get the Arab lion to lie peacefully with the Israeli lamb. An astonished visiting diplomat asked Kissinger to explain this remarkable achievement. "Don't tell anyone," the former secretary of state whispered, "but I change lambs every morning." Nearing Hebron, I tried to appreciate Dov's gallows humor.

Accompanied by Mischa, our gruff but friendly escort from Kiryat Arba, we drove into Hebron, past the looming Machpelah enclosure, along narrow streets bordering on the casbah, to the restored Avraham Avinu quarter. The synagogue had only recently been rebuilt after decades of desecration, neglect, and, finally, destruction. Soldiers guarded the entrance; others were stationed on a nearby roof. Standing with the market behind us, Mischa provided some historical information. It made me uneasy to realize that three Jews wearing *kippot*, with their backs turned, might be tempting targets. How easy it would be for someone to pull a knife or throw a Molotov cocktail before disappearing into the casbah. It would not be the first time that had happened in Hebron.

I was relieved to finally enter the synagogue, where Mischa recounted the horrors of the 1929 massacre, the compulsory evacuation of survivors by the British, and the more recent murders of yeshiva students. But he also reminded us of the Arab sheikh who took Jews into his home to protect them and, nearly forty years later, led Jews back to the ruins of Avraham Avinu, its floor covered with excrement. Mischa opened the *aron* to display Torah scrolls enclosed in the beautiful wooden cases that are customary in Sephardic synagogues.

On our way to Beit Hadassah, which I had last glimpsed from a bus window nearly fifteen years earlier, Mischa updated me on its recent history. By now, it had become home for a dozen Jewish families whose young children darted playfully through the spacious entrance hall. As we walked along the narrow balcony that surrounds the building, Mischa pointed to adjacent houses, now vacant, where Jews once had lived but now were excluded by the Israeli government. The message was evident: just as the Avraham Avinu synagogue had been restored for Jewish worship and the old Beit Hadassah medical clinic had been reclaimed for Jewish occupancy, so other property would be returned to Jewish habitation. I was beginning to learn about the fierce tenacity of Hebron Jews, still attached by an umbilical cord of memory to biblical antiquity and to their own history in this beleaguered city.

Leaving Beit Hadassah, we wound our way up the hill to Tel Rumeida, the likely site of biblical Hebron. On the hilltop, in the newest cluster of Jewish homes, half a dozen small caravans housed Jewish families. As we arrived, a young Orthodox man stepped outside. After brief introductions, Chaim invited us for conversation and refreshment. It was a pleasure, he assured us; it is, after all, in the tradition of Abraham to welcome strangers in Hebron. I asked him why he lived here, in such a dangerous place, surrounded by so many hostile Arabs. Because, he responded, Jewish history began here. "The tree with the deepest roots," he explained, "is the strongest tree."

Hebron, I had learned, is layered with competing historical memories and religious claims that can be traced back to the biblical rivalry between Abraham's sons Isaac and Ishmael. Here several hundred Jews tried to live normal lives. But if threatened or attacked, they would respond in kind; in Hebron, justice still meant *ayin tachat ayin* ("an eye for an eye"). Did it matter that Jewish history, as Hebron Jews invariably remind visitors, began here? If not, why did it matter that the Jewish state be built in the Land of Israel rather than in Africa or South America? Can a people ever relinquish the attachments formed by its deepest memories?

When these glimpses of my previous visits to Hebron finally subsided, I slept fitfully. We returned to Machpelah for the morning service, with the reading of *Chaye Sarah* that 20,000 people had come to Hebron to hear. Recounting a simple real estate transaction, *Chaye Sarah* irrevocably connects Jews to their promised land—and to Hebron. Inside the densely packed Isaac Hall, there was a surge of anticipatory excitement. When the Torah scroll was removed from the *aron* and carried through the room to be reverently touched and kissed, it pulled everyone forward like a magnet. A cluster of rabbis and community elders gathered at the *bima*. I edged as close as I could get to the reader, whose strong voice began to chant the opening words:

> Sarah died in Kiryat Arba—now Hebron—in the land of Canaan (Gen.23:2)

With his purchase of a grave site, Abraham became a landholder, with legal rights of inheritance that his descendants would claim, in perpetuity.

> So Ephron's land in Machpelah, near Mamre—the field with its cave and all the trees anywhere within the confines of that field—passed to Abraham as his possession.... And then Abraham buried his wife Sarah in the cave of the field of Machpelah, facing Mamre—now Hebron—in the Land of Canaan. (Gen. 23:17-20)

Chaye Sarah recounts the precise moment when the attachment of the Jewish people to the Land of Israel and to Hebron was forever sealed. Its annual reading affirms the unbroken link of identification between present and past. That morning in Hebron, the power of the deepest historical memory of the Jewish people was palpable. I was standing on the bedrock of Jewish history, directly above the burial cave in the field of Machpelah, in Hebron, in the Land of Israel, as it is described in the biblical text. At this most venerable yet vulnerable Jewish holy site in the world, I felt enclosed, for that moment, within a community of Jewish memory.

If the Hebrew Bible is the ultimate source for Zionism, as David Ben-Gurion affirmed to British royal commissioners some seventy years ago, then Zion surely includes Hebron. Once Jews relinquish their right to live in Hebron, they implicitly undermine their claim to live anywhere in their biblical homeland. To abandon Hebron is to surrender the claims of memory that bind Jews to each other, to their ancient homeland, and to their shared past and future.

Jewish prayer resonates with pleas from the prophet Jeremiah for the return of his people "within our borders." Immediately preceding the affirmation of the *Sh'ma*, Jews recite, "Bring us in peacefulness from the four corners of the earth and lead us with upright pride to our land." During the concluding *Musaf* service, Jews implore God to "bring us up in gladness to our land and plant us within our boundaries." These ancient religious pleas, as it happens, also define the essence of Zionism. For the Jews of Hebron, Judaism and Zionism are inseparable. In Hebron, in *Me'arat HaMachpelah*, on Shabbat *Chaye Sarah*, an exuberant community of religious Zionists revealed the enduring power of Jewish memory.

31 · Anti-Semitism With White Gloves

Wellesley College opened in 1875 to educate young women "for the glory of God and the service of the Lord Jesus Christ." In the sylvan setting of Henry Fowle Durant's sprawling estate fifteen miles west of Boston, students learned that "Christian character" was "the most radiant crown of womanhood." There they engaged in "the war of Christ...against spiritual wickedness in high places." Wellesley women were encouraged to live their lives "in humble imitation of Him who 'came not to be ministered unto, but to minister'" (Matthew 20:28).

Wellesley architecture reflected and reinforced Christian devotion, literally carving it in stone. The massively elegant College Hall, the first building, was designed to resemble a double Latin cross. The spacious five-story entry Centre reminded one observer of "medieval convents." Consistent with the founder's principles, for nearly a century every trustee, faculty member and officer was required by College statute (although not always honored in practice) to belong to an evangelical church.

Like its Big Brothers—Harvard, Yale and Princeton—and the other Seven Sister colleges, Wellesley designed admission policy to cultivate and perpetuate a white Anglo-Saxon Protestant elite. To be sure, some Jewish girls were sufficiently respectable to gain admission, but in small numbers. They tended to come from wealthy and assimilated German-Jewish families with meager Jewish knowledge or identification. One alum from the Twenties recalled that she "went to church with her friends regularly"; another knew that she benefited from not "looking Jewish"; and still another, who dutifully attended the College chapel service every morning, seemed relieved that other students believed her to be Episcopalian. Questions about religious identification, designed to identify Jews, were part of the application process. So, too, were geographical distribution preferences, personal interviews, and photographs.

Wellesley prejudice occasionally deepened Jewish awareness. A member of the Class of 1928 was infuriated to discover that Jewish students had been grouped together at one end of a hallway in her dormitory. The dean justified the arrangement, saying: "I thought you'd all be so happy together." More than sixty years later, a Jewish alumna still remembered the oblivious freshman classmate who had complained to her: "Isn't it awful how Jews turn up everyplace and

---

"Anti-Semitism with White Gloves," *Anti-Semitism on the Campus: Past & Present* (2011), 23-37.

how they have horns." Another student explained their exclusion from clubs: "Jews tend to look a certain way...all funny and unkempt...with big noses."

In the mid-Thirties College president Mildred McAfee evasively conceded: "I presume there is a sense in which it is true that we have a quota." Then she acknowledged: "We try to keep the number [of Jewish students] within approximately 10 percent of the number of students admitted." Wellesley's policy of discrimination was couched in her rhetoric of respect and tolerance. Jews, she acknowledged, "are our best students." But Wellesley, after all, was "a Gentile community." Too many Jews would create problems. Better to reject qualified students, President McAfee insisted, than "to create a condition on campus which would produce discrimination." At Wellesley, tolerance of Jews required discrimination against Jews....

Wellesley was especially inhospitable to Orthodox Jewish students. Molly Myerowitz, admitted in 1960, encountered what she subsequently described as "the peculiarly polite yet inhumane brand of Wellesley anti-Semitism." Because her religious obligations prohibited her from working on the Jewish Sabbath and holy days, she was compelled to postpone examinations scheduled for those days. The College solution was to incarcerate her in the infirmary for the duration, without access to books or friends lest she benefit from an "advantage" denied to other students. There Miss Myerowitz was served non-kosher food that she could not eat and a nurse was assigned to accompany her to the bathroom. Unable to endure life at Wellesley beyond her sophomore year, she transferred to Radcliffe. Only years later did she finally realize that "the failure was Wellesley's and not my own."...

Anti-Semitism infested virtually every corner of Wellesley life. Admissions officers systematically avoided recruitment at predominantly Jewish high schools. Professors routinely denied student requests to postpone exams and assignments scheduled on Yom Kippur, and openly expressed their displeasure when Jewish students missed class for holy day observance. College events were scheduled with blithe disregard for the Jewish calendar. In dormitory dining halls, Jewish students often confronted forbidden pork products as the only available main course—for both lunch and dinner. When one mother requested that the dietician offer simple alternatives—cottage cheese, cereal—she was told: "My dear woman, if we start providing for the dietary needs of our Jewish students, before long we shall have to provide for Indian girls who don't eat meat."...

In September 1983 the Boston *Jewish Advocate* published its lead story documenting the long history of anti-Semitism at Wellesley College. Once its dirty linen began to be washed in public the facade of institutional denial finally began to crack.

In Academic Council—the faculty governing body—a resolution was introduced condemning and repudiating "the history and legacy" of anti-Semitism at Wellesley. After hours of excruciating debate stretching across three acrimonious faculty meetings, the faculty (amid thunderous administrative silence) finally decided to decide. It acknowledged and condemned the persistence of anti-Semitism at Wellesley, committed the College to obliterate discrimination against Jews in recruitment, admission, employment, and promotion, and declared that insensitivity toward the obligations of religiously observant Jews was impermissible. To placate universalistic colleagues, who could not tolerate condemnation of anti-Semitism alone, the faculty also dedicated Wellesley College to the eradication of all forms of racial and religious discrimination.

But the Board of Trustees dug in its heels. Jewish alumnae on the Board demonstrated that their deepest loyalty was to the college that had deemed them worthy of admission. Declining to endorse the faculty resolution, it refused to mention Jews by name and denied the history of anti-Semitism at Wellesley College. Instead, they fabricated and celebrated a mythical "history of dedication to diversity" and affirmed "the moral imperative of the Founder," which, of course, was the bedrock of Christian exclusivity at Wellesley. Only a sustained torrent of public criticism, from inside and outside the College, finally nudged the Trustees to the minimum concession that anti-Semitism had indeed been an enduring problem at Wellesley and that it was deplorable.

During Academic Council debates it had become evident that the struggle to frame an acceptable condemnation of anti-Semitism had also exposed acrimonious intramural Jewish conflict among the faculty. A bemused, or indifferent, majority watched the spectacle of Jews against Jews, with every dismal stereotype from centuries of Jewish diaspora history on display.

There were Court Jews who reflexively aligned themselves with their Wellesley benefactor, even when it discriminated against Jews. Jewish universalists, who were passionately committed to every worthy liberal cause, could not bear to identify and condemn discrimination only against Jews. Self-hating Jews, inclined to identify as Jews only to legitimate their criticism of Israel, endlessly reiterated the complexity of the issue, the better to deny the reality of anti-Semitism. Finally, there were the Jews of silence, who could not rouse themselves to utter a word in public against anti-Semitism....

Wellesley's Jewish problems lingered. In the English Department a young woman hired to teach Yiddish and Jewish literature encountered hostility to her research topics and teaching plans. Colleagues informed her, "loud and clear, that work in Yiddish wasn't valuable." Her American literature syllabus was criticized for including three Jewish authors: Saul Bellow, Cynthia Ozick, and Bernard Malamud. She was advised to eliminate the Jews, refocus on early modernism, and add Nathanial Hawthorne and Henry James. She soon resigned her position.

By the Nineties Wellesley, like so many academic institutions, had made a strong commitment to affirmative action and multicultural diversity. The special admissions consideration that once was confined to Christian applicants now was reserved for African-American, Latina, Asian and Native-American students—and, of course, the daughters of alumnae. Young Muslim women were attracted to the gendered insularity of a women's college. A small Jewish Studies department was established. But Jewish students, with every reason to anticipate the benefits of heightened tolerance, found themselves marginalized as members of the white majority and available as scapegoats for the grievances of other minorities....

After the September 11th terrorist attacks the battleground for Jews at Wellesley shifted. President Diana Walsh forcefully reminded the Wellesley community to show respect for Muslim students, lest they be held guilty by association with Muslim terrorists. But she said nothing to reassure Jewish students, who encountered malicious allegations, on and off campus, of Israeli responsibility for the terrorist outrages and mendacious claims that several thousand Jews, forewarned of the attacks, had not reported for work at the World Trade Center that day.

Not long afterward, a swastika was painted at a bus stop near the College. The Office of Religious and Spiritual Life, the center of College multicultural sensitivities, sponsored a three-faiths panel discussion about Jerusalem—which it scheduled on Yom Kippur. Blatantly anti-Semitic email postings by Muslim students on College conferences angered their Jewish classmates: an anti-Israel poem repeated centuries-old anti-Semitic canards about Jews as "Judas," while a photograph of three Israeli soldiers bore the caption, "Three Jewish Animals."

In characteristic Wellesley fashion, College administrators responded by bracketing egregious examples of anti-Semitism with "other" forms of prejudice, of which there were no recently recorded complaints. The implicit message was clear: anti-Semitism alone was not sufficiently offensive to warrant condemnation. This double standard made a mockery of Wellesley's oft-repeated claim of multicultural sensitivity. Nothing was heard from President Walsh about the insulting Muslim student posts. When asked explicitly whether she would speak publicly to Jewish concerns, as she had done for Muslim students, she declined to answer. The most she would say was to caution against "hateful or harmful speech" at a time of anti-Semitism "and other ancient hatreds." No other "ancient hatreds" were identified.

For Jewish students, Wellesley often provided their first bitter encounter with anti-Semitism. After Angela Davis roused a campus audience with an impassioned endorsement of the vicious hostility directed at Israel and Jews at the Durban Conference against Racism (2001), a Jewish student acknowledged, "I do not feel accepted here. I feel ignored." A rising leader in the Jewish student community (who would become a rabbi) wrote pointedly in the College newspaper: "I did not come to Wellesley expecting to learn what it felt like to be hated or demonized because I was Jewish," while College administrators "stand idly by."

Some Jewish students began to realize that Wellesley Hillel, impaired by years of limited funding, unassertive rabbinical leadership, and the loyalty of its Advisory Board to the College, was part of their problem. Early in the new century a student rebellion erupted within Hillel, leading to the resignation of the incumbent rabbi. She was replaced by an amiable social director who famously complained, several years later, that "male voices" too loudly supported beleaguered Jewish students.

Leaderless, powerless and uninspiring, Hillel was more likely to antagonize than attract strongly identified Jewish students. For the most important holy days—Rosh Hashanah, Yom Kippur, and Passover—Hillel usually confined its energies to directing and transporting students to religious services at Brandeis, Boston University and Tufts. When the organization finally roused itself to deplore an episode of anti-Semitism, its preferred source of authority was Ralph Waldo Emerson.

Jewish students dutifully internalized Wellesley's Jewish problem as their own. "We wanted to be accepted by our peers," explained a student leader. "We didn't want to rock the boat or have our classmates dislike us." The result was described as "a culture of fear in which the Jewish students were afraid to stand up for themselves for fear of being blacklisted or disliked by their friends and classmates." In the face of persistent hostility, another student confided: "I'm scared and confused and wonder if maybe I'm doing something wrong by being Jewish."

Jewish students assuaged their discomfort by internalizing their hurt. One student was astonished to discover "how lonely Jewish students were feeling." Another confided: "After banging my head against the wall, tiptoeing around, walking on eggshells avoiding stating any of my beliefs so as not to make anyone uncomfortable, to find out the fact that I am religious offends someone else was too much. It's why I hate Wellesley so much but can never leave it." Torn between their Jewish identity and their desire to belong at Wellesley, it was difficult for Jewish students to realize that when Wellesley made them feel uncomfortable, frightened or confused about being Jews, it meant that something was wrong with Wellesley, not with them.

32 · The Clock and the Scale

When my father finally sold his partnership in a small jewelry manufacturing company hardly anything of value remained. The residue of good will, an accretion of 30 years of traveling salesmanship, was not marketable, and the inventory of rings and watches was sorely depleted. His office had never contained much more than the bare essentials; desks, chairs, files, and telephones; a huge safe, with multiple dials, wheels, and handles, for overnight storage of precious gems and metals; and a quaint little bell that every visitor rang, prompting someone to peer through a small window to determine whether the locked security door should be opened.

The office was located on West 47th Street, long the hub of the American diamond industry. A teeming community of buyers and sellers, almost all of whom were Jewish, it seemed to have been transplanted, intact, from Eastern Europe. Some years ago, when I last conducted an informal census, standing for five minutes outside the entrance to my father's building, one-third of the businessmen (the only women were customers) were Hassidic Jews; one-third were second-generation Americans like my father; and one-third were the newest Jewish immigrants, Israelis (joined by a sprinkling of Russians) who seemed to commute between the diamond exchanges in Tel Aviv and New York.

The street, which functioned as an open-air market, always was tumultuous. Amid the bustle and din, diamonds were scrutinized through jewelers' glasses, stones and rings were passed in little manila envelopes and hundred-dollar bills were more commonplace than fives or tens. Hands moved constantly as pockets drained of cash were filled with diamonds, and—as Molly Goldberg would say on my father's favorite television program—versa visa.

The world was viewed through facets and measured in carats. The language of 47th Street, whether Yiddish, English, or Hebrew, was cryptic, I never overheard a complete sentence. Diamonds might be forever, but selling them was a frenetic activity. No one walked, talked, or ate slowly. I sensed a palpable, almost manic, energy, edged by anxiety hinting that deals must be completed quickly lest tomorrow bring calamity. It was easy to imagine some menacing, but undefined, tremor emptying the entire street as instantaneously as when the flocks of resident pigeons suddenly took startled flight. The diamond business, historically, was perfectly suited to Jews, who could pocket all their assets

---

"The Clock and the Scale," *The Jewish Advocate* (August 9, 1990).

at the first rumble of a pogrom and flee for their lives, to prosper another day if they survived that one.

Occasionally, after a frenzied twenty-minute lunch, my father would take me inside one of the diamond arcades. In those sprawling warrens of display cases, with their endless rows of neatly arranged rings, watches, bracelets, necklaces, earrings—shining gold and glistening stones everywhere—I felt overwhelmed by vulgarity. So many people, merchants and customers alike, thrashing in the same stocked pool of avarice. Yet I could not help but respect businessmen whose shared bonds of trust enabled my father to depart with thousands of dollars of jewels in his pocket—"on consignment" in the magic phrase—without a deposit or even a receipt. On 47th Street, members of the diamond community were bound to reciprocal integrity by their handshake. Disputes might erupt, but they were never litigated by lawyers or adjudicated in court. They were resolved, instead, by the Diamond Dealers Club, within its own peculiar synthesis of Talmudic principles and the bottom line. The most extreme penalty, as in any closed community, was ostracism and expulsion, with instant notification of the identity of any transgressor to diamond clubs worldwide.

Not even this self-contained enclave could resist the inexorable pressure of modern business consolidation. Industry monsters, from their Texas lairs, either swallowed or mortally wounded companies like my father's. Each road trip became more arduous for him than the last, for he needed to travel further and work longer to sell the same number of rings and watches, even to customers who, during three decades, had become friends. As the life of his business ebbed, attended in its terminal stages by a lawyer and an accountant (a father and son, the only "outsiders" who were privy to business secrets), I fixated upon three objects in the office that I craved as mementos. The most valuable, surely, was the framed photograph of Hank Greenberg, the baseball star. But it was inscribed to my father's partner, Hank's brother, so I understood that it was not mine to claim.

Fortunately, no one else cared about the other artifacts. There was an old pendulum time-punch clock, framed in oak, which had registered the arrivals and departures of every factory worker during nearly half a century. Made by the International Company, a parent of IBM, it functioned as long as my father kept it wound, compensating for its erratic timekeeping (unlike everything else on the street, it was always slow) with incessant, quite audible, ticks, tocks, and clicks. Less important, but still worth salvaging, was the jewelers scale, enclosed in a cumbersome wood and glass case.

For reasons unknown, I loved to discover old balance scales. This one, made by a company founded in 1857, was not nearly as distinguished as my majestic English grocer's scale, nor at all funky like my marble-based *balance* from a Parisian flea-market. But it certainly qualified as an authentic repository of family sentiment, like the old photographs and sea shells that I periodically examined with archeological fervor. So, for several years, the clock ticked on in our dining room, endlessly fascinating my young daughters and their friends, who still delight in pulling the time-punch lever to elicit its noisy clang. But the scale languished in the basement, competing for limited space with snow tires and storage trunks.

Like my father, I dutifully wound the clock. I even played my own games with it, for it never was entirely predictable, within a maximum seven-day cycle, precisely when it would wind down. So I made calculated guesses, trying not to be too eager, while determined never to be tardy. For I had associated the clock tick with my father's heartbeat, thereby foolishly arrogating to myself responsibility for keeping my father alive. From time to time, mercifully, I was reminded that I was powerless to sustain life with a clock key. But I never discarded the sense of obligation, or compulsion, to keep the clock wound, especially once my father, in his eighty-sixth year, began his inexorable slide toward death.

As the only child, I bore full responsibility for deciding what life-prolonging surgical procedures, if any, my father's deteriorating condition justified. Anyone who has endured the agony of such decisions knows the torment involved; no one who has been spared can imagine it. Family members who are deeply concerned with the quality of a life, I learned, are likely to encounter doctors who are relentlessly committed to its prolongation at any cost. The surgeon advised me that my preoccupation with how my father's life would be lived, without a limb or much of a mind, was irrelevantly emotional. My fury was only slightly tempered by the realization that he was professionally programmed to be ethically and morally obtuse.

During the course of my wrenching debate, simultaneously internal and external, I encountered ambiguity at every turn, which only deepened my own ambivalence. Even the doctors, projecting such boundless assurance about the wisdom of ever more assaultive procedures, surely were making their own calibrated assessments of risks and benefits. As a son, I still wanted my father to tell me what to do, to express *his* preference. But we had done our elaborate family pirouettes around that issue for years, and I knew that he would tell me, as he finally did, to do whatever I thought best. When I needed to know what wisdom traditional Jewish sources conveyed, I learned that life must be preserved at all cost; quality of life decisions were excluded; *but* when a person was in the status of *goses*, in the process of dying, then life should not be prolonged because the angels of death, sent by God, were already waiting.

So the answer begged the question: When, precisely, was a person in the process of dying? I suspected that there were as many answers as there were rabbis. I eagerly awaited direct divine guidance, but I only heard silence, punctuated by the ticking of my father's clock. The message, I intuited, was that the decision was mine.

During my indecision, quite coincidentally, my wife happened to relocate my father's scale to a more conspicuous place near the door to my study. Early one morning, during a respite from the unceasing telephone calls, when my concentration span for any single task had declined to seven minutes, I decided to remove the scale from its unwieldy case and remount it, the better to see it from my desk. But I could not precisely level it. Perhaps it was inherently tilted, or the baseboard was warped, or my study floor sloped. I may even have stumbled upon a deeper truth: that it was humanly impossible to weigh life and death decisions with precision.

Yet with the scale slightly off level, I confronted the challenge, aided by a variety of minuscule jeweler's weights, to rectify its imbalance. I tested various possibilities for several days but the needle continued to oscillate past the center, slightly to the right, then slightly to the left, and then back again. I persisted, shifting the delicate weights in the scale while I finely adjusted my own calculation of the consequences of either decision that I would make about my father's fate. I added and subtracted medical opinion, my sense of my father's wishes, Jewish sources, insights from family members and friends, filtering them all through my own love and fear. Although I managed, finally, to balance the jeweler's scale exactly, that equilibrium was impossible to replicate emotionally. A decision had to be made; silent postponement, itself a decision, was too passive for me. I informed the doctors that I would not authorize further surgery. They assured me that my father would die within a month.

The day after my decision, in welcome vindication, I discovered a card, buried deep in my father's wallet, signed by him some years earlier, requesting that he "not be kept alive by artificial means and heroic measures." The message concluded with a plea "that you who care for me will feel morally bound to act in accordance with this urgent request." I was grateful for his belated guidance. As my father slipped away, suspended between life and death and truly in the process of dying, his jeweler's scale finally was balanced, in tranquil equilibrium. And, to be absolutely certain that I did everything possible, I was as vigilant as ever about winding the clock.

33 · My Desk: Archive of My Victorian Self

In the new era of cyberspace, scholars have become flagrantly indifferent to the aesthetic of their desks. Indeed, the very notion of a "desk" now seems as quaintly archaic as a quill pen. I had a heliotropic colleague who migrated incessantly throughout his house, laptop in hand, to maximize his exposure to sunlight. When I heard that, I knew that I had become an incorrigible survivor of a vanishing species, soon to become extinct. For my desk remains an intricately resonant extension of my writing self.

In a whimsical moment of self-indulgence forty years ago, when I was a graduate student struggling to complete my first published article, I purchased a turn-of-the century oak roll-top desk. I was enchanted by its array of drawers, shelves, cubbyholes, pen niches, and ingeniously concealed hiding places. For me, as for its erstwhile owner, this desk expressed a discernible yearning for stability and order. It seemed a most appropriate acquisition for an aspiring historian who was determined to spend much of his time in the past.

Amid the assorted furnishings—including, if I must date myself, hi-fi components and ashtrays—that my expanding family accumulated, the roll-top desk remained the one material object that was indisputably mine. It was where I wrote—literally, by hand—all the letters, lectures, articles, reviews and books that defined my professional life. Packed with old correspondence, discarded calendar diaries, cancelled checks, and assorted artifacts from my travels, my desk became my itinerant archive. After several moves, I learned to dismantle and reassemble it with military precision.

My children, in turn, were enchanted by its recessed crannies. In the "treasure drawer," they discovered my random accumulation of foreign coins, unmatched locks and keys, seashells, and assorted souvenirs, each with its own memories and associations: an autographed baseball; the combination lock from my father's traveling salesman's case; a rabbit's foot; an Adlai Stevenson campaign button; and my teen-age identification bracelet from when I least knew myself. In time, they added their own distinctive donations: hand-crafted birthday cards, sculpted animals, and painted stones.

My desk was where my professional life as a historian and my interior life as a writer were transformed, by the alchemy of pen and paper, into language. It was my virtual office and I remained fiercely committed to it, and to the con-

---

"My Desk: Archive of My Victorian Self," *Chronicle of Higher Education* (March 23, 2001).

cealed order beneath the messy array of notes, folders, writing pads, and index cards—to say nothing of accumulated postage scales, wax seals, ancient Israelite coins, brass weights, Persian boxes, and turtle fetishes that flourished there like mosquitoes in the tropics. Long after my friends and colleagues had become computer literate, I remained mired in the Victorian obsolescence that my desk so vividly evoked.

I accepted the nicks and scratches that were its signs of aging with more or less the equanimity that I tolerated my own. Eventually, if apprehensively, I submitted to modernity, learning to use a computer and, to the astonishment of dubious friends, even praising its virtues. But it reposed on a nearby table, not my desk, which retained its place of honor in my affections. I fully expected my desk and I to remain partners for the duration of my writing life.

Then, in a stunning moment of avarice a few years ago, I spotted a far more majestic, unusually elegant, antique roll-top. Everything about it, from the golden finish of its fine oak to the subtly carved handles, from quarter-sawn writing slides to concealed drawers, from recessed shelves to curved panels, expressed the distinctive Victorian oxymoron of conspicuous refinement.

Suddenly I confronted the unimaginable: a burst of fickle acquisitiveness in which I would relinquish my venerable, but comparatively pedestrian, writing companion. I worried that my old desk might have taken on a talismanic quality, which would prevent me from writing anywhere else. Had a writer as committed as I was to an idiosyncratic bond with a desk assumed certain unspoken obligations of fidelity? I had experienced divided loyalties over parents, friends, lovers, and even nations. But desks?

My old desk, I appreciated, had become the most enduring transitional object of my adulthood. Every working morning for three decades it had been my safe harbor, enabling me to embark upon my prolonged interior journeys of discovery. Even after my writing had shaded inexorably into word processing, I still dallied there, fiddling with my calendar and papers, even revising by hand, before moving with a twinge of resignation to my computer. Could another desk provide the same reassurance?

I finally yielded to my irrepressible yearning. But for days, I was thoroughly miserable. My own desk, for the last time, must be emptied. As files, letters, family photos, and the detritus of three decades piled up nearby, I felt like a traitor. Not merely to my desk, of course, but to myself—to all those fragments of autobiography and memory that time had rubbed into the textured grain of associations that this desk had always evoked for me. It was small consolation that my venerable writing companion, relocated to my wife's study, remained nearby.

After my new-old roll-top arrived, I sent my young daughters on a treasure hunt to discover the identification numbers that are finely etched into its kneehole flank. Within thirty seconds they were pounding breathlessly back upstairs. Yes, they reassured me, they had instantly spotted the metal identification tag. What metal tag, I wondered, as I followed them down to my study. There it was, high up on the rear panel of the kneehole, precisely at a child's eye level once she crawled inside and made herself at home. "Package Manufacturing Company," it read, identifying the desk's previous owner, a century ago. This grand desk surely was fit for the company president, whose correspondence had arrived through curved mail slits cut into its side panels. Now my words would be manufactured and packaged here.

My new desk, it turned out, more than filled the spatial and emotional void. At first I admired it covertly, like a schoolboy smitten with puppy love, while I arranged and rearranged my writer's tools and toys. Near the letter pigeonholes, I even managed to balance my 18th century Flemish jeweler's scale. Perhaps I needed it as a symbol of equilibrium after all the interior turbulence that my newest acquisition had generated. But my collection of antique scales is another story.

I am not sure what it means that so many writers are indifferent to their desks, while I remain devoted to mine. In a cursory browse through reflections by contemporary authors into their writing habits, I found none who thought that their desk even deserved mention. Only in a design magazine could I locate any reference to the strong attachment that a desk (in this particular case, however, an ordinary door) might provide in a "sensually correct" contemporary study.

It seems that a new breed of home-office engineers has transformed desks into wheeled carts (doubling as cocktail trays), collapsible modular components (which can be concealed beneath dining room tables), and portable caddy trolleys (easily confused with the airport "wheelies" that I scorn). The desk, ever expressive of shifting American values, has become transient, mobile, streamlined, multipurpose, and dispensable. No wonder I prefer the Victorian era.

I am reminded, occasionally, of those captivating photographs of Freud's Viennese study, taken just before he fled the Nazis. They show a substantial writing desk, crowded with his remarkably evocative collection of antiquities. As I excavate historical memory at my new-old desk, I know there must be a good explanation for the fervor of my attachment, one that any true Victorian would understand and respect.

34 · Victory Lap

Driving across the Triborough Bridge from Manhattan to Queens 46 years ago I was terrified. It was not the height of the bridge, but the prospect of teaching my first class at Queens College, that tormented me. In panicked avoidance of an opening-day encounter with Plato in my Western Civilization course I had spent the entire summer preparing a lecture about ancient Egypt. That night, exhausted from my miserable debut, I read Plato.

Over the years I cherished what academic life, at its best, should be about: reading, writing, thinking, learning, and teaching. (And, as baseball umpire Bill Klem famously declared: "You can't beat the hours.") To be sure, my teaching anxieties returned more than occasionally. But I remembered the wise admonition from my undergraduate mentor: when the anxiety vanishes, it may be time to retire.

Last January, I began my final semester of teaching. Or, as I preferred to call it, my victory lap, after 40 years at Wellesley College. I fired up my motivational engines and forged ahead. Within 10 minutes of my first class, students had displayed all the familiar responses, from eager attentiveness to bored distraction. (I took it as a good sign, however, that no cellphones rang.) But in my seminar, with nine enthusiastic students sitting around a table prepared for thoughtful conversation about the history of Israel, I was instantly reminded of my own most rewarding college experiences.

During the semester several colleagues kindly inquired whether I would be giving a "last lecture," already something of an academic tradition among those who take pleasure in celebrating themselves. But I always remembered my visit to Professor Mark Van Doren's last class at Columbia University, 50 years earlier. A gentle and learned man, he entered the classroom, sat at his desk, and quietly resumed a conversation with his students about *Don Quixote*. At the end of the hour, without fanfare, he left. I wanted my last class to be like that.

By mid-semester I had begun to empty my office of now-worthless paper accumulated over the decades. As I lugged each basket down the hall to the recycling bin, I felt pleasurably released from the minutiae that had grown around me like barnacles. After each class session, I also discarded my lecture notes. I enjoyed my new freedom from encumbrances.

Meetings, surely the bane of academic existence, reaffirmed the wisdom of

---

"Victory Lap," *Chronicle of Higher Education* (September 16, 2010).

my decision to retire. At one, no worse than so many others over the years, my colleagues and I were instructed to discuss which "goal," among several equally foolish ones, to impose on our two handfuls of senior history majors for them to demonstrate their competence (and, presumably, ours). It was an absurd exercise, designed by administrators who insistently claim that they can—and must—bureaucratize liberal-arts education.

With a month of the semester remaining, I felt twinges of sadness and loss as my contact with students neared its end. The day after my World War II class, a student stopped by my office to show me a *Life* magazine photograph of Buchenwald survivors, with her grandfather standing in the second row. I was touched that she had shared it with me. Another student came by—ostensibly to discuss her paper, which we did—but really to talk about her difficulties at Wellesley. There had been many such moments of trusting contact with students during four decades.

As the end approached, I was frequently reminded of my own best college teachers who, in their varied ways, had burrowed under my intellectual skin. Teaching, for me, had never meant grand pronouncements and sweeping generalizations. If I could pose questions—while implying that asking questions is what education should be about—I was content. A former student, learning of my pending retirement, wrote to tell me that what she remembered most from our time together was: "Q & A: Question and Analyze." It was the highest teaching compliment that I could receive.

I wanted at least part of my final survey class to be open and spontaneous. In brief concluding remarks, I referred to the pleasures of uncovering the past while trying to make sense of it to students in their very different present. Then we had a delightful conversation. Inevitably, a student asked where I was during the 1960s, and what I had done to save the world. When I replied that I had spent most of my time in the library stacks at Columbia, she was incredulous. Another student perceptively contrasted my having lived through events (if from a distance) with her learning about them decades later. It was a poignant, if unintended, reminder of the passage of time.

As always, my seminar was special for its moments of intimacy and intensity. Near the end of each semester I would welcome the class to my home, which evoked fond memories of my own Oberlin experience. That meant a lot to me then, and I wondered whether any of my students would remember it, as I do, after 50 years. For a historian, after all, memory is immortality.

For our last seminar meeting—my final class—we gathered on a warm, sunny May afternoon on a shaded lawn beneath the iconic campus tower. I noticed that students instantly recreated their seating pattern from the classroom. I wondered whether, like me, they were having difficulty letting go. Our pleasurably meandering discussion wandered from their reactions to a video about Israel that they had watched with evident delight (as had I) to an intense discussion of the centrality of "the land" in the Biblical narrative and modern Jewish history. It was a perfect ending.

With graduation behind me, I began to dwell on a sobering reality: I had entered the final stage of my life. It took a kind friend to ask "But what about old age?" for my uneasiness to subside. I knew that I was not there yet.

My cohort of closest academic friends, all of whom I have known for at least 40 years, is now easing into retirement. We were not the "lost" generation, nor can we claim to have been the "greatest." But as members of the "silent" generation we have left our legacy in less flamboyant, more private, ways during our privileged academic careers. With abundant opportunities, given the small size of our cohort and expanding enrollments to absorb the baby boomers, we enjoyed a great run.

By late August, as the children of younger friends began to drift back to college and I had not had my annual pre-semester anxiety dream, I felt the wonder of it all: I was free! I experienced the joyful absence of the academic calendar that had structured my life for 70 years. In the waning days of summer I felt the presence of that absence, and I cherished it.

35 · At Home

For a year [1974-75], Jerusalem was my constant companion. Exploring the city, I finally began to encounter myself as a Jew. I frequently retraced my steps to the Western Wall, pulled inexorably back by memories from my first night in Israel. There I would sit, sometimes for hours, watching the Hasidim endlessly form and reform their *minyanim* for prayer. With my beard, I must have seemed a likely recruit, for I was occasionally asked to join, or invited to wrap *t'fillin*. Too embarrassed to display my ignorance, since I did not know what to say or do, I always declined. I wanted to be left alone to observe, not to participate.

On the damp, chilly days for which Jerusalem winters are notorious, I often retreated inside the high vaulted stone chambers adjacent to the Wall, beneath Wilson's Arch. There, in the dim light, I was invariably lulled into dreamy contemplation by the rhythmic murmur of prayers, and by the choreographed rituals of the men who drifted in and out to recite them.

Late one Friday afternoon, I was roused from my repose by a haunting cantorial melody, sharply penetrating even from a distance. Its ecstatic cadences held me enthralled. As the *chazzan*, a bearded old man wrapped in a *tallit*, approached, his voice pierced deeply into my memory. Instantly I was transported back to the Friday evenings of my childhood, when Cantor Gorsky had proclaimed the arrival of the Sabbath through our living-room wall. As voice and memory merged, they reverberated through the caverns of my buried Jewish self....

I surround myself in my American home with antiquities dug from tombs in Hebron, Shechem, and Jerusalem; centuries-old maps of biblical Israel; family relics; and books that trace my scholarly itinerary from American history, through law, to American Jewish history and, finally, to Israel. There is also my assortment of antique scales (including a tiny jeweler's scale made three centuries ago by another Jew named Jacob who lived in Cologne, not far from the village of Auerbach). They help me to weigh and balance the conflicting claims that engage me....

There are other photographs nearby, triggering memories of what I never knew but cannot forget. One, from Romania, shows a horse-drawn hearse outside a Jewish cemetery on a bleak, snowy day. A hunched old man, the only

---

Jacob's Voices (1996), 51, 156-57.

visible mourner, shuffles toward the open gate. He might as well be the last Jew in Romania. The horse has turned its head back to watch, as though in silent witness to the death of Romanian Jewry.

Another picture, quite well known, is from Warsaw. Taken during the last days of the Ghetto, it preserves the look of haunted terror on the face of a young boy exiting from a bunker with his hands raised in abject surrender to Nazi storm troops. He is carefully dressed—cap, coat, shorts, knee-socks, school bag—as though his mother had prepared him for a trip, his final journey as it turned out, surely to Treblinka. We were the same age when the photograph was taken. He reminds me of who, but for Jacob, I might have been. In his face I see my own reflection as a young boy, when Jacob came to visit. I know that if Jacob had not left Romania, this Jewish boy and I might have died together. Perhaps, it sometimes tortures me, he died in my place.

Finally, there is a photograph of the Western Wall, taken during the years of the British Mandate. Some Jews lean against it in prayer, others huddle nearby. I recognize the cracks and crevices in those courses of ancient stones, for I, too, have touched them. Although the faces are hidden, I know that I have seen them here, in Jerusalem by the Wall, many times. For nearly two thousand years, Jews have come here to come home, to remember.... If I do not remember, my children will surely forget.

Author's Note

Due to space limitations, footnoted sources in the original texts have not been replicated here.

Once again I appreciate the willingness of Alan Childress and Quid Pro Books to work with me on this project and bring it to fruition.

Michele Veade enthusiastically, patiently and expertly transformed photocopied pages into the Microsoft Word document that became this book, and designed the interior of the print edition.

Pasha never let me forget that his visits to my study took priority.

My family, as always, sustained me: my wife Susan, our daughters Shira and Rebecca; my son Jeff and daughter Pamela; my grandchildren Cole, Dalia and Jonah; my vision of grandchildren yet unborn; and all who will follow them, adding their own blossoms to our family tree. For those yet to come for whom I will, like my grandfather Jacob, be only a name and an imagined memory, know that I will be with you, always, with love.

JSA
August 2011

Permission Acknowledgment

Permission to reprint my writings is gratefully acknowledged to the following publishers and organizations:

"The Best Men and the Best Opportunities," *Unequal Justice: Lawyers and Social Change in Modern America* (1976), pp. 17-39. Reprinted with permission of Oxford University Press, Inc.

"From Rags to Robes: The Legal Profession, Social Mobility, and the American Jewish Experience," *American Jewish Historical Quarterly*, 66 (December 1976), pp. 256-62, 265-74. Reprinted with permission of the American Jewish Historical Society.

"Law and Acculturation," *Justice Without Law? Resolving Disputes Without Lawyers* (1983), pp. 76-94. Reprinted with permission of Oxford University Press, Inc.

"Liberalism and the Hebrew Prophets," *Commentary*, 84 (August 1987), pp. 58-60. Reprinted with permission of *Commentary*.

"'Exodus' and Return," *Jewish Spectator* (Winter 1992-93), pp. 45-47. Reprinted with permission of *Jewish Spectator*.

Are We One? Jewish Identity in the United States and Israel (2001), pp. 26, 82-87, 113-15, 171-83, 189-92, 200-02. © Rutgers University Press. Reprinted with permission.

"Are We One? Menachem Begin and the Long Shadow of 1977," in Allon Gal (ed.), *Envisioning Israel* (1996), pp. 340-51. Reprinted with permission of The Hebrew University Magnes Press.

"Rest in Peace: Zionism, 1967-1993," *Jewish Spectator* (Spring 1994), pp. 32-34. Reprinted with permission of *Jewish Spectator*.

"Israel's Shadow Line," *Midstream* (April 2003), pp. 12-15. Reprinted with permission of *Midstream*.

"Are Settlements Illegal?" *Midstream* (Spring 2009), pp. 4-7. Reprinted with permission of *Midstream*.

"Hebron Letters," *Midstream* (January 1996), pp. 12-14. Reprinted with permission of *Midstream*.

"Inventing 'Palestine,'" *The Jewish Press* (August 10, 2011), 1. Reprinted with permission of *The Jewish Press*.

" '*Altneuland*' Revisited," *Jewish Spectator* (Spring 2000), pp. 36-39. Reprinted with permission of *Jewish Spectator*.

"Woodrow Wilson's 'Prediction' to Frank Cobb: Words Historians Should Doubt Ever Got Spoken," *Journal of American History*, 54 (December 1967), pp. 608-15. Reprinted with permission of the *Journal of American History*.

"New Deal, Old Deal or Raw Deal: Some Thoughts on New Left Historiography," *Journal of Southern History*, 35 (February 1969), pp. 18-30. Reprinted with permission of the *Journal of Southern History*.

"Means and Ends in the 1960s," *Society* (Sept.-Oct. 2005), pp. 9-13. Reprinted with permission of Springer Science+Business Media.

"Thomas Friedman's Israel: The Myth of Unrequited Love," in Edward Alexander (ed.), *With Friends Like These: The Jewish Critics of Israel* (1993), pp. 58-74. Reprinted with permission of Specialist Press International Books.

"Edward Said's Silence," *Congress Monthly* (Nov.-Dec. 1999), pp. 12-14. Reprinted with permission of the American Jewish Congress.

"The Corruption of Historians," *Society* (Nov.-Dec. 2002), pp. 38-43. Reprinted with permission of Springer Science+Business Media.

Explorers in Eden: Pueblo Indians and the Promised Land (2006), pp. 1-14. © 2006 University of New Mexico Press. Reprinted with permission.

"American Jew," *Judaism*, 32 (Summer 1983), pp. 263-66. Reprinted with permission of the American Jewish Congress.

Hebron Jews: Memory and Conflict in the Land of Israel (2009), pp. 189-96. Reprinted with permission of Rowman & Littlefield Publishers, Inc.

"Wellesley College: Anti-Semitism With White Gloves," in Eunice G. Pollack (ed.), *Anti-Semitism on the Campus: Past & Present* (2011). Reprinted with permission.

"The Clock and the Scale," *The Jewish Advocate* (August 9, 1990). Reprinted with permission.

About the Author

JEROLD S. AUERBACH was born in Philadelphia in 1936. He attended the Horace Mann School in New York, graduated from Oberlin College (1957) and received his Ph.D. from Columbia University (1965).

He is the author of nine books: *Labor and Liberty* (1966); *Unequal Justice: Lawyers and Social Change in Modern America* (1976), a *New York Times* Noteworthy Book; *Justice Without Law?* (1983); *Rabbis and Lawyers: The Journey From Torah to Constitution* (1990, 2010); *Jacob's Voices: Reflections of a Wandering American Jew* (1996, 2010); *Are We One? Jewish Identity in the United States and Israel* (2001); *Explorers in Eden: Pueblo Indians and the Promised Land* (2006); *Hebron Jews: Memory and Conflict in the Land of Israel* (2009); and *Brothers at War: Israel and the Tragedy of the Altalena* (2011). His widely published essays and articles have appeared in the *Wall Street Journal, Commentary, Midstream, The New York Times, Jerusalem Post, Forward, Mideast Outpost, The Jewish Press*, history and legal journals, and online publications.

He has been a Guggenheim Fellow, Fulbright Lecturer at Tel Aviv University, recipient of two College Teachers Fellowships from the National Endowment for the Humanities, Meyers Fellow at the Huntington Library, and Visiting Scholar at the Harvard Law School. He is Professor Emeritus of History at Wellesley College, where he taught for forty years.

Visit us at *www.quidprobooks.com*.

www.ingramcontent.com/pod-product-compliance
Lightning Source LLC
Chambersburg PA
CBHW062007220426
43662CB00010B/1265